DROPS OF NECTAR

A Collection of Teachings
By
H.H. Pujya Swami Chidanand Saraswatiji

GANGA

PRESS

Swami Chidanand Saraswati, 2004
Drops of Nectar
ISBN: 978-0-9831490-4-0

Please contact us at:
Parmarth Niketan
P.O. Swargashram; Rishikesh (Himalayas); Uttarakhand - 249 304, India
Ph: (0135) 2440077, 2434301; Fax: (0135) 2440066
swamiji@parmarth.com
www.parmarth.com & www.ihrf.com
Note: from abroad, dial + 91-135 instead of (0135) for phone and fax

Cover design by: Divine Soul Dawn Baillie, Los Angeles, California
Typset by sevaks at Parmarth Niketan Ashram

∞

Dear Divine Soul,

May this book fill your life with
drops of inspiration, drops of guidance,
drops of wisdom, drops of comfort
and drops of divinity.
May you be uplifted and inspired
to follow the Divine Path
every minute and every moment
of every day.

With love and blessings,

Swami Chidanand Saraswati

Table of Contents

Stories to Teach Your Mind, Touch Your Heart & Uplift Your Spirit:

Pieces Sent by Others:

More Information:

Pujya Sant Shri Rameshbhai Oza

DROPS OF NECTAR

Blessings from
Pujya Shri Rameshbhai Oza (Bhaishri)

Jai Shri Krishna!

It is by Lord Krishna's grace that you are holding such a valuable treasure in your hands. They say that a true saint is not one who is simply enlightened himself, but one who brings enlightenment to others. Pujya Swamiji is one of the truest saints I know. His words, his life, his message and his satsang carry *lakhs* of people directly to God.

Pujya Swamiji is one of the rare souls whose life will have enormous impact on all of humanity – today, tomorrow and in the future. He touches and transforms all those he meets. Yet, the arms of his divine influence extend infinitely further. He is not content to only serve those who come to him. Instead, he works tirelessly, yet silently and humbly, to serve every individual creature on the planet, ranging from cows on the streets, to children in schools, to spiritual communities across the globe.

There are many saints who can give divine teachings. But the teaching is not enough. In order to truly inspire people, to touch and uplift the deepest corners of their soul, one must have the divine touch. It is that touch that Pujya Swamiji gives. So, what you have here in this book is not only the word of God. It is the touch of God.

Read this book, then re-read it, then re-read it again. Let its message sink into every corner of your being. Then, if you are open enough, you will know you have been touched by God.

Rameshbhai Oza (Bhaishri)

Preface to the Latest Edition

It has been a great blessing to watch the transformation of this book from a small booklet published during Kumbha Mela, 1998 to the over 300-page tome it is today. In fact, for this edition we had to reduce the font size slightly in order to prevent the book from becoming unweildingly thick. Like the flowers planted in Pujya Swamiji's garden, which blossom and grow under His loving and divine touch, this book has blossomed from a seed of inspiration to a flowering tree of wisdom and insight. The number of printings these five editions have gone through is countless. Over 25,000 copies of the book have been distributed across the world, and the requests keep coming. Emails and letters indicate the profound effect this book has had on people everywhere. Selected quotations from these letters can be found in the back pages of the book.

To me, as I see the insatiable demand for Pujya Swamiji's books across the world, my faith in the future is restored. People have not become complacent, careless, selfish and apathetic. People have not stopped caring or hoping to do the right thing. They are just searching for a guide to show them the path. Directionless, mentorless we go astray. It is like the famous poem by Kabir that says,

A temple roof cannot stay up without rafters;
So without Nam [Divine Truth and Name of God]
how can one cross the ocean?
Without a vessel water cannot be kept;
So without a Saint man cannot be saved from doom.

I have, therefore, come to believe that it is not a diminished capacity for selflessness, compassion and *dharmic* behavior that is leading our world into its current state of self-destruction, but rather a lack of guidance. No one wants our world to plummet into an irreparable state of destruction. No one wants to be doomed, himself, or for his children to be doomed. But, as Kabir says, "So without a Saint, man cannot be saved from doom." It is the presence of the enlightened beings that guides us on the path of righteousness and keeps us from going astray. In the absence of that, we will surely falter if not collapse completely.

I have seen the thirst for Pujya Swamiji's divine wisdom and guidance from adults and youth, Indians and non-Indians, academics, scientists, philosophers and homemakers, rich and poor, Hindus and non-Hindus. Further, I have seen the deep fulfillment which comes to them when that thirst is satiated by the drops of nectar in this book. It has been truly a gift to witness this remarkable, healing, inspiring effect His words have upon all people.

As our world falters more and more on the precarious brink of self-destruction – environmentally, inter-personally and spiritually – the ray of hope I find is in seeing the way that hearts melt, anger dissipates, grudges are dropped and resolutions are made in nearly everyone who reads Pujya Swamiji's books. As His message is spread, by the grace of God, may it be like the 100th monkey phenomenon or the "turning point" in which a major, global shift is sparked by the actions of a single person. May we who are blessed enough to find His words in our hands, make a vow to take them to heart, and to read them not only with our physical eyes, but also with our inner eye, the eye which leads into our soul.

Sadhvi Bhagawati
Rishikesh, India
August 2011

Preface to the Third Edition

It is a great joy and honor to release the new edition of *Drops of Nectar* on the occasion of H.H. Pujya Swamiji's 50th birthday, in June of 2002. When I first met Him, I asked Him His age. I did not know at the time that one should not ask this kind of question to a holy man. He, however, responded simply that He was 45. I was incredulous at how this holy saint, this clear embodiment of the divine on Earth, this timeless, ageless being could simply be "middle-aged." If He had said He was five, I would have believed Him, for His eyes dance and sparkle like a young child's. He moves with the grace and lightness of an angelic, nimble child. Or, if He had said He was five-thousand, I also would have believed Him, for His wisdom, His depth of understanding and His omnipotence speak not of a human but of a timeless Being. Yet, forty-five was incomprehensible.

To this day, nearly six years later, it is equally incomprehensible that He is fifty. His eyes dance and sparkle more vibrantly each day. His steps become lighter, more graceful with each passing year. And yet, simultaneously, His wisdom becomes deeper, more profound, more complete, underscoring everyone's realization that He is simply wearing the clothes of human skin, but is certainly not bound by them.

In fifty years, He has accomplished more than most do in many lifetimes. From nearly ten years of intense *sadhana* in the forests and Himalayas as a young child, to the years as tireless Sant Narayan Muniji who – even in His early twenties – was given the responsibility of running the largest ashram in Rishikesh, to founding and heading the first Hindu-Jain temple in America, masterminding the monumental project of the *Encyclopedia of Hinduism*, traveling as Gorbachav's guest to the Kremlin for a seven-day global forum on Peace and the Environment, presiding over Parmarth Niketan Ashram as President and turning it into a world-renowned spiritual institution, representing Hinduism at numerous international, interfaith conferences, to running schools, free medical programs, ecological programs, and women's vocational training programs, giving prayers and blessings in the General Assembly of the United Nations, meeting with former president Bill Clinton....these are merely glimpses of a life truly lived "in the service of God and humanity."

Whenever devotees, who have not seen Him sometimes in decades, come for His *darshan*, their comments are always the same: "He hasn't changed at all. He looks just like He looked thirty years ago. He's still the same, only better!" Pujya Swamiji seems unaffected by His incredible list of accomplishments and recognitions and remains a humble, pious child of God, owning nothing, draped only in saffron robes, living a life of true renunciation, offering His blessings, His love and Himself to everyone who comes into His presence.

"Mein mast hun, [I am in divine bliss]" has been His answer to "How are you?" for over four decades. Whether living in the jungles or visiting a mansion, whether lecturing to a few dozen devotees in the cold, winter morning prayers at Parmarth Niketan or lecturing to thousands of the world's top religious, political, social and business leaders at the World Economic Forum in New York, whether eating His one begged-for meal a day out of His bare hands as a young wandering *sanyasi,* or eating a twenty-dish meal served to Him on a silver *thali* in the home of aristocrats, whether sleeping in a dirt ditch between fields in the Himalayan forests or sleeping in a four-post, King-size bed at the Waldorf Astoria, He is always *mast.* *"Ast, Vyast, Swast and Mast*...No tension, no depression. Always peaceful, always in ecstasy," is how He describes His life.

That divine ecstasy, that peace, and that stillness is something He not only embodies, but also something He exudes, something He gives out freely to all who meet Him, such that no one who encounters Him is ever the same.

To capture that "touch of God" is nearly impossible in writing, for as He always says, "People need not only divine teachings; they need the divine touch." That "touch" is not physical, however. It does not depend upon physical contact or even physical presence. Rather, the "touch" is one in which your soul quivers in the way that a seed must as it is about to break forth through its shell and become the sprout of a large, flowering tree. The "touch" is not one of a hand to a body, but it is one of a hand to a soul. The souls, which have cried out for years and decades and lifetimes for solace, find it in His presence.

Here, in these pages, the challenge is to give not only the teachings, but also the "touch." This is a task which we have realized is impossible, for words on a page cannot make a soul quiver and burst forth into light unless these words carry within them the spirit of the Master.

Thus, in these pages you will find words that have been written or spoken by Pujya Swamiji. The spoken words have been transcribed as directly as possible from both His informal *satsang* sessions and from His more formal lectures. We pray that within these words you will find not only the teaching for your minds, but the touch for your hearts and your souls.

This book is divided into three sections. The first section is a collection of articles He has written on a variety of subjects, articles which have appeared in various international magazines and yet which are applicable and valuable for all people, in all circumstances.

The second section is compiled of stories – stories He has told to audiences and has followed with moral, divine lessons on how to live our lives. These stories have their origins mostly in the scriptures or occasionally in parables told by other religious leaders to which Pujya Swamiji has added His own special meaning and lesson.

The third section is a potpourri of stories, quotations, letters, and poems which Pujya Swamiji has received via email over the years, which He had marked with a *"save for book"* and instructed me to put into a special file. They are stories and quotations which He felt should be shared with all, which could benefit all. Some of these have known authors, most do not. Some are common and well-known, others are more obscure, but all are things which He felt should be gathered and shared, rather than simply deleted.

The title of this book is *Drops of Nectar*. The "nectar" is a reference to the pot of the nectar of immortality, which is the essence of the story of the Maha Kumbha Mela (the first edition of *Drops of Nectar* was released during the Kumbha Mela of 1998 at Haridwar/Rishikesh). However, the true Nectar is Him. The true, divine nectar is not simply immortality, but rather a connection with He who bestows immortality upon us. To be immortal without Him in our lives would be to live eternally, yet alone.

For those of us who have been blessed to have Pujya Swamiji in our lives, He is that nectar, and it is a great joy and honor to be able to share "drops" of this nectar with all.

Sadhvi Bhagawati
Rishikesh, India
June, 2002

Introduction

I have been blessed beyond words to spend the last year and a half living in Rishikesh and working with Pujya Swamiji. During this time, I have heard so many people ask, "Isn't there anything published with Swamiji's teachings? Isn't there any compilation of His ideas, His wisdom?" The answer, much to my dismay, has been no. The absence of such a work is grievous, for the wisdom that flows forth with His every breath is worthy of being immortalized.

On this auspicious occasion of Kumbha Mela, 1998, I have taken the God-given opportunity to bring together as much "nectar of wisdom" as I could. At this sacred time, people come from every corner of the Earth to bathe in the holy waters, and to imbibe of the divine nectar of immortality. Yet, what is it that truly uplifts us, that truly changes us, that truly brings our souls closer to God? For me, it has been His holy presence in my life. How to encompass, though, divine wisdom and insight in mere pages? The task is obviously impossible. Yet, while the words are a poor substitute for His presence, they carry with them the essence of His teaching and message.

I have, therefore, compiled as many of His written articles (in English) as I could find. In addition to the articles, there are stories, or rather parables, that I have heard Pujya Swamiji tell. I have frequently been blessed to be present at times in which someone has asked Him a question to which He did not directly respond. Rather, on these occasions, His voice took on an even more ethereal tone and His eyes drifted even further away from the Earth, toward the Heavens. He would say, "Let me tell you a story," or He would simply begin to tell it, and we all knew something extraordinary was taking place.

Then, on these occasions, when He had finished the story, He would explain – to we who are ill-equipped to grasp the depth of His wisdom – what the point was. Therefore, these stories have two parts: the story itself and the lesson He gave afterwards. To me, these parables and lessons are like scriptures: words spoken by God which a mere mortal has attempted to capture on paper. I beg the reader to forgive my inadequacies as a scribe. Pujya Swamiji was not as lucky as Vyasji, whose divine wisdom was captured perfectly by Lord Ganesh.

Therefore, the book has two tones. One is literary – writings which have been presented in international magazines or newspapers; the other tone, for the stories, is oral – words which have been spoken. However, while the topics of the articles (or the plots of the stories) differ, the underlying essence of Pujya Swamiji's message remains the same. His message is: Go to God.

Yet, "Go to God; Be with God" is not only the message of His words. It is the message of His life. Every breath He takes is divine; every word He speaks is holy canon; every piece of work He does is Creation. Pujya Swamiji is a saint by title – it is His legal designation. Yet, He is more than that. He is a saint in every pore, every cell of His body. He is not only someone who sends you to God; rather, He is someone whose mere presence carries you to God. However, should one ever try to praise Him, or thank Him, or acknowledge the miraculous nature of His being, His response is always the same: a simple shrug, eyes lifted upwards, palm open to the Heavens, and the words, "It's all God's blessing."

I would like to tell a story of my own. Unlike Pujya Swamiji's, my story is not a parable meant to teach a lesson. It is a true portrait of the man behind this book.

I came to Rishikesh in 1996 as a tourist. I was twenty-five years old, on a three month vacation from my Ph.D. program in California. How I met Pujya Swamiji and moved into Parmarth Niketan is another story, a beautiful example of God's divine plan. For now, it will suffice to say that I was there, alone, and planning to stay approximately one week. During my first two days at the ashram, on the banks of Gangaji, in Pujya Swamiji's presence, my entire being was transformed (and this transformation has not stopped). I was overflowing with joy, bliss and a serenity I never knew. At *Ganga Aarti*, the world would disappear into the blazing fire, into the depth of the voices as they sang, into the setting sun as it bounced off the waters, into the pervasive peace of Pujya Swamiji's presence.

So, the second day, I went to Pujya Swamiji. We sat in his meeting room, alone – He a forty-five year old renunciant, and I a twenty-five year old American girl who could barely see straight I was so filled with ecstasy. "Swamiji," I said. "I feel so incredibly blessed to be here, to have met You, to be able to spend this time on the banks of the Ganges. I feel like You have given me so much. Is there anything I can give You, anything I can do for You?"

A voice in my head that had spent twenty-five years being indoctrinated by the West yelled at me: *"What are you saying?"* After all, there we were, alone in His office. I had only known Him for two days, and I had been warned in America to "stay away from Indian gurus." I was not connected to anyone Pujya Swamiji knew; I was simply an American girl who was staying alone in the ashram for less than a week. And, most importantly, He knew that I did not have the innate Indian understanding of what a saint is and should be.

Pujya Swamiji looked at me, the light streaming in through the windows, casting a brilliant halo around His head. "Anything?" He asked. The voices inside my head screamed, *"No, you're crazy!"* Yet, those voices remained lost inside my head; the voice that actually flowed from my heart to my mouth said, "Yes. Anything."

Pujya Swamiji paused. "You promise?" He asked, staring directly at me as though this were the most serious question in the world. I felt that I would pass out from the intensity of the hold His eyes had on me. Every word I had ever heard in my Psychology of Mind Control classes, every story I had ever read about Indian gurus surrounded by naked women and fancy cars, and every rational thought I could have were swimming in my brain, filling it with fear. *"Don't promise,"* the voices pleaded. I could hear my mother – on the opposite end of the world – saying, *"Just get up and walk out."*

Yet, the two feet between my brain and my heart served as a beautiful barrier, for these words did not even touch my heart. My heart was calm and still, and filled with a sense of security that I had never known. "I promise," I said, knowing that I truly would give this man – whom I had known for two days and who was old enough to be my father – anything He asked for.

The intensity of His gaze lifted and His face broke into the lightest, purest smile I had ever seen. "Okay, then, three things," He said, and even though the divine smile continued to emanate from His face, I knew that what He was going to say would change my life forever. "First," He began. "Get closer and closer to God. Every day get closer. Second, serve the world. Even if it means doing without something you want or something you think you need, give to humanity. Third, be happy. Give all your sadness, all your anger, all your bitterness to me. Give it to me and give it to Gangaji, but don't keep it in your heart. You must be happy."

I sat there, in what felt like a far-off corner of the world, in a place so beautiful it could only exist in fairy tales, in the presence of a man who wanted nothing else from me than to be close to God. The tears streamed down my face, although they were not sad tears. They were the tears of having found Truth.

I could not have told you which was brighter – the morning sun blazing its way through the window or the light streaming from His eyes. I could not have said which was purer – the red rose, still covered with morning dew, which had just opened her petals to the world, or the love pouring forth from His heart. I could not have told you who was God – the formless Almighty Lord my Jewish upbringing had said to worship, or the small, simple man, draped in saffron robes, sitting across from me.

Sadhvi Bhagawati
Rishikesh, India
March, 1998

DROPS OF NECTAR

Articles

Vegetarianism

"Teaching a child not to step on a caterpillar is as valuable to the child as it is to the caterpillar."

We make many choices in our lives without ever questioning "why?" Choices like what religion we believe in, what our values are, what we eat... Perhaps we simply continue to live in the way we were raised; perhaps we automatically adopt our parents' choices. Or perhaps we rebel against how we were raised: our parents made one choice, so we will make the opposite. In either case, we rarely take the time to truly see why we are living the way we are.

In this article, I want to take the opportunity to show why we should live as vegetarians. I want to talk about the deep meanings behind this choice we make each time we put food in our bodies.

I hear so many Indian youth tell me, "But my parents can't even give me a good reason to be vegetarian. They just say that the cow is holy, but if I don't believe the cow is holy, then why can't I eat hamburgers?"

The importance of vegetarianism far transcends a belief that the cow is holy. In fact, although the tenet of vegetarianism is as important as it was thousands of years ago, the reasons why have changed slightly. Some of the meanings and reasons are the same today as when our scriptures were written thousands of years ago. However, many of the reasons are directly related to the world we live in now. While vegetarianism has always been a correct "moral" and "spiritual" choice, today it is more than that.

Today, it is an imperative choice for anyone who is concerned about the welfare of Mother Earth and all the people who live here. Today,

---

it is not only a religious decision. Rather, it is the only way we can hope to eliminate hunger, thirst, rainforest destruction and the loss of precious resources. It is, in short, the most important thing that each man, woman and child can do every day to demonstrate care for the earth and care for humanity.

Spiritual/Religious Aspects of Vegetarianism

One of the most important guiding principles of a moral life is *ahimsa*, or non-violence. There is hardly anything more violent than taking the life of another for our mere enjoyment. It would be one thing if we were stranded in the jungle, starving to death, and we needed the food to survive. But, we live in a world where we can get all our calories, all our vitamins and minerals in other, tastier, less expensive and less violent ways. Hence, to continue to kill the animals is simply to fulfill our desires, our pleasures. It is simply selfish gratification at the incredible pain of another.

More violent than their day of death are the numerous days of their lives. The animals raised for consumption are raised distinctly differently than animals raised as pets, or raised for their by-products (e.g. milk from a cow). Veal is a poignant, yet compelling example. This meat is considered a rare delicacy by people across the world. "Tender veal cutlets" are frequently the most expensive item on a menu. Yet, when we look at the way in which these animals become so tender, we realize that the true price of this dish is far more than what the restaurant charges.

Veal is the meat from baby cows who are separated from their mothers immediately at birth. Cows, as milk-giving/breast-feeding mammals have very strong maternal instincts. It is not a simple coincidence that Hindus worship the cow as mother. A mother cow will keep her calf next to her long after he is born, looking after him, protecting him, and teaching him to fend for himself. But, these baby cows are wrested from their new mothers. I have heard from people who have visited these places that — contrary to what the meat industry will tell you — the mother and baby cows cry in agony for hours after being separated.

It is essential that the babies do not develop any muscle, and if they stand near their mothers, their legs will develop muscle. Muscle is hard; fat is soft and juicy. Fat is tender. The only way to prevent muscle is to prevent use of the limbs. So, these newborn baby cows, screaming for the warmth of their mother's breast, are locked into restraining boxes. Their entire bodies are restrained by chains. If you have ever tried to move a foot or a hand that is chained, you know that it is impossible, so imagine if you are a baby with no muscle. The baby cows are then fed copious amounts of food directly into their mouths – more than babies should theoretically eat – so they will become fat quickly. However, they are never removed from the confines of the restraining box. This torment lasts not one day, not one week, but many months, until they are killed and sold as "tender veal cutlets." So, what is the real price of this dish?

Now, let's look at chickens. Many people (especially in the West) say they are a vegetarian, but they still eat chicken. The lives of chickens raised for food are only scarcely better than the lives of the baby cows. They are put in crates, which are piled high on top of each other. In this way, they are denied space to move, let alone roam around. The crates are never cleaned and the chickens never see the sunlight; the light from the artificial bulbs is enough to keep them functioning.

Chickens — like humans — have natural territory and space needs. Yet, these are unmet in chicken "farms." Rather, these animals are packed together as closely as possible, such that frequently they cannot even move. To have a true understanding of these conditions, picture yourself in an elevator, which is so crowded that you cannot even turn around, let alone move. Picture as well that all the people in the elevator are confused and scared. They do not realize there is no way out. So they cry and bite and kick, in a true frenzy, attempting to free themselves from this claustrophobic terror. Next, imagine that the elevator is tilted, on a slant, so that everyone falls to one side, and it is nearly impossible to move back up. In this elevator, the ceiling is so low that your head is pushed down to your shoulders in order to stand. There is no way to straighten your neck. And you are all barefoot on a wire floor that pokes and cuts your feet — ever so sensitive, for you are probably only a few months old. Finally, imagine that this terror does not end when someone comes to open the door at the "lobby" floor. Rather, this is your whole life, every minute of every day, until you are fried up and served for dinner, with a side of mashed potatoes.

It would be one thing if we were stranded in the jungle, starving to death, and we needed the food to survive. But we live in a world where we can get all our calories, all our vitamins and minerals in other, tastier, less expensive and less violent ways. Hence, to continue to kill the animals is simply to fulfill our desires, our pleasures. There is no need or utility in it. It is simply selfish gratification at the incredible pain of another.

Integrity and Honesty

How many of us consider ourselves honest people? How many of us can say that we do not tell lies? We would very much like to believe that we are righteous, honest people and that we are passing these values onto our children. Well, if we eat meat, we cannot say that we do not tell lies. In fact, our life is a lie. Here is why: if we wanted to be honest and still eat meat, we would have to go outside, chase down a live cow, and bite right into it. Or we would have to go to one of those chicken "farms," take the animal while it was still alive, tear its head off, pull out its feathers and eat it raw. Of course, we do not do that. Instead, we order a "hamburger". We can not even call it what it is, let alone kill it ourselves. So, we call it "beef" instead of cow. We call it "pork" instead of pig. We call it "poultry" instead of chicken. Then, we eat it packaged in neat, nice ways that allow us to forget what we are eating.

How many people stop and think that the thing between the tomato and the bread on a hamburger used to be a living, breathing creature? That it was someone's child? How many of us would eat our cats or dogs between a piece of tomato and a slice of bread? We wouldn't. That is why it is a lie. We cannot even admit to ourselves what we are doing. How then, can we consider ourselves honest people if we are lying every time we eat? Further, these are not lies that only cause misunderstanding; these are not "little white lies." These are lies that are killing our planet, our animals and ourselves.

The Taste of Fear

Eating meat is not only violent to the animal whose precious life-blood we wrest from it due to our insatiable desire for the taste of hamburgers, steak, chicken and fish, but it is also one of the most profound ways we wreak violence upon our own bodies – physically and emotionally.

Each day people come to me and say, "Swamiji, I am filled with anxiety. I am restless. I cannot sleep properly at night. I feel tense and stressed. I suffer from high blood pressure." This is not surprising. Our world today is filled with tension and strife. Heart disease and cancer rates are sky-rocketing. High blood pressure and insomnia affect innumerable lives. The "developed" world is marked by outer busy-ness and inner restlessness.

Much of this of course is due to the lifestyle and culture which propagates success at all costs. However, a large part of our physiological anxiety and anger is due to the meat we consume. Let me explain.

When animals (humans included) are threatened or scared, our adrenal glands secrete a flood of hormones, referred to as *adrenaline*, into our bloodstream. The purpose of the adrenaline is to give our bodies the strength and energy to save our lives – either by fighting off the attacker or by running away. Thus, this hormonal reaction of our sympathetic nervous system is sometimes referred to as the "fight or flight" response.

The effect of the hormones is that our hearts beat quickly, our blood pressure rises, our digestion and reproduction systems shut down in order to send the blood to our extremities, and our physical impulses become very acute and sharp. All of these responses are beneficial if we need to stave off a vicious attack or run to save our lives. Miraculous stories abound of hundred-pound mothers who lifted cars off of their trapped babies, of unfit people who ran miles and miles at top speed while chased by an attacker, of people who scaled trees to save their lives. The "miracle strength" comes from the adrenaline.

When an animal is about to be killed, even if it can neither fight nor flee due to chains, boxes, or restraints, its body still releases the same stress hormones. These hormones course through the animal's blood at the time of death and become absorbed into the tissues of the body. When we eat those tissues in the form of hamburgers or steaks or chicken nuggets, we ingest those lingering hormones. When the meal is digested and the fats, proteins, carbohydrates and nutrients are absorbed by our bloodstream, so is the adrenaline. Thus, the adrenaline is now coursing through our own bloodstream, giving the same messages of "fight or flight" to our bodies, sending the chemical signal to our brains that our lives are in danger and we must prepare to save ourselves.

Our world is becoming more violent each day. Uncontrollable outbursts of anger and tantrums have become common. More and more people are simply out to get ahead, to protect themselves, even at the sake of others. These are the same characteristics that adrenaline and the other stress hormones prepare our bodies for. They are necessary when our very life is on the line. Yet they are counter-productive and detrimental when we want to live in peace, with ourselves and with others.

When we regularly and continuously ingest hormones which send "danger" messages to our body, it is only natural that we will become hyper-vigilant, restless, anxious and angry. Slowly, over time, these hormones change the very nature of our beings and we don't know what has happened to us.

When someone asked the famous playwright George Bernard Shaw why he was a vegetarian, he replied, "Because I don't want to make my body a cemetery of dead animals." Our bodies should be temples, not graveyards.

Perhaps, if we treat this temple that is our body like a temple, it will feel like a temple – pious and pure. When we treat it like a battleground and cemetery, how can we wonder that we feel wars are being waged within?

Vegetarianism and Ecology

Aside from all the compelling moral and spiritual reasons, one can now say that vegetarianism is the only responsible choice in terms of waste and ecology. The natural resources of our planet are diminishing at terrifying rates. More than a third of the world goes to bed hungry each night. We wonder what we can do. Being a vegetarian addresses almost each and every ecological issue.

I believe that being a vegetarian today is the only choice for anyone who is concerned about the health of Mother Earth and all the people who live here. It is the best and easiest way we can help to eliminate hunger, thirst, species extinction, rainforest destruction, deforestation and the depletion of precious resources such as water, land and power. It is perhaps the most important thing that each man, woman and child can do every day to demonstrate care for the Earth and care for humanity.

As you will see from the statistics and details given below, making the choice to be vegetarian is making the choice to live peacefully and *dharmically* in the present and to preserve a world for tomorrow.

Are you concerned about world hunger? Let me give you some facts.

■ It takes sixteen pounds of wheat to produce one pound of

meat. This wheat is fed to the cows who are later killed to make beef. However, it takes only one pound of wheat to produce one pound of bread. So, if we used our wheat to produce bread rather than feed it to cows in order to make hamburgers, we could feed sixteen times as many people.

■ One acre of land can grow 40,000 pounds of potatoes. That same acre, can provide less than 250 pounds of beef if it is used to grow cattle-feed.

■ If Westerners reduced their intake of meat by only 10% (meaning they could still eat 90% as much meat as they do now), we could feed every one of the 50,000 people who die of starvation every day.

■ Every day, 40,000 children starve to death. Every day, the US produces enough grain to provide *every* person on Earth with two loaves of bread.

■ 840 million people go hungry every year.

■ We could feed ten billion people a year if we were all vegetarian. This is more than the human population. There is no need for *anyone* to go hungry in the world – the only reason is the selfishness of the choices we make.

Are you concerned about the Greenhouse Effect/Global Warming?

■ Animal agriculture (raising animals to be killed into food) releases more than 100 million tons of methane gas into the atmosphere each year. Methane gas is one of the worst contributors to global warming. Approximately 50% of the human-induced global warming is caused by methane emissions. This huge production of methane gas from animal agriculture is due to the energy used in clear-cutting the land, the enormous amount of methane released as gas from the animals themselves, and · the energy used in killing them.

■ In addition to the millions of tons of methane released into the air, animal agriculture also produces millions of tons of carbon dioxide, the other leading greenhouse gas. The numbers are breath-taking:

- The average car, if driven all day long, releases three kilograms of carbon dioxide into the air. The production of one hamburger releases seventy-five kilograms of carbon dioxide due to the energy expended in clearing the forest, grazing, etc. **This means that eating one hamburger causes the same damage to our atmosphere as driving your car continuously for three weeks!**

- To minimize greenhouse gases, it is much more expedient to become vegetarian than to simply try to reduce amount of fossil fuel. The lifespan for animals raised to be killed is only one to two years, so a sharp reduction in meat intake would lead to almost immediate drops in methane emissions; on the other hand, the lifespan of a gas-guzzling car, industry, factory or power plant is decades.

Are you concerned about the destruction of the rainforests and other precious land?

One of the leading causes of the destruction of our precious forests across the world is the growing appetite for meat. Millions of acres of rainforest are clear-cut, destroying innumerable species of animals, plants, birds and insects, in order to make room to raise the animals who will end up on our plates.

■ Every second, one football field of tropical rainforest is destroyed to graze cattle who will become hamburgers and steaks.

■ More than 50% of the land on this planet is used to graze livestock. Imagine what we could do with that land if we put it to better use.

■ A great deal of the livestock are raised on forest land. It is estimated that for every hamburger, fifty-five square feet of rainforest land is destroyed.

■ Since 1967, one acre of American forest has been destroyed every five seconds, in order to become "grazing land" for the

---

ARTICLES

animals that will become dinner. If the present trend continues, the country that was seen as the "land of plenty" will be completely stripped bare of all its forests in fifty years.

Are you concerned about poverty in the world?

■ A pound of protein from meat costs $15.40, but a pound of protein from wheat costs $1.50.

   • So, meat costs ten times as much for the same nutritional value.

   • Could we not use that money for much better causes? Is there no more important use for that money than to kill animals?

Are you worried about our rapidly diminishing energy resources?

■ The world's petroleum resources would last only thirteen years on a meat-based diet, but 260 years on a vegetarian diet.

Are you aware of the need to conserve water?

■ The production of one pound of beef takes 2500 gallons of water. This water is used to grow the food for the livestock, to water them, and then to wash their bloody bodies and turn them into food.

   • The production of one pound of wheat or potatoes takes twenty-five gallons of water.

   • So, we would waste one hundred times less water if we ate wheat instead of meat.

■ In an average shower of seven minutes, every day, you would use approximately 2600 gallons of water in bathing over a period of six months. **That means that the same amount of water is used in the production of one hamburger as in showering every day for six months.**

Health Issues

I am not going to use this space to tell you about all the health reasons to eat a vegetarian diet. Every medical text, every health book in every bookstore or library talks about the undeniable link between high-fat diets and heart disease or cancer. It is well known that people who eat meat-based diets have anywhere from two to twenty times higher rates of death from heart disease and cancer than vegetarians.

A recent British study found that vegetarians had a 40% lower risk of cancer and a 20% lower risk of death from any cause than meat eaters.

In fact, Dr. Dean Ornish, M.D. a cardiac specialist in California, USA is the first allopathic doctor ever to be able to "cure" heart disease. Others have slowed the process but never before has it been truly cured. His "cure" consists of a pure vegetarian diet, yoga and meditation.

A health issue less frequently discussed is the antibiotics factor. The animals are loaded up with antibiotics in order to prevent the diseases that their poor treatment causes. For example, more than 20% of the cows and pigs in these farms die prematurely due to disease and infection; 70% of pigs have pneumonia at the time they are slaughtered. The environments are so unsanitary that the animals have a very great risk of developing infections. So, antibiotics are fed to them in great quantity in their feed. When we eat the animals, we ingest the antibiotics as well.

However, bacteria are resilient. They develop resistance/immunity to antibiotics, whether we take the antibiotics themselves or simply eat the meat of an animal who has taken them. So, then when we, ourselves, are sick and actually need the antibiotics, they do not work. This is because the bacteria in our bodies have already developed resistances and mutations to them, through so many years of ingesting these antibiotics through meat.

Each year more and more antibiotics become futile and powerless;

each year there are more and more resistant strains of bacterial infections. Many people believe that the reason for this is that as we consume low doses for so many years through our consumption of meat, the bacteria all have a chance to mutate and become resistant. When Sir Alexander Fleming discovered penicillin, not even one strain of *staphylococcus aureus* (one of the main and most virulent strains of bacteria which causes a wide range of serious infections) was immune to it, but he warned that overuse of the drug would lead to immunity. However, no one paid attention and large doses of penicillin have been fed to animals for decades in their feed. Each year, 24.6 million pounds of antibiotics are fed to animals purely as routine, *not* as a treatment for any illness. Today 95% of *staphylococcus aureus* strains are immune to penicillin and other, newer antibiotics as well.

Another issue has to do with hormones. The animals are fed large doses of hormones to make them fatter, bigger, and "juicier." This is similar to body builders taking steroid hormones to become stronger, even though these hormones are dangerous to their health. We have seen many cases where athletes have suffered serious health consequences and even death from over ingestion of steroids.

Further, there is substantial evidence that over-secretion of hormones within our own bodies leads to disease. For example, over secretion of adrenaline and stress hormones can lead to heart disease. Over secretion of estrogen has been associated with cancer in women. Yet, when we eat the meat, we are ingesting the tissues of animals who have been frequently fed carcinogenic hormones. Between 90 – 100% of US beef cows receive hormones. The rates vary in different parts of the world. This means that we are not only eating meat, but we are also eating hormones that our bodies don't need and that may be putting our lives and health in jeopardy.

There are many other health issues which are rarely mentioned yet very important to consider when making dietary choices.

Conclusion

Across the industrialized world, everyone is talking about what we can do to save the planet. Ecological conservation has become a household word. There are thousands of programs dedicated to feeding the millions of starving children. Yet, while we may talk about wanting to save the planet or feed the hungry, these words are empty if our actions are in stark contrast. We may not be able to carry crates of food to the deserts of Africa. We may not be able to re-plant every tree that has been cut down in the forest. But, we can refuse to allow it to continue. We can refuse to partake of the cruelty. We can strive to make at least our lives and our actions pure and divine.

Instead of a token donation to a hunger campaign or to an environmental organization, let us make our every day, every meal, one that protects not only our own health, but the health of our planet and the health of every person on it.

* Note - see Pujya Swamiji's separate book titled **Vegetarianism: For Our Bodies, Our Minds, Our Souls and Our Planet.** *To order your copy, email to parmarth@parmarth.com or download from www.ihrf.com.*

---

[1]All facts and figures taken from *Diet for a New America,* by John Robbins, 1987, Stillpoint Publishers; *The Food Revolution,* by John Robbins, 2001, Conari Press; and www.earthsave.org.

Overcoming Fear

In one question-and-answer session, a woman asked me with tears in her eyes, *"How do you overcome fear? I live my life so afraid all the time. The object of my fear changes as time passes, but the fear remains."*

In my opinion, this omnipresent fear is the most insidious obstacle to our peace, happiness and progress in life.

When I say fear, I don't necessarily mean terror. Rather, I mean all that makes us anxious, nervous, tense and in need of controlling our surroundings. The root of fear is distrust. We have been betrayed, injured and abused. We decide that the world and those around us cannot be trusted. Thus, we lose that faith which is so crucial.

So what is the answer? The answer to fear is to firmly root ourselves in God (by whatever name, whatever form you choose). When we realize that God is always with us, always for us, we will never be afraid, regardless of the circumstances.

Our family and friends may betray us. They may injure us. But, if we give ourselves to God, if we make our relationship with Him our first priority, then we will never be broken inside; we will always be cared for.

There is a story of a very powerful king. This king prided himself on being generous and caring for all his subjects. He would often boast that no one in his kingdom was hungry or cold or impoverished. Once, a holy man came to see the king. The king told the holy man how he provided for everyone in the kingdom so well. The holy man asked the king to come for a walk. While they walked in the forest, the saint picked up a large rock by the side of a stream. "Break the rock," he ordered the king.

The king looked surprised but immediately told his servant to smash the rock. As the rock broke open they saw a small frog, living peacefully in the nutrient-rich water which had gathered inside the rock. "Have you provided this as well?" the holy man asked the king. The king realized that he could not possibly provide something as perfect, as intricate as this food and shelter for the frog. He realized that it is really God who provides for all His subjects.

We must realize that if God can provide for even the smallest insects, He certainly will provide for us.

I heard a beautiful story of a young boy on a ship. The ship was trapped in a large storm and waves rocked the boat furiously. The passengers screamed and cried and held each other for dear life. In the midst of this terror sat a very young boy, calm, composed and angelic. When asked why he did not cry he answered, "My mother is here, so I know everything will be all right."

This feeling we must cultivate. If God is there, if God is with us all the time, then everything will always be all right.

We take out millions of dollars (or pounds or rupees) of insurance to protect our homes, our property, and our cars. But, what about our lives? Who will protect our lives? We must remember our Divine Insurance Company. We must place all of our faith in Him. He will never betray us, and we will rest assured knowing that we are in the best of hands.

One time, many years ago, when I first started going to the USA, I was on an airplane flying to Chicago. It was winter time and the plane hit a great deal of turbulence and stormy weather. The captain's panicked voice came over the loudspeaker that everyone should assume crash position. The passengers screamed; some even fainted. Cries of, "We're going to die!" could be heard coming from all directions. I was sitting next to a very respected professor. As everything descended into chaos I was calmly writing on my notepad. "What are you doing?" the professor asked me. "How can you work? The plane is going to crash! What could you be possibly working on?"

I told him, "Professor, I am working on my speech. See, I know that I will be all right. I have perfect faith in God. But, as everyone else seems convinced that they will die, it means I will be the only survivor. Therefore, I will have to give a speech on what it was like to survive this crash. And, as I will have to give the speech in English, I thought at least, before you die, I could ask you any questions I might have about English vocabulary."

We must realize that we are God's children. Just as a child is never afraid when his mother is near, so we must never fear. Fear immobilizes us. It freezes us. It prevents us from thinking clearly. Most of all, it serves no purpose. No tragedy has ever been prevented by fear. No catastrophe has ever been averted by anxiety. Calm, serene, wise understanding of the situation coupled with undying faith is what is needed.

There is a beautiful story from the life of Swami Vivekananda. His message to the world was, "Stand up. Be fearless. God is with you." To test his faith, some people staged a scene during one of Swamiji's lectures. In the middle of the lecture gun shots rang out and bullets whizzed past Swamiji's head. The audience screamed and ran for cover. Some dropped to the floor to protect themselves. Only Swamiji remained perfectly calm and composed. Later, he explained as follows: "The bullet which is not meant to take my life will never hit me, even if fired from point-blank range. The bullet which is meant to take my life will kill me, even if I am protected by one hundred guards."

So, let us renew our faith in the Supreme. Let us give away our fears, our anxieties. Let us put all our insurance in the Divine Insurance Company. Let us realize that everything is just as it is supposed to be. We are in the lap of our Mother. How can anything go wrong?

Desires & Desirelessness

One of the greatest plagues on us as human beings is our insatiable desires. We truly never feel satisfied. We never feel that we have had enough, and are always looking for more and more. This pertains to almost every area of our lives. Obesity, diabetes and heart disease are sky-rocketing because we always want "just one more" *ladoo, gulab jamun* or piece of chocolate cake. Our bank accounts are growing bigger and bigger, yet our lives are becoming emptier as we are always striving to close "just one more deal" or to take on "just one more project," thereby sacrificing the precious time that we could spend on spiritual pursuits or with our families or engaged in the service for others. Talking to my young friends around the world, I hear about their boyfriends and girlfriends, who seem to change by the month! "He was nice but he was not smart enough." "She was sweet but not as beautiful as I would like." "He was perfect but half an inch too short."

Families with four people have five Mercedes in the driveway! Everyone has only two feet, yet I know people with hundreds of pairs of shoes. We have one body, but closets full of clothes. What is the need? Nothing other than the futile attempt to satiate our desires.

There is a beautiful line in one of the prayers we sing each morning. It says:

> *Zindigi ki dora saunpa, haath Dinaanaath-ke*
> *Mahalon me rakhe chahe, jhopri me vasa de*
> *Dhanyavad nirvivad Rama-Rama kahiye*
> *Jahi vidhi rakhe Rama, tahi vidhi rahiye.*

It means, "Surrender your life to God. Give Him the reins to your chariot. Wherever He leads you, be happy. Whether He puts you in a palace or a shack, just stay there and be thankful. Be always grateful to the Lord, without any argument and without any doubt. Be happy, ever happy, in whatever condition He keeps you."

This is the only way to live. It is through surrendering to Him that we become desireless. Through being desireless we attain peace and joy. We think, mistakenly, that it is by fulfilling our desires that we will attain joy. However, it is the exact opposite. Fulfillment of desire leads to temporary happiness *not* because the object of desire was attained, but simply because the desire has now temporarily disappeared! If I am craving a new car and I get a new car, then my desire for a new car has gone away. It is not the new car itself that gives me the joy, but rather it is the fact that I am now free of the desire for a new car. The diminishment of desire is what brings joy to us. But the way to diminish our desires is not to rush around and try to fulfill them. There are always more. They are like weeds in the garden of our mind. No matter how many we pluck, there will always be more. For a short while we are satisfied, and then the fire of desire begins burning again.

I remember when I was on my first trip to the United States, over twenty-five years ago, and I was staying in Los Angeles. The family I was staying with had a beautiful Rolls-Royce car. We were driving in the Rolls-Royce one day and the man said to me urgently, "Swamiji, look, look, do you see that car?" He frantically pointed out a car driving near us on the freeway and made sure that I knew which one he was showing me. As we were in the middle of a serious conversation on another topic at the time, he did not elaborate further. However, later when we returned home, he said to me, "Swamiji, I need your blessings. Do you remember that car I showed you as we were driving? That is the model of Rolls-Royce I want. Please bless me that I can get that model of Rolls-Royce." I was amazed! Here we were sitting in a Rolls-Royce, and he was dreaming about a different Rolls-Royce! Yet, the truth is, life is always like that.

We must renounce our desires. That doesn't mean renounce enjoyment or renounce possessions. Rather, it means savor everything. Enjoy whatever God gives you, as much as He gives you, however He gives it, and wherever He gives it. Use whatever you have for the benefit of the world. Rest peacefully in the realization that you have exactly as much as God wants you to have right now. You are in exactly the place and exactly the position where He wants you. Do not let your life go to waste always thinking, "If only I had that, then I would be happy." Wherever God is, that is where true richness is.

Look at Hanuman. After the war in Lanka, Ma Sitaji presented Hanumanji with a beautiful, precious pearl necklace. Hanumanji proceeded to carefully examine each and every pearl – from top to bottom, from left to right. Then, he began to take the pearls off the string, one by one, bite them in half, again examine them thoroughly, and then throw them on the ground. Ma Sitaji could not watch this. Finally she said, "Hanuman, what are you doing? That is a very expensive, precious necklace I have given to you. Why are you pulling off the pearls and breaking them?"

Hanumanji replied, "I am looking for Rama. You have said these pearls are priceless and precious. If so, they must have Rama inside them."

Pearls (and diamonds and rubies and cars and money) are only precious if they are filled with God. If God is not there, it doesn't matter how expensive the diamond is, it is empty and useless. God's presence in your life can turn stones to diamonds, but without God your diamonds are as worthless as stones.

So, let us vow that we will desire God and only God. Wherever He is, everything is. Let us vow not to waste any more of the precious moments of our lives in the endless and futile pursuit of more and more pleasures and possessions.

What is True Love?

Across the world, people spend billions of dollars each year on cards, chocolates, flowers, balloons, candle-lit dinners, and other material things to express love. However, we often miss what love actually is. What is true love? True love is something that cannot be bought, bribed, begged, manipulated or forced. It can only blossom from deep within the heart.

Love is simultaneously the purest and one of the most complex emotions we find. True love at its purest is just that – pure, true and love. It is unpolluted, untainted, unencumbered by desires, expectations, needs or wants. Love is content just to love. As Khalil Gibran says, "Love has no other desire but to fulfill itself." Love needs no reciprocity. Love needs no appreciation. Love loves for the very sake of loving. Loving is its own reward.

It is of course essential to clarify that I am not talking about lust or passion, which are completely unrelated to love.

Love dissolves the very borders and boundaries of who you are as you melt into its vast ocean. Love takes you from time to timelessness, from separation to divine union. Love is the sunshine which coaxes open the petals of the flower. Love is the water that causes the seed to sprout. Love causes those who love – whether they are people or flowers – to blossom and grow.

Unfortunately, too few people are able to really reap the physical, emotional and spiritual benefits of true love as they are incapable of either giving it or receiving it. Love is not glue which puts together that which is broken inside of you. Love is not a filler for the holes within you or a band-aid for inner wounds. Love does not complete you, heal you, or make you whole. In fact, true, pure love can only be experienced between two people who are both already whole and complete. As long as you are looking to another – whether it's a parent, a child, a friend, a spouse, a Guru or anyone – to fill that within you which is empty, to heal that within you which is hurt, to put back together that within you which is broken, you will never be able to experience true love.

Many people mistake need for love. "I need you" is very different from "I love you," yet too many people mistake the former for the latter. Love gives, need takes. Love accepts, need demands. The poet Khalil Gibran said, "Love possesses not nor would it be possessed; For love is sufficient unto love." When you find yourself criticizing your loved ones, finding fault in what they are doing or not doing, when you complain and sulk, you are moving away from love. Not only does the love within your own heart become diminished, but the beloved's feelings toward you change. No one on Earth likes to be nagged or criticized. No one likes to hear the same complaints over and over. No one likes to see sulking, grumpy or cranky faces day in and day out.

We think tragically that we can change people, that we can make them love us more or better or differently (or at all, in some cases). Hence, we manipulate, we cry, we complain, we sulk, we do all sorts of things which we think will turn the beloved in the direction we want, toward us. But, it actually backfires. You may succeed in changing your beloved's actions. Depending upon the relationship, many people may find it is a lot easier to just amend their behavior to suit their spouse, friend, parent, child or other person who loves them. Yet that is only behavior. The heart cannot be molded, stretched or pulled according to our wishes. In fact, the more you nag and complain to loved ones, the farther they move internally away from you. To quote Khalil Gibran again: "And think not you can direct the course of love; love, if it finds you worthy, directs your course." Love is one of the greatest blessings and greatest mysteries on Earth.

Take a moment and examine whether you are truly loving, whether your love is full of acceptance, gratitude and giving, or whether your love is riddled with complaints, criticism, condemnation and comparisons. Take the opportunity not merely to eat chocolates or enjoy a candle-lit dinner from a loved one, but to truly find the source of pure, divine love within you – the love which asks nothing in return, the love which is content just to love.

The Essence of Spirituality:
Service of Others

Spirituality is the essence of life. It is the light that shines on our lives, illuminating our paths, bringing light to the darkness, joy to the sorrow, and meaning to the incomprehensible. And the essence of spirituality? The essence of spirituality is service. As one goes deeper and deeper on a spiritual path and as one gets closer and closer to Realization and Enlightenment, one realizes that the Divine resides in all. One begins to see God's presence in every person, every animal, and every plant.

The first line in the *Ishopanishad* says:

> *Isha vaasyamidam sarvam*
> *yat kincha jagatyaam jagat*
> *Tena tyaktena bhunjeethaa*
> *Maa gradhah kasya svid dhanam*

This mantra tells us that God is manifest in everything in the universe. All is Him, and all is pervaded by Him. There is nothing which is not God.

When one realizes this Truth deep in one's heart, one becomes filled with an insatiable desire to care for and serve all of God's creation. Typically, we sit in our *mandir* and ever-so-carefully bathe the deity of God. We gingerly and lovingly perform the *abhishek* ceremony, caressing His body lovingly with sandlewood and rose water, and adorning Him in the finest clothes. We offer food to Him before we eat; we distribute the sweetest sweets as *prasad* and we offer our hard-earned money as *daan*.

However, as one's spiritual path deepens and as one gets closer to the state of God-realization, one sees God's form in everything.

Thus, the feelings of care, love, sacrifice and devotion which we feel for the deity in the temple begin to blossom in our heart for all of creation.

Every widow, every orphan, every homeless leper, every wandering, malnourished animal, every deforested piece of land, every polluted river – all become as precious as the marble image of Shiva or Krishna or Durga in our *mandir*. Thus, from our hearts we are called to do as much as we can to remedy the world's tragic situation.

Many people think a spiritual life means that one retreats to the mountains, performs meditation and then lives peacefully forever in one's own enlightened cocoon. However, that is not true, deep spirituality. That is not the essence of Enlightenment. Yes, solitude, silence and intense *sadhana* are crucial in order to establish the connection with God, in order to make the leap from a material life to a spiritual life. It is difficult, initially, to connect deeply with God while one stands in line at the supermarket or while one is stuck in traffic on the road home from work. Thus, in the beginning, one must retreat temporarily in order to lay the ground work. It is like wiring a house for electricity. In the beginning, when the house is being built, one must carefully lay all of the wires. Much time is spent on this initial electrical wiring. However, once the lines have been laid, once the electrification work is complete, then one simply has to plug the cord into the socket and the lamp immediately illuminates! One does not have to re-wire the house each time!

The same is true on a spiritual path. Solitude, silence and extensive *sadhana* are required, as a parallel to laying the electrical wires. But, once the deep connection with the Divine Powerhouse is established, one simply has to close one's eyes and one connects with God.

Look at Lord Buddha – he left the world in order to go into the forest and practice meditation. But once he attained Enlightenment under the bodhi tree, he did not stay in the forest, reveling in his own Enlightenment. Rather, he returned to the world to spread the message, to spread the light, to spread compassion, to serve the needy. He had attained Enlightenment and once having attained the Enlightened state, he was able to see the Divine in all and thus dedicated his life to spreading light, wisdom and compassion to all.

Ramakrishna Paramhansa, one of the greatest saints in history, used to bow down in *pranam* to prostitutes and worship them as the Divine Mother. He would lay in the grass and talk to snakes and rabbits. He saw the Divine just as clearly in the impure prostitutes as in the image of Kali in the temple!

In the *Bhagavad Gita*, Bhagwan Krishna says, "I am the Self, O Gudakesha, seated in the hearts of all beings; I am the Beginning, the Middle and also the End of all beings." When we embark on a spiritual path, or as we walk on the path, we must dedicate ourselves to cultivating the divine vision and awareness with which we can see the Divine in all.

Once we see every being as Divine, we cannot walk by someone who is suffering without helping them. We cannot sleep at night unless we have done our best to lessen the pain of our fellow beings, just as we could not sleep if we neglected to perform the *aarti* in the *mandir* or if we forgot to offer food to the deity of Krishna Bhagwan. We cannot see sick, starving animals wandering on the road or watch toxic chemicals dumped into our precious rivers, any more than we could tolerate watching someone toss a *Shiva Linga* onto the pavement.

So, ultimately, if the spiritual path is true, it culminates in an insatiable urge to serve all, to help all, to give to all, and to live for all. This does not mean that one forgets one's personal meditation or *japa*. Rather, the two go hand-in-hand. There is a beautiful line in our prayers that says, "*Mukha mein ho Rama Nama, Rama seva haath mein*...Our lips keep chanting His name, and our hands keep doing His work."

It is also important to note that "service of all" can take a variety of forms. For some, it may take the form of working hard at their profession every day and donating their income to humanitarian causes. For others, it may take the form of founding organizations or foundations which directly work to alleviate various aspects of suffering. For some, it may take the form of giving lectures or writing books on spirituality which bring inspiration and upliftment to the masses. For some, it may take the form of being a spiritual guide or Guru who brings the light of awareness to all of his/her devotees. The possibilities are endless. But the central core is the same – all of these people have a deep realization that all beings are Divine and that God resides in all. Once one has this realization, one feels unity with all creatures and beings on the planet; thus one hears the internal call to help and serve in whatever way possible.

Peace – Internal and External

We constantly talk about peace – it is one of the most popular topics of world discussions today. Peace between nations, peace in our societies, peace in our schools, peace in our families, peace within ourselves. Yet, although billions of dollars and millions of hours are spent each year on think-tanks, brainstorming sessions and international conferences, this much-desired peace continues to elude us.

Without peace – both inner and outer – all else is meaningless. We can spend millions of dollars building posh downtown centers in our cities, but if we are at war with another country, they will bomb that center to ashes in a second. We can spend thousands of dollars building beautiful homes, but if our neighborhood is violent, our windows will be smashed and our new lawns destroyed. We can work hard and successfully at our jobs, but if we come home to turmoil in the house, there is no joy in the success obtained at work that day, for there is no one with whom to share. We can devote ourselves to obtaining high education, top credentials and a beautiful figure. However, if we are miserable inside, no outer achievement will ever pacify us.

The root to success in life on all levels – personal, familial, societal, national and international – is first and foremost to be in peace. But how to attain peace? What is the secret to finding this elusive treasure?

Calm Your Pose

Once, a woman came to see me when I was visiting Chicago. She told me that she was stressed and tense. In order to sleep at night, she took pills called Compose (a medicine for anxiety and insomnia prescribed in India). But, I told her that she did not need to take Compose. "Just calm your pose," I said, "and you will sleep beautifully at night and be peaceful all day. You do not need Compose. You need only to calm your pose."

If we are peaceful, humble and sincere inside, then nothing outside can take away our peace. So, the first message is, *"Calm your pose and you will never need to take Compose."*

Usually, though, we do the opposite. We pose our calm. We put on airs of being wise, aware, centered and peaceful. We want others to look at us and think that we are calm and serene. However, inside we are steaming; our anger, greed and envy have grabbed the reins of our lives and are steering us in violent, corrupt, dishonest, *adharmic* and anxiety-ridden directions. Let us, therefore, really and deeply calm our pose instead of posing our calm!

I Want Peace

The mantra of today seems to be *"I want peace."* Every day people tell me this. They all say, "Swamiji, all I want is peace. Tell me how to find it."

The obstacle and the solution are buried in the statement. Listen: I want peace. What do we have? An "I", a "want" and a "peace." If you remove the "I" and the "want", what is left? Peace. You do not have to look for peace, find peace or create peace. All you have to do is remove the "I" and remove the "want," and peace stands there in its full glory for all the world to imbibe. It is the "I" and the "want" which obscure this treasure from our view. So, how to remove these?

REMOVING THE "I"

"I" is one of the greatest obstacles to peace. I is our ego. I is our sense of ownership, doership and pride. This "I" says, "I want to be in the center." Isn't it true? We always want to be the ones getting the glory, the appreciation, and the prestige. Even when we don't do anything, we still want to be appreciated. This is our downfall.

We have everything these days. Everything is set. We have tea sets, TV sets, sofa sets, video sets; but we, ourselves, are upset. Everything is set and we are upset. Why? Because of this "I" that tries to keep us in the center of everything.

So, ideally we remove this "I", which is dividing us from our own true selves, dividing families and dividing nations. Yet this is very difficult. Living in the world today, it is nearly impossible to completely remove the sense of "me," "mine," and "I." So the next best option is to take this "I" and change it.

When "I" stands vertically it is an obstacle. It creates borders, barriers and boundaries between ourselves and others. But, if we take this "I" and turn it sideways, making it horizontal, it becomes a bridge – a bridge between our families, our communities, and our nations. Let this "I" become a bridge in the service of the world. If we keep standing so straight and tall and proud as the vertical I, then we will always stand alone. If, however, we turn this "I" sideways, we say, "Let me be a bridge, let me bridge chasms instead of creating them, let me stand smaller than others instead of always trying to stand tallest, let me put others in the center instead of myself." Then we will stand united and peaceful.

This "I" is so proud. It thinks, "Oh, I am so successful. I am so good." Yet, the truth is that we only go to work, it is God who works. We can do nothing without His grace. One minute we may be at our desks, acting like king of the world, and the next minute, just one microscopic nerve in our brain could fail and we would no longer be able to speak or write. One small blockage in one tiny blood vessel, and we would not even be able to go to the bathroom by ourselves. We would have to be fed and taken care of for the rest of our lives.

So, what is there to be proud of? God works, we just go to work. As soon as we realize this, we can take our little I and merge it in the big I, the universal I, the divine I. Then, we surrender our lives and our every action to Him and say, "God, let my tiny drop of water merge with Your great ocean. Let me be a tool for Your will and Your work."

It is through this selfless surrender to Him that the pain of the "I" is removed and all our troubles and unrest disappear.

We must aspire to be like the sun. The sun gives and gives and gives with no vacation. The sun sets in India and we think, "The sun has gone to sleep." But, if you call America they will tell you, "The sun is shining brightly." So, with no rest, no vacation, the sun shines, bringing light and life to all.

The sun gives with no discrimination. It doesn't say, "I will only shine on Hindus," or "I will only shine on Muslims, or on Christians." The sun is for all. Anyone who wants to open their window and go outside will find the sun there, shining and waiting.

The sun shines with no hesitation. The sun does not wait for you to pay your bills. All day, all year it shines and never sends a bill. If you don't pay your electric bills for one month, they will turn off your electricity. But, not the sun. The sun never sends a bill.

We must be like that – always giving, with no vacation, no discrimination and no hesitation. That is the way to merge this "I" into the divine I, freeing ourselves from pride, ego, and tension and becoming peaceful and ever blissful.

REMOVING THE "WANT"

The next obstalcle is the "want." Our wants, our perceived needs, our desires—what obstacles these are to peace! The more we have, the more we want. People always think that if they attain something more, whether it's more money, a better job, a degree, or a good husband, then they will be happy.

But, it never works like that. Happiness and peace are found not in the acquisition, but rather in the renunciation of our attachment. I always say, "Expectation is the mother of frustration and acceptance is the mother of peace."

It is not having or not having that is the issue. The issue is wanting, yearning and expecting. These external things never bring any lasting happiness.

The key to life is sacrifice. One of the most common Hindu rituals is a *yagna* fire. People sit around the fire and place offerings into the fire. With each offering, every time we make an oblation to the *yagna*, we say, *"idam namamah."* It means, "Not for me, but for You. Not for me, but for You."

The purpose of this is to remind ourselves that although we may be performing the ritual for some benefit of our own, perhaps a wedding or the opening of a new business, or just for inner peace, everything is for God. We must offer every thought, every action, every breath, at His holy feet.

So, in order to know true joy and peace, we must give more and want less. But how to become selfless? How to learn to give more? Prayer. Peace comes through prayer. It doesn't matter what name you use for God or what language you pray in. You can pray to Allah in Arabic, or you can pray to Jesus in English, or you can pray to Adonai in Hebrew, or you can pray to Buddha in Japanese, or you can pray to Krishna in Sanskrit – it doesn't matter.

There was once a little boy who went to temple with his father. He heard all the people chanting many prayers in Sanskrit. For hours they chanted many different prayers and mantras and slokas. Then, at the end, the priest said it was time for silent prayer. The little boy was nervous. He didn't know any of the prayers. But, he loved God and wanted to pray to God. So he closed his eyes and silently said, "God, I don't know any of the Sanskrit prayers. I'm only a little boy. The only thing I know is the alphabet I learned in school. But, I know that all the prayers come from this alphabet. So, I will sing you the alphabet and then whatever prayers you like best you can make from this alphabet." He started to sing, "A, B, C, D, E, F, G…"

Let me tell you, God is happier with that little boy, with his devotion, purity and piety, than He is with all the people who chant the prayers like robots.

ARTICLES

The point is: love God. It doesn't matter what name or form you use. It doesn't matter what language you pray in. Just pray. Then you will see the magic.

The fruit of prayer is faith. The fruit of faith is love. The fruit of love is devotion. The fruit of devotion is service. The fruit of service is peace.

Through this – prayer, faith, love, devotion and service – we will all, inevitably, attain that sought-after state of inner peace. Then, when we are at peace inside, that harmony will radiate out to all those around us, bringing peace to our relations, peace to our communities, peace to our nations and finally peace to the world.

Note: For a deeper discussion of ways to attain peace—for ourselves and for our world—please see Pujya Swamiji's book titled, Peace—For Ourselves, For Our Families, For Our Communities and For the World. *To order your copy, email to parmarth@parmarth. com or download from www.ihrf.com.*

How to Be A Yogi 24 Hours a Day

The secrets of the ancient science of yoga were passed down from our *rishis*, saints and sages who came to these very Himalayas for divine inspiration. Through their meditation, austerities and prayers, a treasure chest of wisdom was bestowed upon them for the benefit of humanity.

Yoga is not a religion. It does not require you to believe in a certain God or to chant certain mantras. It is an ancient science which leads to health in the body, peace in the mind, joy in the heart and liberation of the soul.

These days people take yoga classes to learn all about the various techniques of *asanas*, *pranayama*, and meditation. But yoga is more than that. Yoga is a way of life, and its teachings should penetrate every aspect of your being – from your actions to your speech to your thoughts.

An *asana* session has a beginning and an end. You start at 8:00 for instance, and you finish at 9:00. Your *pranayama* has a beginning and an end. You start at, say, 6:00 and you finish at 7:00. Even meditation – at least in the beginning – has a fixed starting point and a fixed ending point. You sit in meditation for a certain number of minutes or hours each day.

But, what about the rest of the time? How to live yoga even when you are not doing *asanas*, *pranayama* and meditation? How to practice yoga in the grocery store? How to live like a yogi with your family, in your work place, when you are stuck in traffic?

Yoga is an eight-fold path. *Asana* is one part; *pranayama* is another;

meditation is still another. Two other aspects of this path are called *yama* and *niyama*. These can be loosely translated as righteous living. These are the rules for life. By following these moral, ethical, and spiritual guidelines, one's entire life becomes yoga.

In general, *yama* is exercising restraint over our lower, baser, animal-like instincts; for instance, overcoming greed, lust, anger, and envy, and definitely never acting based on these impulses. *Niyama* can be seen as the embrace of higher, spiritual, humane values, such as being generous and selfless, cultivating piety, devotion, compassion, loyalty and humility.

The concepts of *yama* and *niyama* can be summed up as, "Do good and be good; do divine and be divine; have the Lord's name in your heart and on your lips, and do His work with your hands."

These moral and ethical principles affect us whether we believe in them or not. People may say, "But, I'm not Indian" or, "I'm not Hindu, so I don't have to follow these ethical laws." Yet this is not true. Yoga is not a religion. Not one of the eight aspects depends upon one's spiritual belief system. Just as *shirshasana* is beneficial whether one "believes" in it or not, similarly these moral and ethical laws of the universe affect us whether we believe in them or not.

They are like the law of gravity. One can certainly stand on the top of a ten-story building and say, "I don't believe in gravity so I am going to jump." Perhaps as one falls through the sky, one temporarily thinks they have succeeded in defying this pervasive law. Yet, inevitably, they will hit the ground and their life breath will be immediately whisked away.

Similarly, people may live lives full of greed, anger, lust, arrogance, and disregard for their fellow humanity for many years, thinking they are immune to these natural laws which affect us all. However, eventually they too will hit the ground and be destroyed.

I remember once, when I was abroad, I saw a sign that said, "Follow the rules and enjoy your stay." It is like that in life as well.

There are so many things we do that perhaps we realize are not right, but we do them anyway. We lie, we covet things which are not ours: "Oh, how I wish that beautiful car were mine instead of his." We harbor bad thoughts about each other: "Oh, if only he would fall sick, then I could have his job." We deny these to ourselves or we rationalize them with excuses. However, if we are going to live truly yogic lives then we must subject every area of our life to scrutiny.

To Eat Yogically

One thing we must examine is if our diet is in concert with a yogic life. People are learning a lot about *sattvic* food, which means food that is fresh, easily digestible and leads to health of the body and peace of the mind. Rather than talking to you about the intricacies of a *sattvic* diet though, I am simply going to ask: Are you vegetarian? Do you teach vegetarianism to your children? There is virtually nothing we can do to our bodies that is more contrary to the yogic life than to eat meat.

How can we be true yogis, full of life, if our bodies are graveyards for dead animals? How can we be at peace if our food choices bring pain and suffering to others?

Additionally, one of the most important aspects of yoga for daily life is honesty. How many of us consider ourselves honest people? How many of us can say that we do not tell lies? We would very much like to believe that we are righteous, honest people and that we are passing these values onto our children. But, if we eat meat, we cannot say that we do not tell lies. If we wanted to be honest and still eat meat, we would have to go outside, chase down a live cow, and bite right into it. Or we would have to go to one of those chicken "farms," take the animal while it was still alive, tear its head off, pull out its feathers and eat it raw.

Of course, we do not do that. Instead, we order a "hamburger." We cannot even call it what it is, let alone kill it ourselves. So, we call it "beef," instead of "cow," "pork" instead of "pig," and "poultry" instead of "chicken," and we eat it packaged in neat, nice ways that allow us to forget what we are eating. How many people stop and think that the thing between the tomato and the bread on a hamburger used to be a living, breathing creature? That it was someone's child? We can't. We cannot even admit to ourselves what we are doing. How then, can we consider ourselves honest people if we are lying every time we eat? These are not lies that only cause misunderstanding; these are not "little white lies." These are lies that are killing our planet, our animals and ourselves.

This is what the true yogic life is – contemplation, introspection. We must ask ourselves, "What right do I have to take the life of another?" We must pause and think about the decisions we make.

Additionally, a yogi is calm; a yogi is centered; a yogi is in peace, not in pieces. We cannot be calm and in peace if we eat meat. Bloody food leads to bloody thoughts. When animals (humans included) are threatened, we secrete large amounts of hormones. These numerous hormones are frequently referred to as *adrenaline*. Their purpose is to prepare our body to fight, to save our lives. Have you ever noticed that when you get scared, a lot of things happen inside you? Your heart beats fast, your digestion stops, your palms sweat and your physical impulses become very good and sharp. These are the result of the hormones, and they prepare us to either fight or run away. Thus, they are sometimes called the "fight or flight" hormones.

When an animal is about to be killed, its body is flooded with these stress hormones which remain in the animal's tissues. So, when we eat those tissues, we are ingesting those hormones (which are the same as our own bodies make). Thus, our own bodies become flooded with these "fight or flight" chemicals, making us even more prone to simple survival instincts.

Thus, the saying "you are what you eat" comes alive. Eating an animal with stress hormones coursing through it leads to stress in us. If we eat stress hormones, then we are eating terror, and it is no wonder that we cannot find peace in our lives.

So, if you are a vegetarian, great. It will not only improve your health, but it will change the very nature of your being. If you are not a vegetarian, then at least think about it. The yogic life is one of contemplation, honesty and integrity.

Additionally, how our food is prepared is as integral to our overall health and peace as what we eat. It is very important our food is prepared with love, with devotion and with purity. The energy of preparation is absorbed into the food, and — just as the animal's stress hormones affect our own bloodstream — we are physiologically affected by the energy of the cook and the place of preparation. Thus, chant, sing, meditate while you cook and encourage devotion in those who cook for you. Eat pure, fresh food. Then, you will see the magic of it.

So, if being a vegetarian and taking care of the food you eat is all you can do right now, then do it. But, let me go further and explain how to let yoga saturate every aspect of your life. For, remember there is both *yama* and *niyama*. Remember what we said about "follow the rules and enjoy your stay."

But, how to put these laws into daily practice? How does one truly live and breath yoga instead of simply following a set of rules like a robot? Let me give you three capsules – a multivitamin – you can take every day. If you take all three every day, and let them deeply saturate your being, then you will experience true health of body, mind and spirit. Then, you can say you are truly practicing yoga.

Multivitamin of Spiritual Health

MEDITATION: Meditation is the best medication for all agitations. People have so many troubles today, mainly related to the stress in their lives. To address this anxiety, this sleeplessness, this inability to simply be content, they may take pills or fill their lives with excessive material pleasures. For example, when people feel stressed they may attempt to forget about it by going to the movies, or by getting drunk or by indulging in simple sensual pleasures. Yet, these are not solutions. They do not address the underlying issues. They are simply band-aids to a wound that runs deep below the surface.

Meditation will truly calm the mind, fill the heart with joy and bring peace to the soul; the serenity and joy the comes from meditation lasts throughout the day and throughout your life. Meditation is not a simple diversion which works only as long as you are actively engaged in it. Meditation is not a pill which quickly wears off and carries unpleasant side-effects. Rather, meditation brings you into contact with God; it changes the very nature of your being. It brings you back to the world from which you come: the realm of the Divine. As you sit in meditation you will realize the insignificance of that which causes anxiety; you will realize the transient nature of all your troubles. You will realize the infinite joy and boundless peace that come from God.

You will learn (or perhaps you have already learned) meditation techniques. Do not worry if you can't do it perfectly, or if it is difficult, or if you can't remember everything. The point is to do it. Make a time that is "meditation time." It's okay if it's short. Don't worry, just do it. Do not say, "Well, I don't have an hour to sit so I won't bother." Commit five minutes to meditation each morning, and you will begin to see the magic of it.

Then, let this meditation become your life. Yes, of course, one should have a time set aside for meditation, and there should be a quiet, serene place in which to meditate. However, even when it is not "meditation time" or even if you are away from home, away from your "meditation place," do not think that you cannot meditate. Take five minutes at work to simply close your eyes, watch your breath, focus on the oneness of us all, and connect with the Divine. Let your life become meditation.

NO REACTION: We must learn to be calmer in our lives. We must learn to remain still and unaffected by all that happens around us. We must be like the ocean. The waves come and go, but the ocean stays. Even a large rock thrown from a great distance with great force will only cause temporary ripples in a small area. Most of the ocean will remain unaffected. Yet, we are always jumping into the ocean, right into the waves, letting them carry us. This is our choice. We must learn instead to be like the ocean itself, unaffected by these small, transient things.

So many times we act as though we are the waves of the ocean. Up one minute, down the next, changed by every gust of wind and every passing boat. In our lives there are waves of anger, anxiety, jealousy, greed, and lust that are just as vast, just as strong, and just as restless as the waves of the sea. Yet, we are not these waves.

We are not waves, pulled this way and that by every passing breeze, by the daily changes in the moon. Yet we act like that.

We act as though we are light bulbs and anyone who wants to can simply switch us on or off. The slightest comment or look or action of another can change our mood 180 degrees. It is so frequent that we are in a wonderful mood, but then someone at the grocery store is rude to us, or someone on the freeway passes in front of our car, or a friend is cold and distant, and our mood immediately switches. Any of these things can immediately switch our mood as though we were light bulbs.

So many times I hear people say, "Oh, I was in such a good mood, but then Robert called and told me what Julie said about me," or, "Oh, that phone call just ruined my day." The same works the other way. We are sad or depressed and we get a nice phone call or letter in the mail or we eat some good cookies. Then we feel better.

How is that? How can one phone call or one rude comment from a person have so much control over us? Are we so volatile in our emotions that others have more power over our moods than we, ourselves, do?

Aren't we more than this? Aren't we bigger, more divine, and deeper than this? Isn't there more to this human existence than the law of action and reaction? We must learn to keep that light switch in our own hands and to give it only to God. Otherwise, we are switched on and off, on and off, all day long and the only effect is that the light bulb will burn out!

ARTICLES

Let us take whatever comes as *prasad*, as a gift from God. Let us remain calm and steady in the face of both prosperity and misfortune. We must not lose our vital energy in this constant action and reaction to everyone around us.

But how to remain unaffected by the waves of life? This is called spiritual practice! I always say that one of the best ways to learn "no reaction" is through silence. When we are anxious, angry, tense or frustrated, we tend to say things which we later regret; we tend to let our words fuel the reaction in our hearts. So, let us learn the power of silence. Silence on the outside will lead to silence on the inside. This is why so many saints and other spiritual people have periods of silence; it is a time of remembering that we are more than our reactions, a time of tuning in to the Divine Insurance Company, a time of charging our inner batteries.

So, let us learn to meet life's waves with silence – that will make "no reaction" much easier to achieve.

There was once a huge elephant crossing a wooden bridge high above a raging river. The bridge was old and rickety and it shook under the weight of the elephant. As the elephant was crossing the bridge he heard a voice saying, "Son, Son!" The elephant looked around him, but he was all alone. "Son, Son!" the voice continued. When the elephant reached the other side of the river, he saw a small ant crawl onto his nose. "Son!" the ant cried. "We almost collapsed that bridge, didn't we? Our weight was so great, so immense that the bridge almost collapsed beneath us, didn't it son?" The elephant of course knew that the ant's weight had been completely irrelevant to whether the bridge would have collapsed, and he of course knew that the tiny ant was not his mother. However, what good would it have done to engage in a battle of egos with the ant? Instead, the wise, calm elephant simply said, "You are right, Mother, our weight almost broke the bridge."

The elephant retained his serenity, peace and joy. The ant, for what it's worth, was allowed to continue believing in its own greatness. But, how many of us could be like the elephant? Aren't we always trying to prove ourselves to others? Aren't we always ready to shoot down anyone who trespasses on our egos?

We must emulate the grace and divinity of the elephant who knew that only harm would come from a fight. We must make "no reaction" the *sutra*, the *mantra* for our lives. Then, and only then, will we know real peace.

INTROSPECTION: So in the morning we begin with meditation. All day we practice no reaction. And at night? Introspection. At the end of the day, a good businessman always checks his balance sheet: how much has he made, how much has he spent? Similarly, a good teacher reviews her students' test scores: how many passed, how many failed?

By looking at their successes and failures, they assess how well they are doing. Are the businessman's profits greater than his losses? Are most of the teacher's students passing the exams?

In the same way, each night we must examine the balance sheet of our day: what were our successes, what were our failures? For all the successes, all our "plus-points," we must give credit to God, for we have truly done nothing but let Him work through us. All credit goes to Him. He is the one who saves us, who maintains our dignity and maintains our success.

Just imagine if God had put one television screen on our foreheads and everything we thought was broadcast for the whole world to see! All our reactions, all our inner sarcastic comments, all our judgments, all our weaknesses....just imagine! We would never succeed nor would we have many friends! Isn't it true?

It is by His grace that the world does not see our thoughts, that only He sees our thoughts. For this, we thank Him. We can say, "Thank You, God, for bringing success to this venture," or, "Thank You God for letting me truly make a difference in someone's life today," or simply, "Thank You God for all that went well today."

We must also give our failures to Him. The fault is definitely ours, yet He is so forgiving and so compassionate that He insists we turn these over to Him as well. We must say, "God, please take these minus points. You know that I am weak, you know that I am nothing. See all my failures, all my minus points for even just one day. I cannot go even one day without accumulating so many minus points. But, still You love me. Still You protect me from having the world see all my minus points. I am so weak, but You protect me." In this way, each night we check our balance sheet, and we pray to God to help us have fewer minus points, to make us stronger, to make us better hands doing His work, to give us more faith and more devotion.

If we practice these three points every day then our lives will become beautiful. Just as a serious daily *asana* practice can bring the glow of health to our body, a serious daily practice of meditation, no reaction and introspection can bring the glow of peace, joy and divinity to our lives.

The Eight Limbs of Yoga

Yoga is not only about making our bodies healthy, strong and flexible. It teaches us to make ourselves healthy, strong and flexible.

The secrets of the ancient science of yoga were passed down from the divine *rishis*, saints and sages who came to the Himalayas for divine inspiration. Through their meditation, austerities and prayers, a treasure chest of wisdom was bestowed upon them for the benefit of humanity.

The sage Patanjali is the one most renowned for compiling this treasure chest of yogic wisdom for the benefit of the world.

Yoga is not a religion. It does not require you to believe in a certain God or to chant certain mantras. It is an ancient science which leads to health in the body, peace in the mind, joy in the heart and liberation of the soul.

These days people take yoga classes to learn all about the various techniques of *hatha yoga*, *pranayama*, and meditation. But yoga is more than that. Yoga is a way of life, and its teachings should penetrate every aspect of your being – from your actions to your speech to your thoughts.

A *hatha yoga* session has a beginning and an end. You start at 8:00 for instance, and you finish at 9:00. Your *pranayama* has a beginning and an end. You start at, say, 6:00 and finish at 7:00. Even meditation – at least in the beginning – has a fixed starting point and a fixed ending point. You sit in meditation for a certain number of minutes or hours each day.

Yoga as Union

Yoga encompasses *asana* (the postures) and *pranayama* (the breathing exercises), but ultimately the word *yoga* means union. Union of what? Union of the self to the Divine. That oneness with the Divine is what we are striving for in our lives.

Lack of unity is the cause of all problems in the world – both on a personal level and on a global level. Personally, we are not united with ourselves. We are constantly at war between our mind and our heart, our desires, our fears, and our confusions. There is no balance, no harmony, and no unity within ourselves. We feel alone, we feel scared, we feel that everything is on our own shoulders. The divine union is not there.

In our families unity is not there. Frequently we are fighting with each other, manipulating each other, and criticizing each other.

In our communities unity is lacking. "I do Iyengar yoga. I do Anasura yoga. I do Bikram Yoga. I do Kundalini Yoga. My type of yoga is better than your type of yoga." Even though we are all practicing the art of union, we are still divided!

And of course in our world we are divided – by nations, by religions, by color. Yoga therefore, in its fullest and most complete meaning, is truly the *panacea* for all that ails us and for all that divides us, from the most basic personal level to the most complex global level.

So how to find that union? How to become united?

8 Limbs of Yoga

In his compendium of wisdom, inspiration and insight titled the *Yoga Sutras*, Patanjali explains yoga as an eight-limbed tree, with the highest branch being *Samadhi*, the ultimate, divine bliss and ecstasy which comes from a complete, transcendental union with the Divine.

The foundation of the tree are the *yamas* and *niyamas* (the moral and ethical code of conduct). Afer this foundation, one begins to move upward through *asana* and *pranayama,* which use the body and the breath as the medium, then into the aspects of yoga in which one's mind becomes fine-tuned and united with God, ultimately to the state of divine liberation.

When I talk about attaining liberation, I am not talking only about an abstract and vague concept in which – after death – you merge into Oneness with the Divine. I am talking about liberation here on Earth. Liberation while living. Liberation every moment of every day. What is that liberation? It is liberation from anger. Liberation from greed. Liberation from worry. Liberation from desires. Liberation from despair. Liberation from depression.

One has to begin at the foundation and move upwards. Let us take these eight limbs of the tree of Yoga – the tree of Divine Union – one by one and see what they mean for us in our lives.

Yamas and Niyamas

We begin at the foundation with the *yamas* and *nimayas.* Oneness with God, unwavering peace, ecstatic joy, and ultimate fulfillment in life – of our external, physical desires as well as our internal, spiritual desires – can only come if we abide by the natural laws of *dharma.* These laws are delineated simply and comprehensively in the first two "limbs" of the *yamas* and *niyamas.*

The five *yamas* are the moral restraints and injunctions which, when followed with dedication and discipline, help us become the master of our bodies, minds and lives. The five *yamas* are:

1. **Ahimsa – non-violence.** This is the fundamental, most basic and crucial tenet of living as a good human: do not cause pain or injury to another. However, *ahimsa* does not pertain only to our physical actions. It does not simply mean, "Thou shalt not kill," or, "Thou shalt not hit." Rather, it encompasses all forms of violence – violence in thought, violence in speech and violence in deed. We must think pure and loving thoughts. We must speak pure and loving words, and we must practice pure and loving acts.

Further, *ahimsa* does not only call upon us to live peacefully with other human beings. Rather, the meaning of *ahimsa* encompasses all beings, all creatures, all life on the planet. It includes the animals as well as Mother Nature. This means of course that one should be a vegetarian and shun products which are made through violence to animals (either through using animal products or through cruel testing on the animals). It also means that one must take care of Mother Nature, protecting and preserving our natural resources.

Moreover, the law of *ahimsa* goes even deeper than that which we do to others. It also includes that which we do to ourselves. When we smoke cigarettes, take drugs, eat food that we know leads to heart disease or diabetes, get involved in relationships in which we are abused, victimized and suppressed, or when we simply waste our precious time engaged in meaningless activity – these are all ways in which we injure ourselves.

2.   *Satyam – truthfulness*. This tenet also goes deeper than its surface meaning. Yes, of course we must speak the truth. But, that is not enough to say we are practicing *satyam*. We must also live the truth. Our thoughts, our values, our words and our actions all must be aligned. So many times we say one thing in front of others, or in the temple, or to impress people, but we act in a different way. I have even heard parents tell their children, "Do as I say, not as I do." This is not *satyam*. *Satyam* means: "As I say, so I do." *Satyam* means being true to our promises and vows, fulfilling our word to ourselves, to others and to God.

But *satyam* doesn't mean we have to tell everything. I have seen, particularly in the West, people who are on a spiritual path think that being truthful means telling 100% of the truth in all circumstances to everyone. This is not the case. Our scriptures clearly say that we should practice that speech which is truthful *and* kind and beneficial. So, if the truth is neither kind nor beneficial to the listener, then it should not be spoken.

3.   *Asteya – non-stealing*. *Asteya* is not as simple as refraining from stealing a possession that belongs to someone else. We steal much from others without realizing it. We steal people's time by wasting it engaged in idle gossip or complaints. We steal people's credit by claiming to have done something that actually was accomplished by someone else. We steal from Mother Earth by using more than we need – by driving cars that are too big and use too much fuel, by building homes larger than our requirements, by purchasing more and more unnecessary possessions which are made using natural resources and whose production pollutes the atmosphere. We steal the dignity, the safety and the health of the poor when we purchase things that were made by indigent people in deplorable conditions. Further, if God has blessed us with prosperity and we have enough to help others, it is stealing if we do not share our wealth. We must realize the joy that comes from sharing with others. Life is for sharing and caring. Life is for giving.

4. Brahmacharya – sensual restraint. *Brahmacharya* is frequently translated as celibacy or abstinence, but its meaning is actually more comprehensive than refraining from sexual activity. Rather, it actually means one who is *brahma-acharya*, one whose actions are all dedicated to God, one whose actions are all pure and holy. It means one whose attention, energy and life are focused on God. These *yamas* and *niyamas* are not applicable only to celibates, *sanyasis* or monks. Rather they were laid out for all times, for all of humanity. The law of *brahmacharya* pertains to those on the householder path.

So what does it mean? It means restraint. It means moderation. It means realizing that the purpose of life is much greater and far deeper than continually fulfilling one's sexual urges. It means that all of our relationships should be ones in which we are moving closer and closer to the Divine. We should not entertain any relationships in our lives which are taking us off the track of our spiritual growth. By over-engaging in sexual activity, our minds and attention gets diverted and our vital energy gets dissipated. So, even if you are married, still one must try as much as possible to move beyond the realm of the body to the realm of the spirit. We must ensure that those relationships we have, which do include physical intimacy, are loyal, are honest, are loving and are dedicated to bringing us closer and closer to God.

5.   *Aparigraha – non-accumulation*. *Aparigraha* literally means "non-hoarding." It means not taking more than one needs in any area of life. Mahatma Gandhiji said beautifully, "There is more than enough for everyone's need, but not enough for any man's greed." It means, live simply. Use only that which you require. Purchase only that which is essential. It doesn't mean that everyone must live like a wandering monk, but it means that we must cultivate a sense of moderation and simplicity; regardless of our financial means, we should not live extravagantly or surround ourselves with unnecessary possessions.

Travel light! If you came here for the weekend and brought ten suitcases full of different fancy yoga clothes, fashionable suits for every activity, and other unnecessary items, you would go through a very difficult time at the airport! They would charge you for all the excess baggage, and you would hurt your back and arms trying to lift everything! Then, it would take you a very long time to get from baggage claim to the car, from the car to the hotel, from the hotel to your room, and so on. Your room would be cluttered with so many suitcases and you would never be able to find what you were looking for!

But, if you came with just one small bag with the bare necessities – clean clothes for each day, your bathroom articles, a good book to read – you'd pass easily through every step of the journey. You would never be weighed down, slowed down, or inconvenienced, and you wouldn't hurt your back!

The same is true in life also. The more we try to accumulate, the more we acquire, the more we get bogged down and the more difficulties we face. So, travel light in life and you will find that you progress quickly and easily.

Aparigraha also means that there should be no sense of "mine" in life. We must realize that everything is God's and we have simply been lent a certain amount for a temporary period of time. In *yagna* ceremonies, after each mantra, the priest chants *"idam namamah."* It means, "Not for me, God. It is for You, God." This is *aparigraha.* Nothing is mine. Everything is His. Everything is for Him.

We also have five *niyamas* – the spiritual and ethical observances which, once we have mastered our bodies and minds through the practice of the *yamas*, will take us higher on the spiritual path. In Sanskrit, the word *"niyama"* means a rule, a law or a standard practice. These five *niyamas* are internal laws, rules which we set for ourselves to live a spiritual, ethical, and *dharmic* life.

1. Suacha – purity. *Suacha* means "cleanliness and purity," but it does not simply imply that one must bathe each day and keep one's fingernails clean. Rather, it pertains to a deeper level of purity – purity on the inside, purity of thought, and purity of action. We must purify our thoughts through *japa*, meditation and the practice of positive thinking. We must purify our lives by ensuring that our actions are models of integrity, *dharma* and righteousness. *Suacha* also pertains to that which we allow to enter our bodies and minds – what food we take through our mouths and what "food" we take through our ears and eyes. True *suacha* means refraining from putting anything impure into our being – this includes everything ranging from drugs and cigarettes to negative gossip to violent music lyrics to pornography. Practicing *suacha* is like taking perfect care of your brand new car. If you had a $100,000 new Mercedes, you would only put the most expensive, purest quality gasoline in the tank. You would never fill it up with cheap, bad quality gas and you certainly would never dump mud into the engine! Yet, our divine selves are more valuable than the most valuable car, and we continually fill them with low-quality, impure junk!

2. Santosha – contentment. In life, it is tragic that no matter what we have, we always want more. It is a disease of the human mind: we are rarely, if ever, satisfied. The irony is that even as we earn more and more, buy more and more, acquire more and more, and achieve more and more, our hunger for possessions and achievement only grows! It is a disastrous paradox. Our scriptures say that whatever we are given we should accept as *prasad* from God. One of the most important personal characteristics toward which

---

we should strive is the "attitude of gratitude." In our prayers that we chant each morning, there is a beautiful line which says, *"Sita Ram, Sita Ram, Sita Ram kahiye, jahi vidhi rakhe Rama, tahi vidhi rahiye."* It means that we should be thankful to God and keep chanting His holy name regardless of the condition in which He keeps us. We should accept more and expect less. Expectation is the mother of frustration and acceptance is the mother of peace and joy.

3.   *Tapas – austerities or* **sadhana**. Through the performance of regular *tapas*, we learn to be the master of our body and mind. Due to our lifelong and misguided identification with *maya* (illusion), we spend our lives entrapped by the belief that we are at the beck and call of our mind, emotions and senses. We unconsciously yet readily hand over the reigns of our lives to our volatile mind and insatiable senses! *Tapas* puts the control back into our hands, into the hands of our higher Self. *Tapas* does not mean only doing *japa* or fasting or doing a certain number of *ahutis* in the *yagna*. *Tapas* can extend to every area of our lives. *Tapas* is being nice to our mother-in-law. *Tapas* is not shouting back when our husband or wife gets angry. *Tapas* is the practice of tolerance.

In our lives, we tend to act based only on instinct, like animals. When the feeling of anger washes over us like a wave, we yell and lash out at others. When the feeling of hunger creeps into our stomachs, we eat. When we are overcome by feelings of lust, we engage in sexual behavior. Through practicing *tapas*, we learn to have control over ourselves so that we can choose whether to act or not. *Tapas* teaches us that we are not merely lightbulbs which can be switched on and off by the incessantly vacillating mind and senses.

4.   *Swadhayay – sacred study*. *Swadhayay* typically means study of the scriptures. It is very important to read something spiritual and inspiring every day. This helps us to stay on track and keep our mind pure. Otherwise, we tend to get lost in our own mind's sea of confusion. However, it is important to remember that scriptural study – although it is crucial – is not, by itself, a complete spiritual path. It is only one of the ten *yamas* and *niyamas*. Simple reading of the scriptures does not take you to *Samadhi*. One must also put

these readings into practice. One must *live* the scriptures, not just read a few chapters every morning or every evening.

Further, *Swadhaya* also means self-study. Introspection is one of the greatest tools of a spiritual path. Our egos, our fears, our desires, our misconceptions and even just the hecticness of our lives keep us from truly examining our own lives. Each night we must ask ourselves, "Where do I stand? Am I progressing further and further on the spiritual path?" A good businessman always examines his balance sheets in order to see whether he is in the red or in the black. Similarly, we must examine the balance sheet of our lives.

5.   *Ishwara pranidhana – devotion or surrender to God.* This is the final, ultimate commandment of leading a *dharmic* life. It doesn't matter what name or what form of the Divine you worship. What matters is that you are surrendered fully to God. Only through living for Him and dedicating all our actions to Him can we find peace, joy and meaning in life. There is a beautiful mantra in our scriptures which says:

> *Kaayena vaachaa manasendriyairvaa*
> *Buddhyaatmanaa vaa prakriteh svabhaavaat*
> *Karomi yadyat sakalam parasmai*
> *Naaraayanaayeti samarpayaami*

It means, "Oh Lord, whatever I have done, whatever actions I have performed – whether through speech, through thought, through my senses, through my mind, through my hands or through just the nature of my existence – I lay it all at Your Holy Feet. Every aspect of my life and existence are completely surrendered to You."

Universal Rules

These moral and ethical principles affect us whether we believe in them or not. People may say, "But, I'm not Indian," or, "I'm not Hindu, so I don't have to follow these ethical laws." However, this is not true. As I mentioned, yoga is not a religion. That means *none* of the eight aspects depends upon one's spiritual belief system. Just as *shirshasana* is beneficial whether one "believes" in it or not, similarly these moral and ethical laws of the universe affect us whether we believe in them or not.

They are like the law of gravity. One can certainly stand on the top of a ten-story building and say, "I don't believe in gravity so I am going to jump." As one falls through the sky, one may temporarily think one has succeeded in defying this pervasive law. Yet, inevitably, one will hit the ground and one's life breath will be immediately whisked away.

Similarly, people may live lives full of greed, anger, lust, arrogance, and disregard for their fellow humanity for many years, thinking they are immune to these natural laws which affect us all. Yet eventually, they too will hit the ground and be destroyed.

I remember once, when I entered customs in Japan, I saw a sign that said, "Follow the rules and enjoy your stay." It is like that in life as well.

Asana

After we master the do's and don'ts of a yogic life, we are ready to move into *asana*. *Asana* is typically translated as the physical postures, the parts we associate as "yoga." But actually, *"asana"* means a seat upon which you sit. This is a very, very important distinction.

There is a line in the sixth chapter of the *Bhagavad Gita* in which Lord Krishna, as He explains to Arjuna about yoga, says the following:

> *Tatraikaagram manah kritwaa yatachittendriyakriyah;*
> *Upavishyaasane yunjyaadyogamaatmavishuddhaye*

It means the following: "There, having made the mind one-pointed, with the actions of the mind and the senses controlled, let him, seated on the seat, practice *yoga* for the purification of the self."

Do you see the distinction? *Asana* is the seat upon which one sits to practice yoga! *Asana* is *not* the yoga. It is just the preparation for the yoga. The same is true whether you translate *asana* as a seat or as a physical posture. In both cases it is just the preparation for the true yoga – the union of the Self!

The posture are very important. In order for one to truly be able to practice the depths of yoga, the *asana* must be perfect, but we must realize it does not stop there.

One cannot sleep if one is standing up, one must lie down. But, that does not mean that the *asana* of lying down is the same as sleep. It just readies us for sleep. Sitting at the table with our food in front of us is not the same thing as eating dinner. Sitting is important. One shouldn't eat standing up or running around or driving one's car! But, sitting at the table in the proper posture with the spoon in hand is not the same as eating! It just prepares us to eat dinner. Similarly, we must not stop with the *asana*. The *asana* readies us for the higher limbs of yoga.

Another important point about *asana* is that it must be graceful, stable and done with ease. Patanjali says *"Sthira sukham asanam"*: that which is stable, that which is comfortable, is *asana*. He doesn't say, "That which is the most complex, most difficult, most strenuous, and most impressive-looking is *asana*," but rather, "That which is stable, that which is comfortable." So, even though we may be learning advanced postures, we must never lose the stability, the grace or the comfort which is an inherent part of *asana*.

Pranayama

As we learn to get in touch with our breath – our *prana*, our lifeforce – we come into contact with the very divine force which sustains our existence and unites us with the rest of the world. *Prana* literally means "the life force," the energy which flows through all. It can be physical energy, mental energy, intellectual energy or even magnetic or heat energy! *Ayama* means "to expand." So, *pranayama* is the extension, the stretching, the prolonging of our life force and energy.

Pranayama teaches us to be calm, collected and centered. As the breath becomes still, slow, deep and steady, we find that in our lives also we become steady and still. We learn not to be ruffled by the ups and downs of life. We feel deeply connected to the very force that flows through each of us, giving us life.

Pratyahara

After *pranayama* is *pratyahara*, which is withdrawal of the senses. In life, we are aware of so many things – all that we see, hear, smell, touch and taste. We are filled with millions of sensory antennae all over our bodies which are constantly perceiving sights, smells, and sounds. In fact, we are flooded with sensory perceptions, so much that we frequently feel overloaded. "I need some quiet. I feel claustrophobic. I have a headache. I need to be alone. The world seems to be spinning." These are all examples of sensory overload. The more we are focused on outward awareness, the less time and energy we have to be focused on internal awareness.

Pratyahara is like taking all the millions of antennae all over our body and turning them from outward to inward – a total and complete withdrawal of all the senses, of all the organs of perception.

It is important to realize that *pratyahara* is not a dulling of the senses. Rather it is simply turning the object of our senses from the external to the internal. Thus, with the same keen awareness that we perceive the outside world, we are able to perceive the internal world.

Dharana

Dharana – the next step – is single-minded concentratio, single-pointedness. *Asana* taught us to control the body. *Pranayama* taught us to control the breath. *Pratyahara* taught us to control the senses. *Dharana* teaches us to control the mind.

There are a wide variety of objects of concentration one can use in *dharana*. A burning candle, an image of the divine, the ocean, the tip of one's own nose, the center between one's eyebrows, the sound of a mantra – these are all common objects. The point is to focus, to stop the incessant wanderings of the mind, to channel all thought-power in one direction, to teach us to be the masters of our own minds.

Usually our minds are the masters and we are the slaves. Our minds are filled with anger, jealousy, lust, greed, fear, and desire, and we run around like servants answering every beck and call of the fickle mind. Through *dharana*, and then even more through *dhyana*, we learn that we are the masters and the mind is the slave.

Many people think that on a spiritual path one has to "overcome one's mind." This is not true. The mind is a wonderful thing. The mind, in many ways, is what makes us human rather than animal. It allows us to think, to plan, to have compassion, and to create. The problem comes when the mind becomes in charge! The mind should be a tool, just like the tongue is a tool. The tongue helps us to eat and thereby keeps us alive. But one would never turn over control to the tongue! Could you imagine? The person next to you in a restaurant is having an ice cream cone. Your tongue likes the taste of ice cream, so you automatically start to lick the person's ice cream cone. Or, your best friend walks into a party wearing a horrible, ugly dress. Your mind and heart know that you should not tell her it's ugly because she will be hurt. But if your tongue were in charge you would automatically shout, "Oh Mary! That is the ugliest dress I've ever seen!"

See what trouble we would be in if we gave control and power to any of our other senses? The same is true with the mind. It is a tool, and a helpful tool, but it should not be allowed to go wherever it wants and do whatever it chooses and control the whole show!

Dharana helps teach us that we are in charge. We are the boss. The mind is only a tool.

Dhyana

The last step before *Samadhi* is *dhyana*—meditation. I always say, "Meditation is the best medication for all agitations."

People frequently confuse concentration with meditation. They confuse *dharana* with *dhyana*. In concentration, there is a subject and an object. You, the subject, are concentrating on a candle, or an image of God, or the tip of your nose. These are the objects of your concentration. In meditation, the object disappears. The subject disappears. All becomes one. Rather than focusing on a mantra, you and the mantra become one.

In meditation, all borders, boundaries, and separation between ourselves and the universe begin to disappear. We begin to realize the inherent oneness of all beings and all of creation. There is a famous mantra that says "*So hum.*" It means: "I am that. I am one with the universal energy. I am part and parcel of all that exists. I am one with God." Through meditation, we catch a glimpse of that realization.

Meditation gets us back in touch with our true, divine nature and the deepest core of our being.

There is so much that has been written and taught on meditation and different meditation techniques. But, the important thing is that it is not so important which technique you use. Each of us is different. We all have different temperaments, different sensibilities. Therefore, different techniques will work for different people. There is no right or wrong way to meditate. What is important is that you are becoming more and more One with the Divine, that you are becoming more and more peaceful, more and more blissful, less and less affected by the waves in the ocean of life.

One thing is important to remember about meditation techniques: they are only techniques! A boat is very important to get you across the river to the other bank. But once you reach the other bank, you don't need the boat any more.

There is a funny story told of three men who were seen walking in the city carrying a canoe on their heads. When they were asked why they carried a canoe through the city, they answered, "We used to live in a small, poor village across the river from the city. We yearned to come to the city so we built this boat which ultimately took us across the river to the city."

"But why are you still carrying it?" they were asked. They replied, "We are so grateful to it for bringing us to the city that we do not want to let it go!"

We are the same with our meditation techniques sometimes. The technique is to get us to the state of meditation, but it is not the meditation itself! Meditation is very much like wiring a house. In the beginning, while the house is being made you have to spend a lot of time and a lot of energy putting down all the electrical wires. But, once it has been properly wired, then if you want to turn on the light you only have to plug it in! You do not have to re-wire the house! The same is true for meditation. Meditation is learning to plug yourself into the Divine Powerhouse, The Divine Energy Source! In the beginning, we need the technique; we are not connected. But once we are connected to the Divine, then we just have to close our eyes and we are there. Or, even with our eyes open, we are there.

So, do not hang on unnecessarily to one technique or another. They are all good. They are useful. They are necessary in the beginning. But realize the technique is just a technique to get you across the river. Once you've reached the other side, let go of the boat.

Samadhi

Last is *Samadhi*. Divine Union. Ecstasy. Bliss. *Samadhi* literally means "to merge, to come together. Here, the subject is completely lost. The object is completely lost. There are no boundaries, no barriers, and no separation. The lover and the beloved become one. Every cell of our being becomes saturated with God. We are no longer looking for Him or praying to Him. Rather we merge into Him like the rain drop merges into the ocean. All identity is lost. We are One with the Source.

Sometimes people think *Samadhi* means trance, a time in which all sense is lost and one becomes so immersed in the Divine that one loses all awareness of the outside world. This is also a definition of *Samadhi*, but it is not only in a trance.

One cannot live in a trance! The question and the key is how to attain a state of *Samadhi* that is with you all the time. Divine trance is beautiful, it is wonderful. But I want more than that for you all. I want you to attain a *Samadhi* that exists even when your eyes are open, even when you're moving in the world. That is possible.

When we attain *Samadhi* our lives become peaceful, joyful, and problem-free. Obstacles still come, but we are not affected by them. Ups and downs are there in life, but we do not go up and down. *Samadhi* is the divine shock-absorber! No matter how rough the road of life may be, we are smooth and shock-free.

Samadhi means that we have the reins of our lives only in our own hands, we cannot be switched on and off like lightbulbs by other people. We know that we are one with God and that oneness fills us with such peace, such bliss, such stability that nothing else can affect us.

Samadhi means, essentially, that our lives are lived in peace, not in pieces, and that is the ultimate goal of yoga – Divine Union.

I pray to the Lord Almighty that you may all walk the divine path of yoga with strength, courage and steadfastness, and that you may all stay committed to the goal. I pray that, through your practice of the seven limbs with devotion and perseverance, the grace of *Samadhi* may be showered upon you. You will then not only experience the path of yoga in a yoga class, but your life will become a path of yoga.

Pearls of Wisdom

Every day people come to me with problems for which they would like guidance. While the details vary from person to person and situation to situation, there are common themes that run through much of what ails us. The deeper questions, the questions beneath the questions are always the same: how can I be happy? How can I have meaningful relationships with others? There are so many deeply important principles to live by, so many lessons to be learned in this life on Earth. Below of just a few of these lessons.

I) Devote Your Life to God, Not Glamour

Every day people go out, go to work, earn money and become more and more prosperous. Yet, at the end of the day, when they return home, they are not happy. At night, when they lie in bed to go to sleep, their hearts are not peaceful, their minds are not at ease. There seems to be no correlation between the amount of money we earn, the number of possessions we buy and our sense of inner peace. Yet, if you ask people what they want most deeply out of life, they will say, "To be happy." How then can we find this happiness that appears so elusive? What is the true secret to internal peace and everlasting joy?

The secret is God and God alone. In India, in all villages, there is a temple. I remember when I was growing up, and it is still mostly true today, that first thing in the morning, everyone would go to the temple. Before beginning the day's tasks, everyone went to the temple, did *pranam* to God and took three *parikramas* (walking in a circle around Bhagwan). The point of this was not merely ritual. Rather, the *parikramas* signified, "God, I am about to go out and perform my worldly tasks, but let me always keep You in the center, let me remember that all work is for You." Then, they would take *prasad* – from their tongues to their souls God's sweetness would spread – and they would leave.

In the evening, before returning home, once again everyone went to the temple. "God, if during this day I have forgotten that You are the center of everything, please forgive me. Before I go home to my family, let me once again remember to Whom my life is devoted."

This still occurs in almost every village, especially the small ones, every day. People in those small villages have very little in terms of material possessions. Most of them live below the Western standards of poverty. Yet, if you tell them they are poor, they won't believe you, for in their opinion they are not. They have God at the center of their lives. Their homes may not have TV sets, but they all have small *mandirs*; the children may not know the words to the latest rock and roll song, but they know the words to *Aarti*; they may not have computers or fancy history textbooks, but they know the stories of the *Ramayana, Mahabharata,* and other holy scriptures; they may not begin their days with newspapers, but they begin with prayer.

If you go to these villages you may see what to you looks like poverty. But, if you look a little closer, you will see that these people have a light in their eyes, a glow on their faces and a song in their hearts that money cannot buy.

So, what is the meaning of this? It means, acquire possessions if you want to. Earn money if you want to. There is nothing wrong with being prosperous. It's wonderful. But, remember what is truly important in life, and that is God. Only He can put the light in your eyes, the glow on your face and the song in your heart.

II) Giving is Living

There is an old adage that says, "It is better to give than to receive." Yet, how many of us actually live by this? How many of us would give to another before taking for ourselves? It is not simple sacrifice I am talking about. Sacrifice implies some level of suffering.

It implies that one is forsaking something one wants out of duty to another. While there is a great deal of spiritual value in the lessons of sacrifice, this is not what I am talking about. For, in true giving, there is no suffering. One does not forsake anything. The giving itself becomes its own reward. People talk about cycles of life. For me, the true cycle is: giving is living, living is learning, learning is knowing, knowing is growing, growing is giving and giving is living. This is the true cycle of life.

The poet Khalil Gibran said beautifully, "All that we have will some day be given away. Let us open our hearts and give with our hands so the joy of giving is ours and not our inheritors'."

This is truly the message to live by. Embedded within this phrase are many important factors. The first is the fact that we can take nothing with us when we leave this Earth. We expend so much time, mental energy and physical energy to acquire material possessions. Yet, we come into this world with nothing and we leave with nothing but the *karma* accrued from the lives we lived. Hence, we must re-evaluate the drastic measures we take and the stress we go through to acquire more and more fleeting wealth. That which marks our life, that which lives on after we have departed, is that which we gave while we lived.

The second important message in the above phrase is the idea of the "joy of giving." Giving truly is a joy. We think we will be happy if we get this or get that. But, that happiness is transient. Watch a child with a new toy, for this is a beautiful example of the happiness which is possible through material wealth. The first minute, the child is ecstatic. Nothing else matters in the world; he can barely contain his exuberance. Within a mere few minutes though, you can see the child start to get a little bored. He looks around; what else does this toy do? Are there any other parts that came with it? Within a matter of hours the toy is lying behind the couch, and will only be picked up by the child's mother or father in an attempt to either straighten the house or re-stimulate the child's interest.

Yet, when the child's interest is completely faded, watch the child give this toy to a younger brother or sister. Watch how he loves showing what the toy can do, how he loves telling everyone that "I gave this toy," and how he loves watching his sibling enjoy it.

Isn't this how life is? The pleasure you get out of an old sweater, or a dress you wore once, or some mechanical appliance that you just "had to have," is minimal. Yet, take those clothes or appliances to a homeless shelter; donate them to someone in need – you will then know real joy, the joy of having given to someone else. This is a joy that will last. It will stay with you and never fade. In fact, it will inspire you to give even more. So many times we regret having bought something. "Oh, why did I waste my money?" we say. Yet, I have never once heard anyone regret that they gave something to someone in need. I have never heard anyone say, "Oh, why didn't I let that child go hungry?" or, "Why did I help that charity?"

So, remember, old adages may have a great deal of meaning for today. "It is better to give than to receive" is one of those adages.

III) Leaving is Always Losing

So many times in life, when something is not going our way, we attempt to solve the problem by leaving the unsatisfactory situation. Sometimes this works, but usually it doesn't.

The real lesson in life is to live with it, not to leave it. It is by living with situations that seem difficult that we can truly attain peace and non-attachment. It is in these circumstances that we learn that happiness can only come from God, not from one environment or another.

If you are with God, everywhere is Heaven, and you would never want to leave anywhere. You would see every place as an opportunity to learn, to grow or to serve. However, that is not how we usually live our lives. Instead, we say, "Oh, this is Hell!" and we leave. Yet, if He is with you, how can you be in Hell? Hell is due to lack of Him. If the spiritual corner in your heart is not there, you will be cornered everywhere. So, the goal of life is to develop that spiritual corner, to be with Him, not to leave where you are.

IV) *Be Devoted on the Inside, Perfect on the Outside*

Your mind should be always with Him, yet your hands should be doing His work. People think that in order to be spiritual, or to "be with God," one must be sitting in lotus posture in the Himalayas. This is not the only way. In the *Gita*, Lord Krishna teaches about *Karma Yoga*, about serving God by doing your duty. It is the duty of a few saints to live in *samadhi* in the Himalayas. Their vibrations and the global effect of their *sadhana* are extraordinary. However, that is not what most people's *dharma* is. We must engage ourselves in active, good service; that is truly the way to be with Him.

In one of our prayers, it says, *"Mukha mein ho Rama-nama, Rama-seva hatha mein."* This means, "Keep the name of the Lord on your lips and keep the service of the Lord in your hands." Let your inner world be filled with devotion to Him, and let your outer performance be filled with perfect work, perfect service.

I once heard a story about a man who spent forty years meditating so he could walk on water. He thought that if he could walk on water, then he had truly attained spiritual perfection, that he was then "one" with God. When I heard this story, I thought, why not spend forty rupees instead, sit in a boat to cross the water, and spend the forty years giving something to the world? That is the real purpose of life.

However, there must be both devotion and service. We cannot develop one at the expense of the other. We can't be truly perfect on the outside unless we are devoted on the inside, for only then will God's work shine through us in a beautiful and perfect way. Similarly, we cannot say we are truly devoted on the inside unless we are doing perfect work on the outside.

The pearls I have given you are only a few. However, like any precious jewels, they are priceless, regardless of the size. If you follow these and let them purify your life, they will bring you more prosperity than all the diamonds in the world.

Fasting

A fast is:	*A fast is not:*
About God	About food
A time of reflection	A time of hunger
For peace of the body, mind and spirit	For *pakoras, phalahari chapatis,* and *puris*
A day of discipline	A day of dieting
To purify you	To frustrate you

Today, fasting has become a great trend across the world. In any bookstore you will find volumes of literature extolling one fast or another – juice fasts, water fasts, fruit fasts, and so on. Fasting is frequently heralded as the "miracle weight loss" for those who have tried all else without success.

Connection with the Divine

However, while fasting is certainly of great health benefit, to define it merely as a type of "diet" is to undermine one of the oldest and most sacred spiritual practices. Fasting has been used for millennia by the *rishis*, saints and sages in order to purify their bodies, minds and souls and to bring every cell of their bodies into connection with the Divine.

A True Fast

A true fast, undertaken with understanding and discipline, has the ability to restore all systems of the body. The nervous, circulatory, digestive, respiratory and reproductive systems are all regenerated. The toxins and impurities in our blood and tissues are eliminated and our system becomes rejuvenated. The majority of all today's terminal illnesses are rooted in over-consumption, so a fast purifies our bodies from the excess of not only food but also preservatives, chemicals and toxins.

A fast also is one of the best ways of controlling our mind and senses. Fasts have been used for millennia to subdue passion, anger and lust. They allow us to withdraw our senses from the outside world and become refocused on our own divine nature and our connection to God. Additionally, during this period of *sadhana*, austerity, and restraint one realizes that one is truly the master of one's body, not vice versa.

Unfortunately, many people in the Indian community seem to have forgotten much of the purpose of a fast. Today, you will see people with plates overflowing with *puris* and *pakoras* who say they are fasting. There are *phalahari chapatis*, *saboodana kichari* and so many other hearty foods that we barely even notice it is a fast. I have heard that there is even a recipe for *phalahari* pizza dough!

On the one hand, it is wonderful to see such a proliferation of the idea of *phalahar* (the taking of foods not made from cereals, such as fruits), and I am glad to see that observing weekly fasts, or fasts on Ekadashi, are rituals which have not been lost as we enter the 21st century.

However, it is crucial to pause and reflect on what we are calling a "fast," for although the idea of fasting is still upheld with great fervor, its true meaning and purpose can be obscured by the latest *phalahar* recipes.

Upvas

In Sanskrit, the word for fast is *upvas*. *Upvas* literally means, "sitting near to." Sitting near to whom? Near to God.

Fasting is a time in which our bodies are light, a time in which our vital energy is not being dissipated through the process of consumption and digestion, a time in which we are free from the heaviness and lethargy resulting from over-indulgence.

However, a fast is not meant to be merely a refrain from eating. In fact, it is not necessary to refrain entirely from food on the day of a fast. Fruits and milk enable our bodies to remain strong and active while simultaneously giving us the benefit of a "fast." *Upvas*, however, is not as simple as reducing one's caloric intake or avoiding certain foods. *Upvas* is not a time in which only our stomach is free from excessive external stimulation. It is not a time of mere restraint of the tongue. *Upvas* should be a time in which all of our organs are restrained. It should be a time in which all of our organs are purified, a time in which every sense is turned toward the Divine.

Our tongues should refrain from both indulgence in food and drink, as well as from indulgence in speech. A fast should be a time during which we observe as much silence as possible, for we lose much of our vital energy in speech, and through speech our focus becomes diverted outward.

A Fast For All Senses

We tend to think that we only "eat" through our mouths, that our meals are the only "food" our bodies get. However, what we hear, what we see, what we touch – all these things are taken into our bodies as food. Just as pure, wholesome food brings us health of the body, pure wholesome sights, sounds and other stimuli bring health to the mind, heart and soul. Therefore, when we undertake a fast, we must be equally as aware of purifying the food that we take in through our eyes, ears and hands as we are of the food that we take in through our mouths.

During our fast, our ears should refrain from hearing anything other than chanting of the Lord's name, positive conservation which is peaceful, pious and beneficial, or the quiet of our own thoughts. During a fast we should not listen to music with harsh lyrics, watch TV, or be part of idle gossip. So frequently we see people at temple who have spent the whole day "fasting" who then come to the temple and huddle together, gossiping and chatting. Their bodies may be hungry, but their souls have not fasted.

Additionally, that which we see – frequently without even noticing it – penetrates our minds and hearts and changes our perspective. The simple sight of a woman's bare leg may arouse lust in an otherwise simple and pious man; the sight of blood might cause nausea and panic in one who is usually calm; the sight of a enemy might immediately evoke animosity in one who is usually peaceful and loving.

When we fast we must limit all stimuli which we perceive. That is why we should "sit near to God." Sit at the temple – either the temple in your home or in the actual *mandir*. Or, if you prefer, be with nature. Just make sure that as much as possible the sights and the sounds which you "imbibe" during your fast are pure, pious, loving and filled with divinity. Even if you go to work or to school during your fast, try as much as possible to avoid those situations in which you will see or hear things that are arousing, disturbing or distracting. If there is a way to drive to work or school that may be perhaps a few minutes longer but takes you through a tree-lined road rather than the packed freeway, take the nicer drive. If you can spend your lunch break walking in a park or with your eyes closed in meditation, do that instead of sitting in a cafe with your friends. Remember, a fast is not every day.

A day of fasting should be a special day of purification and remembrance of God. Try to take steps that remind you throughout the day that you are "fasting" all of your senses.

During a fast we should also try to quiet our minds as much as possible. So much of our energy is drained each day in our cease-less, incessant thought process. Frequently this leads only to more confusion and more questions. Therefore, as we give our bodies a rest from digesting food in our stomachs, as we give our ears a rest from digesting impure thoughts, and as we give our eyes a rest from digesting over-stimulating or sensual sights, let us also give our minds a rest from having to digest our thousands upon thousands of thoughts each day.

Weekly Fasts

Many people fast on a particular day of the week. You will notice, for example, on Monday that many people will say, "This is my fast."

The days of the Indian week are in honor of a particular deity or aspect of the Divine. Monday, Somvar, is the day dedicated to Lord Shiva. Tuesday, Mangalvar, is the day dedicated to Hanu-manji. Thursday, Guruvar, is the day dedicated to the Guru. It is said that on these particular days, that aspect of the Divine is in the nearest reach of the devotee. So, for example, devotees of Lord Shiva will observe a fast on Mondays in order to offer their respects to the Lord and to seek His blessings. Seekers who are strongly devoted to their Guru will observe a fast on Thursdays, in order to feel "one" with the Guru and to remember Him throughout the course of the day.

However, sometimes we see that these fasts have become merely ritual; the spiritual aspect has been lost in many cases. People ob-serve fast because they've done it for years, or because their parents did it, or because they were instructed to do so. It is a rare and truly divine devotee who truly remembers, throughout the course of the day, that aspect of the divine for whom they are fasting.

Indian culture and Hindu tradition are meant to bring us into close contact with the Divine. They are meant to open up the infinite, glorious channel between us and God. These rituals were given to help us step out of the mundane world and re-realize our divine connection.

The point of a fast is to be light so we can sit comfortably in meditation. The point is to have our energy turned away from food, away from the mundane world and to the divine. The energy which our body saves on digestion gets channeled toward both physical repair of the body as well as toward vital spiritual *Shakti*. The point of being a little hungry is that it reminds us of why we are fasting.

I heard a beautiful story of a great saint who could cure lepers of their oozing wounds. One day, a very sick man came to the saint and she carefully laid her hands over his gaping wounds, and they each instantaneously healed beneath the touch of her divine hands. However, when she sent him away, she had left one wound untreated. Her devotees questioned her, asking why. Since she clearly had the ability to cure all the wounds, why would she leave one bleeding? Her answer was beautifully apt. She said, "Because it is that one bleeding wound which will keep him calling out to God."

Our lives are extremely busy and filled with so many small errands, appointments and pleasures that we rarely find the time to remember God. I always say that we tell our loved ones, "Oh, I miss you, I miss you," if they are gone for only a few days. But, do we ever find ourselves, with tears streaming down our faces because we are missing God? Those who do are very rare and very divine. Typically, we tend to remember God when there is adversity. Our child is in the ICU after a car accident and so we start to religiously chant mantras. We find a lump in our wife's breast, and we start going religiously to the temple. We are hoping for a promotion at work and so we perform *yagna*. This is not wrong. It is human nature. We are very busy the rest of the time, and we mostly find ourselves turning to God when we need Him.

So, when our *rishis* and saints urged people to fast, part of the reason was to remember God. As we are hungry, we remember, "Oh, yes, today I am fasting." This rememberance that we are fasting then makes us remember God. Even if we cannot take the day off work to sit in *puja* or meditation, the constant feeling of mild hunger in our bodies will still keep us connected to the reason for the fast, and thus we will be reminded of God throughout the day.

That doesn't mean we must starve ourselves completely. Those who are working or going to school or whose health does not permit them to fast should not worry. Take fruit, take nuts, take milk. However, try to take as little as is necessary for you to do your daily tasks. Try to leave enough empty room in your stomach that the emptiness causes you to remember that you are fasting. If we fill our stomachs with *pakoras* and *ladoos* and fried potatoes, are we likely to remember God? Try to eat only those things which are easily digestible and thus preserve the vital energy of the body.

The ideal is to remember God all the time. The ideal is that He should be ever with us, ever such an integral part of our minute-to-minute, moment-to-moment existence that we never feel separate. But, this is rare for people, especially for those who are living in the West (or in Westernized India) and are constantly inundated with tasks and jobs and propaganda telling them that they must buy more, own more and obtain more. Amidst all this, many, understandably, find it difficult to keep God in the center of their lives. That is the beauty of the fast – even unconsciously, you are reminded every moment that "Today is a special day. Today I am fasting for Hanumanji [or for Lord Shiva, or for my Guru.]"

If we satiate our hunger with platefuls of *phalahar*, then in many ways we have defeated the purpose.

Ekadashi

Twice a month we observe Ekadashi. The eleventh day of each lunar cycle (both lunar fortnights) is observed as a special Ekadashi fast. There are many Ekadashis during the course of the year, each with a slightly different significance. The importance of observing Ekadashi is written in both the *Puranas* as well as in the *Upanishads*. It is said that by observing one Ekadashi fast with reverence, devotion, purity and strictness, one attains all of the benefits of performing a wide range of extended austerities.

However, Ekadashi is of an importance far greater than simply the restraint from rice and grains. It symbolizes the control of the mind.

Our *Upanishads* say that to control the mind is the greatest task and the greatest accomplishment. They say that when the mind is under control, all else – the senses, the body – will follow. *"The body is the chariot, the senses are the horses pulling the chariot, and the mind is the driver with the reigns in his hands."* So, if the driver is calm, pious and peaceful, he will drive the horses, and thereby the chariot, toward peace, love and God. But, if the driver is tempestuous and intractable, then the horses jump and buck wildly, leading the chariot to thrash here and there, eventually collapsing upon itself.

Our scriptures say we have ten sense organs, and the mind is the eleventh. Ekadashi stands for the eleventh, and since the moon is symbolic of the mind, the eleventh day of the lunar cycle thus becomes especially conducive to practices which teach us control of the mind.

Ekadashi is, therefore, a fast for the control of the mind. It is said that if a seeker observes even one Ekadashi with true commitment, faith and devotion and if the seeker keeps his mind entirely focused on God during the course of the Ekadashi, this seeker will be free from all *karmic* cycles of birth and death.

The *Puranas* encourage complete fasting on Ekadashi, but they allow those who are weak to take roots, fruit, milk and water. This is important, because the scriptures specifically state that this is only for those who are weak. Today, however, we can also extrapolate from that to mean those who would become weak (and therefore unable to perform their tasks) if they abstain completely from all food. There are many students and others whose jobs or studies are so taxing and straining that the body requires some caloric intake. For these people, it is fine to take fruit, juices and milk. But, unless it is necessary, people should refrain as much as possible from eating at all on the Ekadashi fast. When it is necessary, fruits and milk should be taken in their purest, simplest, most unadulterated forms.

Further, it is said that the day of Ekadashi is meant to be spent chanting the holy names of Vishnu and performing sacred Vishnu *puja*. If we are able to take the day off of work and do this, it is wonderful. If not, we should be sure that at least some time is spent in the morning before leaving home, in meditation on the holy form of Vishnu and chanting His name. If we must be at school or work during the day, let us vow that at least every two or three hours we will take a five minute break and sit silently, chanting God's name. Let us also vow that when we return home at the end of the day we will spend special, extra time in meditation and in prayer. A fasting day should feel more divine and more holy than other days, but it is up to us to make the choices and decisions which will lead to that special feeling.

If we truly want to reap the spiritual and physical benefits of fasting, we must follow the principles laid out by the sages and saints. These principles urge us to refrain from filling any of our senses (mouths, eyes or ears) with that which is unholy, and urge us to spend our "fast" engaged in contemplation of the Divine.

Let us all vow to observe fasts. What exactly you eat or don't eat is not as important as the spirit in which the fast is done. Unless you are performing a very specific fast for a very specific occasion or ritual, the little details are not so important. What is important is that the day of the fast is a day that you are with God. Be light. Be restrained. Be disciplined. Be focused.

Worship of the Mother

(Note: This article was distilled from a speech by Pujya Swamiji addressed to Indians living abroad.)

One of the most important aspects of Hinduism is reverence for the Divine Feminine, the *Shakti*, in all Her myriad manifestations. However, although there are truly infinite ways to thank and worship the Mother, I feel that three ways are most important.

If we hold three of Her aspects close to our hearts, cherish them deeply and thank God for them every day, we can honestly say that we are worshipping the Goddess.

These three aspects are: your mother, your mother-land, and your mother-tongue.

Your Mother

A mother is truly divine. It is from her womb we have come. Our life is a gift from her own; our nourishment flowed from her body. The love that sustains us, that embraces our soul, ceaselessly streams from her heart.

When I say your "mother," I mean many things. Of course I mean the actual mother who gave you birth. But, I also mean the Divine Mother of all — the Goddess. In this Mother, we find not only our own mothers, but mothers everywhere. We find Mother Nature, Mother Earth, and Mother Ganga.

These Mothers must be seen as divine. For your own mother, this means treating her with respect, with love, and with patience. I know that when we are young, we tend to take our parents for granted, or to become frustrated at their attempts to teach us. We must not do this. We must find, in our hearts, her own blood and her own life. For that is how connected we are.

For Mother Nature and Mother Earth this love and respect means protection. Mother Earth has given us all that we need to sustain our lives, and we are simultaneously destroying Her. Let us treat our Earth as a Mother. If our own mother were sick, we would not let her simply suffer, decay and die. We would fight tenaciously to bring her back to her full state of health and glory. Let us give the same to the real Mother. We must not pollute her or waste her. We must nurse her back to health.

Your Mother Land

Be Western (if you live in the West) when it comes to professional excellence, but be Indian in your domestic life, and in your heart. The West has a great deal to teach in terms of external perfection, especially in professional, business and engineering arenas. But, we must not lose our souls in this attainment of external success. Our bodies and our brains may be in the West, but our spirit must stay with our Mother land.

How to do this? First, have a "happy hour" in the evenings, but make it an Indian "happy hour." Make it an hour whose happiness lasts even when the sixty minutes are up, a happiness without a hangover, a happiness that runs to your soul, not just your bloodstream. The real happy hour is *puja*, *Aarti*, and being with your family. Wevspend so many hours each day being Western-ly perfect. Spend at least one hour being Indian-ly devoted. Then, you will see the real magic.

Maha Laxmi is the Goddess of Wealth. We pray to Her for prosperity. Yet, our real wealth lies in our heritage, in our roots, and in the ancient wisdom of our scriptures. Let us not forsake the everlasting richness of our culture in favor of transient material possessions. Before we pray for more wealth, let us treasure the wealth we have already been given. This is the real prosperity.

Your Mother-Tongue

Your mother tongue is the language of your soul. Your brain may think in English, your mouth may speak English, but your soul speaks the mother tongue (whether it is Hindi, Gujarati, Punjabi, Tamil, Kannad, Sindhi...). Do not cut yourself off from the words of your ancestors, for much of the wisdom and clarity is lost in translation.

A dog does not have to learn how to bark; a cat does not have to learn how to meow. A cow does not forsake her own natural "moo" for the chirping of the birds. It is wonderful that you are learning English and French and Spanish and German. These languages will be of a great help to you in your academic and professional lives. But, your mother tongue is the thread that connects you to your roots, to your family, and to your true essence. Do not sever this connection, for it is the tube through which your life-blood flows. How can you truly know a culture, be part of a heritage, if you cannot speak its language?

The Yagna of Mahatma Gandhi

Each year on August 15th, we celebrate India's independence, and on January 30th, we observe the anniversary of the assassination of Mahatma Gandhi. The former is an occasion for rejoicing, the latter an occasion for somber reflection. We won our independence but lost a beautiful soul, a true *Maha Atma* ("Great Soul"). As we revel in the joy of India's freedom, we must not forget the price we paid. Gandhiji was truly the saint of the century, and our *pranam* to him should be that we never forget the message of his life.

As we reflect on the greatness of Mahatma Gandhiji's life and the tragedy of his assassination, let us look not only at facts but also at meanings. What was the meaning of his life? What was the message of his death? What does he have to teach the world today?

All of these questions can be answered with the word "*yagna.*" *Yagna* was the spirit of his life and the message of his death. Every breath of his life, including the last, was an oblation to his country, his principles and his faith in God. The theme of his life was sacrifice.

Sacrifice for His Country

Mahatma Gandhi could have been a wealthy attorney. He could have had a life of relative ease and prosperity. However, he was a man devoted to his country and to Her freedom. Through his tireless effort and his simple piety he led India to independence. However, in spite of national and international acclaim, he never lost his humility, his dedication and his spirit of sacrifice. Rather, the flames of his true *yagna* to Bharat Mata seemed to only grow until he, himself, was the *poornahuti*, or final offering.

Typically in life, we always want to be the center of everything. We always want the focus on ourselves, the recognition for ourselves and the reward for ourselves. We do not actually work or accomplish anything meaningful, but we expend great effort trying to convince all those around us of our inestimable worth. However, Gandhiji was different. He did everything, accomplished everything. Yet he worked and lived with such humility and such piety that he never put himself in the center. A great message of his life was, "Work, serve with every breath, but remain a simple, humble, unattached child of God."

There is a story of a man traveling by train to Porbandar in the same coach as Gandhiji. However, the man did not know that the old man in his coach was Mahatma Gandhi. So, all night long this man lay down on the seat, occupied the entire bench in the coach, pushed Gandhi, put his feet on him, and left Gandhiji with barely enough room to sit upright. However, Gandhi did not fight, nor did he complain. How easy it would have been to proclaim, "I am Mahatma Gandhi. Give me room in the coach." But that is not the spirit of yagna.

As the train pulled into Porbandar, the man mentioned that he was going to see the famous Mahatma Gandhi. Gandhiji still remained silent. As Gandhiji descended from the train to a welcoming crowd of thousands, the man fell at his feet, begging for forgiveness. Gandhiji of course blessed and forgave him, telling him only that he should be more respectful of others, regardless of who they are.

That is the spirit of *yagna*. That is the spirit of India we must maintain in our hearts.

Another beautiful example of Gandhiji's humility, his selfless sacrifice for his country is how he "celebrated" his victory. When India won independence, when Gandhiji was the hero of the country, he could have been in New Delhi receiving boundless honors and appreciation. However, he was not. He was not in New Delhi, nor was he in Bombay, nor in Calcutta. He was nowhere that would shower him with love and esteem. Rather, he was in East Bengal where Hindus and Muslims were fighting bitterly. He was not content to have "fulfilled his mission." If humans were still suffering, then he still had work to do. So, while the rest of the country celebrated, Gandhiji continued his tireless work to heal the wound between Hindus and Muslims. This is the spirit of sacrifice. This is the spirit of divinity. Even when all external circumstances throw you to the center, you remain humble, you remain simple, you remember for whom your *yagna* is being performed. Gandhi's *yagna* was for his country, not for his own fame.

Sacrifice for the Principles of Right Living

However, his life was not only a sacrifice for Mother India. It was also a *yagna* of morality, of *dharma*, of ethics and of truth. How easy it would have been to fight with weapons; how easy to kill the enemy. How easy it would be to carry a gun to protect himself. Yet, the flames of Gandhi's *yagna* were fueled by non-violence. Wars throughout history had been won with weapons. Gandhi was devoted to proving that peace could only come through peace. People criticized him vehemently for refusing to take up arms; they claimed he was forfeiting India's fight for freedom. Yet, he simply kept pouring truth, piety, and *dharma* into the fire of his life *yagna*, and the flames rose in victory. This is the true meaning of *yagna*, for Gandhi sacrificed an easy win (or a quick loss) for India by refusing to engage in armed warfare. He sacrificed his popularity; he sacrificed his status as a fighter. Yet, the truth prevails and he is now remembered as one of the greatest leaders – both political and spiritual – that the world has ever known.

Sacrifice to God

Mahatma Gandhiji's life was in service to God. His work for his country and his tenaciously held values were part and parcel of his complete sacrifice to the Divine. The *Gita* was his closest companion and his most trusted guide.

So many people today claim that their lives and their work are "God's." Yet, they use this as an excuse to lie, to cheat, and even to kill. At the end it is clear that they merely used God's name in the service of themselves. Yet, Gandhiji was pure and his death is the clearest example. Due to his tenaciously held belief in *ahimsa* and his true surrender to God, he refused to employ a bodyguard. Hence, he was gunned down on his way to a prayer meeting. As he drew his last breath, there was no sign of fight, no break from his lifelong dedication to non-violence and to the Divine. He did not scream, "Who are you? How dare you! Somebody help me!" Rather, the only words that escaped from his lips were, "*He Ram, He Ram, He Ram.*" This is the spirit of *yagna*.

What Can We Learn?

So many people come and go in this world. So many people become famous through valiant efforts to "make a name for themselves." Yet, how many of these people have really left lasting impressions or have really changed the course of history? Very few. When we depart this Earth, when we leave our bodies, what is it that remains? It is that which we have given to the world. It is that for which we have sacrificed. It is the love and the peace that our presence brought to those around us. Gandhiji's name will live eternally not only because he brought independence to India. He will be remembered forever and revered forever because of the *way* he brought peace, because of the message of his life.

When Gandhiji was in South Africa, he was traveling by train and the conductor came, rudely telling Gandhi to leave. "But, sir, I have a ticket," Gandhi replied. The conductor violently threw him from the train and yelled, "You do not deserve to ride on this train!" Gandhi, however, did not raise an arm in his defense. Today, does anyone know the name of the man who threw him from the train? Of course not. But, today the name of that train is the "Mahatma Gandhi Train," and the name of the station is "Mahatma Gandhi Station"! That is the spirit of *yagna*.

Gandhi would not have wanted to be remembered only in history books. He would not want to be remembered only as the politician who led India to independence. He would want his message to live on; he would want his *yagna* to continue burning, to continue bringing light and warmth to all the world. In fact, when someone once asked him for a message, he replied, "My life is my message."

So, as we remember this *Mahatma*, this "great soul," let us take his message to heart. Let us live our lives as a sacrifice to world peace, as a sacrifice to our principles, and as a sacrifice to God. Then, and only then, will our lives truly make a difference.

Biodiversity and Nature: Our Responsibility

The subject of biodiversity is a very ancient, complex topic which is addressed in the Vedas as part and parcel of India's cultural heritage. The entire realm of nature is composed of five basic elements, each one inseparable from the others. These elements are: earth (*Prithvi*), water (*jal*), air (*vayu*), fire (*agni*) and sky (*akash*). However, according to our ancient traditions, these elements are not seen as only bio-chemical compounds. Rather, they are revered, respected and worshipped as divine. As these forces are what give us life and sustain us, we must see them as divine.

Although these five forces can be separated and seen as discrete elements, the entire natural world is inextricably interwoven and interdependent. Nothing exists in a vacuum. The intricate ways in which one species affects another are hard to fathom. They say, for example, that by letting one species of frog from the Brazilian rainforest become extinct, we are causing a cascade of events that could potentially lead to the demise of the human race. It is not the frog, itself, that is so crucial to our existence. Rather, it is the web of life that connects us all. We cannot simultaneously destroy Mother Earth and yet convince ourselves that we have a bright future ahead of us.

A wise man by the name of Chief Seattle once said:

"All things are connected. This we know. The earth does not belong to man; man belongs to the Earth. All things are connected, like the blood which unites one family. Whatever befalls the earth befalls the sons of the earth. Man did not weave the web of life, he is merely a strand in it. Whatever he does to the web, he does to himself."

Yet, in the face of this, we allow (and cause) thousands of species of plants and animals to become extinct each year due to our disrespectful and indiscriminate use of Mother Earth. In addition to providing food, wood for our homes, and the simple beauty of nature, more than 25% of the world's medicines come from our forests. We would not set fire to our own homes. We would not destroy our supermarket or pharmacy. Why can we not show the same respect for our real home, for our real supermarket, for our real pharmacy? We must have more respect for this land which gives us life, nourishes us, protects us, heals us and sustains us.

We call our Earth "Mother Earth," yet we do not treat Her as a Mother. She has given us all that we need to sustain our lives, and we are simultaneously destroying Her. If our own mother were sick, we would not let her simply suffer, decay and die. We would fight tenaciously to bring her back to her full state of glory. We must give the same love and attention to our Mother Earth. We must not pollute her or waste her; rather, we must nurse her back to health.

Additionally, the natural order of Mother Earth must be respected. What do I mean by this? India is a land rich in natural resources, rich in lush, untouched beauty, and rich in its ability to provide food, water and land to its people. Methods of agriculture and farming must be in concert with the natural laws of the land. When we try to impose our own demands on the land, we limit its inherent ability to produce fruitfully and with variety.

The United States is suffering the consequences of attempting to impose its will on the land. The U.S. agricultural service has converted American forests, woods, and fertile areas to grazing land for the cattle that later become hamburgers. More than 260 million acres of American forests have been turned into land for the beef-laden diets of its inhabitants. Since 1967, one acre of forest has been destroyed every five seconds. If the present trend continues, the country that was seen as the "land of plenty" will be completely stripped bare of all its forests in just a few decades!

Yet this tragedy far exceeds the loss of aesthetic, natural beauty. As our forests are destroyed, as more and more species become extinct, as our water becomes less and less drinkable, as our air becomes filled with pollutants, we are pulling apart the web of life strand by strand. Sure, the web will not collapse with the removal of one small strand. However, day by day, we are making what was once a strong, tightly-woven web into a fragile, wispy collection of strands fighting to hold themselves together.

A proverb says, *"The frog does not drink up the pond in which he lives."* We must follow the example of God's other children, and have greater reverence and gratitude for the wealth and diversity in our home.

There is a story that goes as follows: *A man once lived a long and pious life. When he died, God took his hand and said, "Come, I will show you Hell." The Lord took the man to a room where many people sat around a pot filled with food. The pot was deep, so a long spoon was needed. Each person held a spoon, but the spoon was so long that the people could not feed themselves. The spoons were longer than their arms, so — although the people tried various ways — they could not carry the food from the pot to their mouths. The suffering was miserable. The people were famished and weak.*

Next, the Lord said, "Come I will show you Heaven." He then took the man to a room that was identical to the first: many people sitting around a large pot of luscious food. Here the pot was just as deep, the spoons were just as long, but the people were joyous and healthy. "I don't understand it," the man said. "Everything is the same as is Hell, but here all the people are so content and well-fed."

"The difference between Heaven and Hell," God said. "Is that in Heaven people have learned to feed each other."

Let us realize that if we were left alone we would suffer and starve. We depend upon each other – humans, animals, plants, water – to survive. Let us continually remind ourselves of the ocean in which we are only drops. Let us not turn a blind eye to the web Mother Earth has so gently wrapped around us.

ARTICLES

Pariksha, Samiksha and Pratiksha

A spiritual path has three important components: *Pariksha* (tests), *Samiksha* (introspection), and *Pratiksha* (waiting).

The true *pariksha* is not simply passing a test given by someone else. The true *pariksha* is when you start taking your own test. The true *pariksha* is when you start taking your own photo with the camera of your own heart. The true *pariksha* is when you start checking yourself all the time – checking your volume, checking your actions, checking your thoughts, and checking your eyes and ears. We must not simply rely on others to take our test in life. Sometimes we can fool others, but we can never fool God and we can never fool our Guru. So, the true *pariksha* is when you start watching yourself, knowing that God and Guru are always watching you.

There is a beautiful story of a Guru who, nearing the end of his inhabitance in his Earthly body, called his three closest disciples together and said, "I'm giving you a test. To each of you I will give an apple. You must go from here, eat the apple without being seen by anyone and then return as quickly as possible. He who returns first will be my successor. But, be sure that no one can see you."

The three disciples were each given their apple and went off in three separate directions. After a few hours the first disciple returned, "Guruji," he exclaimed. "I went to the top of the highest mountain and ate my apple. Even the birds could not fly as high as this mountain; therefore there was nobody who could watch me." The Guru nodded in silence.

In the evening the second disciple returned, breathless. "Guruji, Guruji, I went into the deepest, darkest cave in the mountainside. There I crawled into the darkness and ate my apple, unseen by any being." The Guru nodded but said nothing.

The night passed as did the following day, but still the third disciple did not return. Finally, on the afternoon of the fourth day, the disciple returned slowly with his head down. "I have failed you, my master," he said. "I climbed mountains, I swam in the rivers, I crawled into the trunks of trees and into deep pits in the ground. But, everywhere I went God's eyes were watching me. There was nowhere I could escape His gaze." The Master said, "You, my child, are the one who shall be my successor, for you are the only one who understands the true nature of God and His omniscience."

When we realize that God is always watching us, then we will never go astray. That is true *pariksha*.

The second aspect is *samiksha* – introspection. We must constantly analyze and re-analyze ourselves. We must never become complacent. At the end of the day, a good businessman always checks his balance sheet: how much has he made, how much has he spent? Similarly, a good teacher reviews her students' test scores: how many passed, how many failed?

By looking at their successes and failures, they assess how well they are doing. Are the businessman's profits greater than his losses? Are most of the teacher's students passing the exams?

In the same way, each night, we must examine the balance sheet of our day: what were our successes, what were our failures? For all the successes, all our "plus-points," we must give credit to God, for we have truly done nothing but let Him work through us. All credit goes to Him. He is the one who saves us, who maintains our dignity and maintains our success. It is only by His grace that our eyes can see the work in front of us, that our hands can perform the necessary tasks, that our brains can understand instructions, and that our mouths can speak. We must never become arrogant; we must never think that it is "we" who have accomplished anything. It is only His grace working through us.

We must also give our failures to Him. The fault is ours, definitely. Yet, He is so forgiving and so compassionate that He insists we turn these over to Him as well. We must say, "God, please take these minus points. You know that I am weak, you know that I am nothing. Please make me stronger tomorrow." In this way, each night we check our balance sheet, and we pray to God to help us have fewer minus points, to make us stronger, to make us better hands doing His work, and to give us more faith and devotion.

A true spiritual seeker introspects frequently and always strives to be better the next day.

Last is *pratiksha* – waiting. One must always wait. We must do our *sadhana*, perform our duties, and then wait for the grace of God to shine upon us. Sometimes I hear people say, "But when will He bless me with a vision of Him?" or, "I have been doing *sadhana* for so long and still my mind is restless." There is no set rule to how quickly one attains the state of spiritual bliss. This is all God's plan. Patience, patience and patience – we must cultivate this in our *sadhana*. However, one thing is certain: His grace *will* come. His grace and blessings *will* be bestowed upon those who dedicate their lives to Him. This is definite. Only the time and the way are in His hands. So, we must just keep doing our *sadhana*, keep surrendering our lives to Him, staying humble and pure, and we must have faith that in the right time the shower of grace will fall upon us.

Corporal Punishment : Is it OK to Hit Our Children?

Corporal punishment is all too frequently used in homes and schools across the world. People seem to believe that children require physical and emotional violence in order to be "well-trained" or to be properly scolded for their bad behavior. This is however a tragic falsehood, one that leads to nothing more than an escalation of violence in our society.

Violence leads to violence. Peace leads to peace. This is a truth that pertains to countries at war as well as to our youngest children. When we raise our voices, when we become angry and aggressive, so our children raise their voices and their fragile bodies flood with anger and aggression. We hope that by becoming aggressive, our children will become calm, repentant and defensive. This is not the way the world works, however. When we act with anger, we create an environment of anger in the home. This negative energy persists, like a toxic chemical, in the home long after the actual fight is over. Our children, at the most receptive time of life, are then breathing in air filled with violence, lack of control, and negativity. We wonder why our world is becoming more violent each day, but really it is not such a mystery.

Additionally, when we hit our children (and this includes slaps and spanks, which many people believe do not count as "violence"), we lose their respect. Children are much more perceptive and insightful than we sometimes believe. As they watch us turn red with rage and then explode in verbal or physical attacks, they know we have lost control. They know we have no other methods by which to teach them. Their respect for us quickly diminishes.

This pertains to teachers as well. It is so important for children to respect their teachers. How else can young, exuberant bodies sit still for so many hours each day? Yet, when they lose respect for us as people, they simultaneously lose respect for what we are teaching. There are so many important lessons to be learned in school that we cannot afford for the students to lose their respect for teachers. We seem to believe that if we punish them severely they will respect us, but this is absurd. Sure, they will fear us, but respect and fear are not even related. We do not want our children's or our pupils' fear. We want their respect.

We complain that our children lie, that they hide from us, that they disrespect us. We ask why, yet the answer is not a mystery. Children are like sponges, voraciously soaking up every aspect of the environment in which they live. If they live with lies, they will tell lies. If they live with disrespect, they will show disrespect. If they live in the vicious cycle of action/reaction, they will only know how to act and react. If they live in a home in which there is neither tolerance nor understanding, they will learn to keep everything to themselves. However, if they live with patience, with love, with tolerance, with a tender touch of teaching, they will manifest patience, love, and tenderness as well as learn the lessons we are trying to teach them.

The keys to divine children lie in changing the nature of how we, as parents and teachers, behave. We must never act in anger or frustration. We must wait until we have calmed down and then, gently and tenderly, explain things to the children. Then, and only then, can we be sure they are only getting the teaching they deserve, and not the brunt of our anger from the office or from the traffic on the way home. How many times have we had exasperating days and come home and taken it out on the children (or on our spouse, who then, in turn, takes it out on the kids)? Too many. What do the children learn from this? Nothing other than low self-esteem and insufficient tools for dealing with their own emotions.

So, the first thing to do is wait until you are in a "teaching" mood, not a scolding mood. For children need not only the teaching, but they need the "touch," and that touch should be velvet, not violent. With a velvet touch and calm mind you can achieve anything with children. You should have "eye" communication. You should be able to simply look at them in a certain way and have them understand. There should never be the need to raise your voice.

Yet, I also understand that this is not easy. It is not easy to be calm when we are full of rage inside. It is not easy to use a velvet touch when our instinct is to hit.

Perhaps we say, "But I was hit by my parents and by my teachers. That is just the way it should be." Yet, we must be better than this. We must not fall into the trap of being like robots, unable to think critically. I, too, was slapped by my first Spiritual Master. He believed it was the way to teach. Sure, at the time I obeyed him. I feared him. But, I can see clearly now that that was not the way to teach me. I can see, in retrospect, how much more I learned through his silence or through his calm (and sometimes stern) words, than through his slaps.

Our scriptures say that a mother and father are enemies of their children unless they teach their children well, unless they fulfill their duties of imparting understanding and values. The scriptures say that these parents are enemies of their children unless they provide real education. Education does not mean simply dropping the children off at school each morning. It means ensuring that they are learning right from wrong, truth from falsehood, and integrity from deception.

There was a man who was caught stealing. As this was the last in a long string of violent burglaries, the judge sentenced the man to death. When the court asked the man what his last wish was, the man replied, "I want to meet with my mother." Thus, as the court always tries to fulfill the last wish of dying men, the mother was called. Upon her arrival, her son touched her feet and then, suddenly, leapt up and bit her face. Blood cam rushing out of her gaping wound. Everyone was astonished. Why would a dying man viciously maim his own mother?

ARTICLES

In explanation, the man replied, "If I am going to die, it is because of her. All that I have become is because of her. When I was a small boy and I used to steal things, I would bring them to her and she would praise me. She never taught me that stealing was wrong, she simply encouraged it. When she was angry with me, she never explained to me what I had done wrong. She never sat me down and tenderly helped me understand. Instead, she would simply beat me or scream at me. In that way, I too learned violence instead of values. So, I wanted to show the world that if I have become a criminal worthy of death, it is because of who she was as a mother."

I do not tell you this story so that we may all simply blame our parents for our own weaknesses. Rather, I tell it to illustrate the crucial nature of the effect parents and teachers have on children.

The children are the future of the planet, and it is our responsibility to help them make that future a bright one. Will we lead the world toward violence, or will we lead it toward love? Will we instill the values of forgiveness in the future world leaders, or will we instill the values of retribution and vengeance? Will we lead the world towards greater calmness or towards greater chaos? We must never take for granted the role we play in the future of the world through what we teach our children.

Significance of Temples

A temple is not merely a building. It is the abode of the Lord.
A temple's strength is not in its bricks.
Its fortitude comes from the dedication of its members.
A temple is not held together by plaster and mud.
Its glue is the piety and devotion of the community.
A temple is not simply a place we visit.
It should be the axis around which our lives revolve.

People may ask, "If God is everywhere, if every living being is a manifestation of Brahma, then why do we need to go to the temple?" There are many reasons. The most important reason is that a temple is not only the home of God; it is a concentration of divine energy.

During the installation of the deities (*Prana Pratishtha* ceremony), the *murtis* become powerful manifestations of God. The priests chant special Vedic mantras and perform special sacred rituals which endow these deities with divine attributes and powers. Therefore, praying before a deity in a temple may give us a greater sense of being in the presence of God than praying in our own homes.

Additionally, the temple building itself is constructed in such a way as to maximize the concentration of positive, sacred and peaceful energies. The actual structure of a temple is said to represent the resting body of the Lord. The sanctum tower (*vimanam*) represents His head, the door of the sanctum is His mouth, the entrance tower (*raga gopurum*) is His holy foot, and other parts represent His limbs. Most importantly, deep inside the main structure is the sanctum sanctorum (*garbha graha*), which is the Heart of the Lord, and it is there that we place the deities.

Ancient *rishis* and saints could realize God through their meditations. They lived high in the Himalayas and in secluded forests. There were few distractions, and their lives were focused on one thing: attaining the Divine vision. They, therefore, did not need temples. Their world was their temple. However, today our lives are flooded with material desires, mundane tasks, and logistic concerns. We must get up each day and go to earn a living to feed our families. We must live in a world that indoctrinates us to crave only sensual pleasures and material wealth. It is very difficult for this world to seem like a temple. Therefore, we must have a place which is sacred, a place which is holy, a place in which our sole purpose is becoming one with God, a place in which we hang up our daily concerns and troubles like coats at the door. We must have a place which focuses our mind on the true meaning in life. The temple serves this purpose.

A university student may claim he does not need to go to the library to do his homework, may say his dorm room is a good place to study. Theoretically, that is true. The books are the same, the material to be learned is the same. However, we know that in a dorm room he will be tempted constantly by ringing phones, knocks at the door, loud music, the desire to gossip with his friends in the hallway.

However, the library is silent. It is a place devoted to academic studies. There, he will not be distracted. In the library, everywhere he looks he will see other students deep in their work. This environment will provide him not only quiet in which to study, but also inspiration from others who are there for the same purpose.

Similarly, we go to the temple for the sacred environment, for the holy energy in the building itself, for the divine presence of the deities, as well as for the inspiration of others who are focused on God.

Yet, a temple should not only be a place in which we worship. It should become the focal point of our lives. The temple should become your extended family; it should be your tightly-knit community. Your temple should be the place where children come to learn about their heritage as well as to play with their peers. Your temple should be your place of celebration during times of joy, as well as your place of comfort and solace during times of grief. Your temple should feed every aspect of your being: your heart, your mind, your stomach and your soul. Then, it will truly be a temple, not just a building.

ARTICLES

Significance of the
Prana Pratishtha Ceremony

A Hindu Temple is a sacred place, endowed with divine energies and powers. At the heart of each temple lie the deities, to whom we bow and pray in worship. Why is it, though, that these statues, these "idols" are worshipped as God? How did they come to be infused with divine characteristics? The answer is the *Prana Pratishtha* ceremony.

People say that Hindus are idol worshippers. We are not. We are *ideal* worshippers. It is not the plaster and marble and stone we revere; rather it is the presence of God which has been transmitted into these otherwise lifeless statues. The rites and rituals of *Prana Pratishtha* are followed strictly according to the Agamic texts. Prior to installation, priests who have been well trained in Vedic rituals, perform specific mantras and *pujas* which have been shown to endow an inanimate object with divine life and energy.

These mantras and rites begin with the simple man who sculpts the stone. He is not an ordinary artist. Rather, he is one who has been blessed with the ability to create a physical manifestation of God. He performs *puja* and prayer prior to and during the sculpting. He maintains, in his mind, the vision of the deity he is sculpting. He prays for this God to come to life in his statue. His work area looks more like a temple than an art studio. So, from the very first moment, the stone is treated with reverence and piety, preparing it to carry the force of God.

Then, when the *murtis* are finished and taken to the temple, the special *Prana Pratishtha* ceremony typically lasts for five days. During this time, numerous special rites and rituals are performed and mantras are chanted. It is after this complex set of sacred rituals that the murtis become infused with divine power and truly embody the God in whose manifest form they are created. At this point, they are no longer *murtis*. They are deities. After this, we no longer refer to the stone or other materials of which they are constructed. For, they have become sanctified and are now only a physical manifestation of aspects of the Supreme Godhead. They are no longer marble; they are now divine. "Whatever form of Me any devotee worships with faith, I come alive in that form," says the *Bhagavad Gita*.

Some people may ask why we need deities, if God exists everywhere. It is very difficult for most people to envision the unmanifest, ever-present, all-pervading Supreme Being. It is easier for us to focus our attention and our love on an image of Him. It is easier to display love, affection and devotion to a physical deity than to a transcendent, omni-present existence. Additionally, through the *Prana Pratishtha* ceremony and through our own faith and piety, this image of Him truly comes alive and becomes Him. So, by worshipping His image with faith and love, we arrive at His holy feet.

In the *Srimad Bhagavatum*, Lord Krishna says, "Whenever one develops faith in Me – in My manifest form as the Deity or in any other of My manifestations – one should worship Me in that form. I exist within all created beings as well as separately in both My unmanifest and manifest forms. I am the Supreme Soul of all." (Canto ll, Chapter 27, Verse 48).

A Prayer to God

(Note: Please go to http://www.parmarth.com/audio/audio.html to hear
Pujya Swamiji sing this beautiful prayer/song.)

Mein to kab se teri sharan mein hun.
Oh Lord, I have been waiting and waiting for You,
for life after life, birth after birth.
When will You come and take care of me?

Meri or tu bhi to dhyaan de.
Please, Oh Lord, I am at Your holy feet, yearning for You.
Please pay just a little attention to me.

Mere man mein jo andhakaar hai.
Oh Lord, my heart and mind are flooded with a darkness known only
to You. You know how weak I am. You know how plagued I am by the
darkness.

Mere Ishwar mujhe gyaan de.
Please, Oh Lord, Ocean of mercy, Ocean of compassion, shine upon
me light which will remove this darkness. Bestow upon me the light of
understanding and wisdom so that I may remain true to You in spite of
the trials and tribulations of life.

Chahe dukh ki rehn mile to kya,
chahe sukh ki bhor khile to kya.
Let me be filled with divine bliss and acceptance in every circumstance,
whether it's the dark night of sorrow or the dawn of joy.

Patajhar me bhi jo khila rahe,
main vo phool ban ke rahun sada.
Make me the flower which always blossoms, whether it's spring, sum-
mer, winter or fall. Even in Autumn, when others are dropping let me
continue to blossom.

DROPS OF NECTAR

Jo lute na fiki pade kabhi,
mujhe vo madhur muskaan de.
Give me the sweet, loving smile which never fades, even during times of
adversity.

Teri aarati ka banoon dia,
meri hai yahi mano kaamana.
Oh Lord, I have only one desire: make me the lamp of Your aarti. Let
me be the flames which burn with devotion for You, and which are so
bright they shine Your divine light on others.

Mere praana tera hi naam lein,
kare man teri hi aaraadhana.
Gunagaan tera hi main karoon,
mujhe vo lagan Bhagawan de.
Let my every breath chant Your name. Let my heart beat only for You.
Let my every action be in Your service. Let not only my lips sing Your
glories, but let my heart also sing Your glories.

Mujhe mein hai raag aur dwesh bhi,
ninda paraayee mein karoon.
Oh Lord, I am afflicted by attachments and jealousy.
I am burdened by the habit of condemning others.

Aahenkaar ko Prabhu har lo tum.
Oh Lord, please remove me from this darkness. Annihilate my ego, my
arrogance, my anger, and my attachments.

Mujhe divyata ka daan do.
Please bestow upon me the gift of divinity. Make me pure.
Make me divine.
Oh Lord, bless me, bless me.

Tera roop sab me nihar mein. Tera darsh sab me kiya karoon.
Mujhe vo nazar Bhagwan de.
Give me that divine sight whereby I see only You, only Your beautiful
image in all I behold.

ARTICLES

Question & Answer:

Rebirth & Reincarnation

1. Rebirth is a philosophy of the Hindu religion. Does any other religion advocate the same philosophy?

Sikhism, Jainism and Buddhism also adhere to the philosophy of rebirth.

2. What is the meaning of rebirth? What relevance does it have to the common man?

The literal meaning of "rebirth" is the act of the soul casting off the body in which it had lived and inhabiting a new body, one which will be conducive to its evolution.

This is incredibly significant for people, for the undeniable implication is that our "lives" are not merely limited to the fifty or sixty or even eighty years we spend in this current body, but rather we will live again and again. Intricately connected to the philosophy of rebirth is the philosophy of *karma*, for it is our *karma* which determines the body that our soul will inhabit next. Our *karma* determines both the positive and the negative situations in which our soul will find itself in the future. Thus, if we cause pain to others in this life, it is likely that we will experience pain, both in this birth and in the future.

Relevance of Rebirth

The belief in this philosophy serves several purposes for people. First, it ensures that we live our lives honestly, compassionately and purely. If we fully understand that our present actions determine our future circumstances, then we will act with discretion, love, peace and generosity. In the same way that people do not speed in their car when there is a policeman present, for fear of receiving a ticket, so we will not speed (or otherwise break the laws) in our lives when we realize that every action is being recorded.

However, the belief in this philosophy also provides hope to people. We see that this life is not our only chance. If someone has lived a life of greed, of lust, of anger and of *adharma,* and if he does *not* adhere to the philosophy of rebirth, then he would feel hopeless and fated to an eternity of "Hell." On the other hand, rebirth offers him another chance. **The laws of rebirth and *karma* say, "Your future begins right now. Change yourself today so that your future may be bright."**

3. *What is the reasoning and purpose behind rebirth?*

There are several purposes to rebirth. The first purpose lies in the realization that as humans, we are weak. We succumb to temptation, to desire and to our emotions. Rebirth offers us a vision of life as a continuation from low to high, from impure to pure, and from human to divine. The law of rebirth allows us to both accept our "human-ness" graciously without feeling damned to a life in Hell, while simultaneously striving to live our lives in a way that will ensure a positive tomorrow.

Second, the purpose of rebirth is to show people the inevitable repercussions of our actions. If you play "hide and seek" with a small child, she will frequently "hide" right in the middle of the room, closing her eyes in the belief that since she cannot see you, you must also not be able to see her. People also live like this, assuming that just because they don't "believe" in the law of *karma* it doesn't affect them. Yet, although our eyes may be closed, the Almighty God can still see us, and His law of *karma* "catches" us regardless of where we are.

So, in the same way, there is no way we can escape the eyes of *karma* or the law of rebirth. Thus, through these laws, God has given us both a never-ending, continuous chance for self-improvement and also an inescapable equation by which we always reap what we sow.

Third, another important point of rebirth is to fulfill unfulfilled desires. As long as we have desires for anything other than God, we cannot attain liberation. In fact, liberation is the freedom from all desires. Thus, until our mind becomes desireless, we will continue to engage ourselves in actions to fulfill these desires. These actions are what lead to *karma* – both good and bad – and thus bind us in the chains of birth and death. Thus, through rebirth we continue to live until we realize that God is the thing worth desiring. Then, falling in surrender at His holy feet, we begin the path toward desirelessness and liberation.

Thus, the most important purpose and reason of rebirth is to attain liberation, to become one with God. People can go astray in one life. People can choose paths of passion instead of piety, paths of decadence instead of discrimination, and paths of hedonism instead of honor. Yet, God wants us all to come to Him. That is the purpose of human birth. So, He gives us more chances. We keep coming back until we learn the lessons of this human birth and until we transcend the limitations and temptations of the flesh. Thus, we must realize that everything we do which is not conducive to the path of God-realization is simply an obstacle we are putting in our own way. Every act we commit which is not honest, divine and pure is simply one more stumbling block we put in our path. It is one more hurdle we will have to cross, if not in this life then in the next.

4. We know about the ten incarnations of Lord Vishnu. In which way does God descend on earth? Does he take birth in the same way as that of the common man or through some other way?

God is God, so He can manifest in any way. He can manifest in human forms or in non-human forms. He is not limited in any way. The rules of man do not apply to God. All of His manifestations are divine.

5. How many times can a soul take birth? Can a soul say, "That's enough, now I do not want to be reborn?" Is this request ever accepted?

A soul will come to Earth in human form as many times as are necessary to attain the final state of liberation. The faster one progresses, the fewer births are necessary. Yes, a soul can certainly decide that this is enough and that it does not want to be reborn. However, simply wanting liberation is not enough. One must work for it. This is the point of *sadhana*, of *seva*, of *japa*, of meditation, of *yoga*. Through these ways, the soul sheds layer after layer of illusion, ignorance, attachment and desire. Once the layers have all been shed, once the soul realizes its true, divine nature, then rebirth is not necessary. Through these disciplines one can break the cycle of birth and death.

Attaining liberation is not merely due to a "request." Rather than just giving us liberation as per request, God gives us the light by which we can see the path toward Him. He gives us the light of discrimination, the light of wisdom, and the light of truth by which we can find our way.

Thus, we cannot simply say, "I want liberation" and then continue to accrue *karma* which will bind us. All actions which are not laid at His holy feet – whether they are good actions or bad actions – result in *karma*. In order to completely break the chain of *karma*, we must lay our entire lives – every thought, every action, every word, and every desire – at His holy feet, realizing that He is the doer and we are merely the vessels through which He acts.

In the *Bhagwad Gita*, Bhagwan Krishna says:

> *Yat karosi yad asnasi, yaj juhosi dadasi yat*
> *Yat tapasyasi kaunteya, tat kurusva mad-arpanam.*
> *Subhasubha-phalair evam moksyase karmabandhanaih*
> *Sannyasa-yoga-yuktatma vimukto mam upaisyasi*

This means, "Whatever you do, whatever you eat, whatever you give, and whatever *sadhana* and *tapasya* you perform, do everything as an offering to Me. In this way you will be freed from the bondage of *karma* and from the results of *karma* in your life. Through this renunciation of everything unto Me, you will be free of all bondage and you will become united with Me."

Further, it is only through becoming desireless that we can stop accruing *karma* and attain salvation. In order to become desireless we must practice *sadhana* to realize God. A child will be very attached to his toys and will desire more toys. However, by the time he is an adult, he will no longer be interested in these toys. "There are more important things than toys," he will say. If you gave him a choice between diamonds and toy trucks, he would choose the diamonds. Similarly, we must reach a state where God is the diamond and all else are worthless toys.

When we perform *yagna* we say, "*Idam Agnaye, swaha, idam agnaye, idam na mama.*" This means, "Not for me, but for You, God." This must be our attitude not only in *havan* ceremonies, but also in every action of our life. Everything must be done as an offering to Him.

6. *The next birth for a saint like you will be progressive and important like this birth. Do you know what will be your next birth?*

For me personally, I am not concerned about where I take birth. I want only to continue to serve God through service to His children. The point of rebirth is not to be concerned with when, where and how, but rather to make Here and Now your Heaven! Liberation can take place now, if only we will work for it.

With the blessings and the grace of God, every moment of every day can be Liberation. In a rat race, you are always a rat. Even if you win the race, you are still a rat. The point of life is to live with Grace, not in a race. Yes, we must perform our duties. Yes, we must try to succeed in whatever way we are able. But, we must live in Grace, not in a Rat Race! That is the point of a divine life.

We should take the divine life of *bhakta* Prahlad as an example. Lord Vishnu offered him anything. What did he ask for? What boon did he request from God? He said, "Regardless of where I take birth, regardless of what form I come in – be it a scorpion, an insect, a tree, an animal or a man – the form and the place and the circumstances are irrelevant to me. I only ask that, in whatever form I take future births, please bestow upon me the blessing of undying devotion for Your holy feet." The only thing he wanted was to live his life with the divine nectar of *bhakti* filling every pore of his body. He wanted to be completely saturated with love for God. This is the point of life.

7. *If someone lives a virtuous life and achieves* nirvana, *does that mean there is no rebirth for him?*

Yes, if one achieves *nirvana*, then that is the goal of human birth and one is liberated from the cycle of birth and death. However, saints may choose to return to the Earth, although they don't have to, in order to ease the pain of those who are living. Yet, the difference between the liberated souls and those who are still bound by the laws of *karma* is like the difference between the prisoner and the jailer. Both live within the confines of the jail. However, whereas the prisoner must live according to the rules of the jail and his every movement is restricted, the jailer is free to move about as he wishes. He is not subject to the rules and no one is monitoring his movements. Further, while the prisoner must stay in the jail until his term is up, the warden is free to leave – either temporarily or even to give up his position as jail warden.

Similarly, the enlightened soul is on Earth, knowingly and by choice, in order to help others attain liberation. He is free and not bound.

8. *Can a person really have any knowledge of a previous birth? If so, is this knowledge beneficial or disadvantageous?*

Usually, people cannot remember previous births. One must perform great *sadhana* or go to the saints or special *jyotishi* (expert astrologer) to learn about previous births. It is usually not advantageous to know, which is why the Divine Plan does not give us easy access to that information. We have enough trouble trying to navigate through one life, with one husband or wife, one mother, one father, and one job! Imagine if we immediately recognized others as our previous parents or spouses or vicious enemies! It would be impossible to remain neutral and unbiased.

Imagine that a man is married to a woman with whom he is not deeply in love. Certainly he loves her but not passionately or deeply. However, due to his duties, he stays married and lives an upright life. Now, imagine that one day he sees a very old woman in the grocery store and immediately recognizes her as his beloved from an earlier birth. He would have great difficulty not leaving his wife and family for an old woman whom he lusted for passionately in an earlier life!

Imagine that an upstanding young man and a young woman fall in love. The man goes to the woman's parents to request her hand in marriage, and the girl's father immediately recognizes the boy as an enemy from an earlier life. He would never allow his daughter to marry the man, although perhaps through the last few lives the man had gone from being a rascal to being righteous.

In this way our lives would be quite difficult if we remembered our earlier births. Additionally, people talk about remembering one's "last life," but how many lives do we want to remember? One, three, ten, fifty? Where would we stop? Eventually, we would be living in a situation where many people we met had played some role in an earlier birth, thus preventing us from treating them fairly and dispassionately in this birth.

9. Why should the soul take birth on earth only? After leaving the human body, can a soul be born in any other form?

When we realize the purpose of rebirth, then it becomes clear as to why the Earth is the best-suited place and why the human body is the best-suited medium. The purpose, as we have discussed, is to work through previous *karmas*, to become desireless (through either fulfillment of the desires or through *sadhana* to eradicate the desires), and to attain God-realization. The human body – with its intellect, compassion, consciousness, yearning, understanding and wisdom – is the most conducive to attaining God-realization. As an animal, our lives would be spent solely in eating, sleeping, protecting ourselves and reproducing. There is not time or ability for *sadhana*. Similarly for plants and other species, consciousness is there in terms of ability to feel pain and to reproduce, but it is not well-developed enough to search for something higher.

However, occasionally, due to the performance of truly evil deeds and the accumulation of significant negative *karma*, a soul will have to come to Earth in the form of an insect or lower life form. However, as soon as the lessons are learned in that life form, then again the soul can come in the form of a human, in order to continue its progression toward God-realization.

10. How many times does a soul have to take birth? Does the same soul always take birth on Earth? When he is born, does he look the same each time?

First of all, the soul never actually takes birth. Rather, the soul inhabits human bodies in order to come to Earth, the *Karma Bhoomi* ("Land of *Karma*"), so that it can engage itself in actions which will lead to its liberation. The individual soul comes to the Earth into situations which will be most conducive for working through past *karmas*, enabling the mind to become pure and desireless, to attain salvation.

People frequently become confused that it is the soul which must work through *karma* or the soul which has desires. This is not correct, as the soul is pure, divine and complete. Rather, it is the mind, the senses, the *pranas*, desires, *sanskaras* and tendencies which form the subtle body and travel with the soul from one gross body to the next gross body and which obscure the true, divine perfection of the soul.

It is like a perfect reflection of the sun (the individual soul as reflection of the Supreme Reality) which becomes distorted and murky due to the dirt and waves in the water in which it is being reflected (the mind and the senses). The reflection (the soul) is perfect. It is only the vehicles of reflection (the mind and senses) which are turbulent and murky, thus making the reflection itself seem less than clear. Once the water becomes clear and calm, the sun will reflect perfectly. Similarly, once the mind and the senses become calm and clear through *sadhana*, association with the saints, and good work, the individual soul can manifest perfectly and attain liberation.

11. If we have good parents, brothers, sisters, friends and gurus,

how can we have the same relatives and friends in the next life?
Does a soul have the right to select his family and friends?

There are two important points. Yes, on the one hand we can hope to be with certain people again in our next life. The only way to do this is through prayer. It is not a matter of the soul having a "right" to choose. But, rather, if someone prays with great sincerity, purity and devotion, God can answer the prayer.

However, the other important point is that the purpose of life is *not* to become so attached to our family and friends that we are already worried about not being with them in our next birth. We have a hard enough time living together in this life! So many times we cannot even get along with our family members in this life! We must focus on loving and caring for each other *now*, rather than be concerned about whether we will be together in the future.

Also, when a soul departs from the body, the soul continues its journey toward God-realization. The scriptures caution us against thwarting the progress of other souls. By begging to stay together with someone, we may be inhibiting his or her own progress and path.

Thus, let us instead concentrate on loving those we are with now. Let us care for all those who come into our path. Let us pray to move forward with each birth, and let us not be so attached that we sacrifice our own or someone else's spiritual growth in order to simply stay together.

12. Does the karma *of this life become useful in the next life? If the present life is happy, does that mean the soul has done good deeds? On the contrary, if this life is full of unhappiness, does that mean the soul is suffering from his own misdeeds of his last birth? Can you please explain the law of* **karma?**

The *karma* we perform and accrue in this life is extremely relevant to our next life. However, the equation is not as simple as just good deeds in one life beget happiness in the next, or bad deeds beget unhappiness. First of all, *karma* can take place immediately; it does not necessarily wait until the next birth. We always reap that which we sow. Therefore, performing good deeds with a selfless motive will definitely lead to positive *karma*, both in this life *and* in future lives.

However, there are a few important points. First, motivation is important. We must perform our duties with no motivation other than to do God's will purely and selflessly. If we simply do good deeds so that we will reap good *karma* (e.g. going to temple in order to pass an exam, or being respectful to your mother so that she will raise your allowance), then we do not really get the long-term benefits. Rather, we must do good deeds because it is the right thing to do. We must perform right action because that is what will lead us to God. We must not concern ourselves with the immediate fruits or results.

Second, it is important to realize that that which may seem to be negative is not necessarily so. For example, if a young, pure, innocent boy dies at the age of ten, people immediately question, "What horrible sin did he commit in a past birth in order to account for the tragedy in this one?" Perhaps the death was due to negative *karma*. However, perhaps he had come very close to liberation in a past birth and only had a few *karmas* to work through before his soul was ready for salvation. These *karmas* may have been quickly resolved during only ten years and thus, the soul is free to be liberated. So, rather than being a tragedy, the early death is a blessing.

13. Can a great soul take birth again to finish his life's work? Are there any such examples? Or if two lovers failed to live together in this life, if they shorten their lives by committing suicide, will they then be together in their next life?

Yes, of course, souls can come back to finish their work. That is why they come back – because their work of attaining divine liberation is not completed. There are many examples through history of proven cases of reincarnation. In fact, when I was young, doing *sadhana* in the Himalayan jungles, I met several people (including very small children) who told me about their past births, down to the smallest detail of the home in which they lived and their previous families. They explained the circumstances of their death and how their work was thwarted by death. These details of their lives have been confirmed through independent sources.

However, to commit suicide in the hope that in the next life our wishes will be fulfilled is a grave mistake. This is true regardless of what our wishes are, whether they are wishes to be with a particular boy or girl or whether they are wishes to succeed in a particular arena. Suicide is never the answer.

God has given us a great gift of life. Through this life we have the opportunity to move closer to Him and closer to the Heavenly Abode. However, if we throw away this opportunity, then we lose the chance. People, especially youth, make the tragic mistake of thinking that suicide will give them a "fresh start" on a new life. But it is the exact opposite. By committing suicide, they condemn themselves to lifetimes of not only the exact problems they faced in this life, but also to the negative *karma* accrued by killing themselves. Thus, their next life will inevitably be even more problematic and even more painful than this one.

14. *Some people donate arms, eyes, and kidneys after death. Some cultures give their bodies to vultures. Do these good deeds at the end of life help the soul for rebirth? Are they beneficial to the soul or does the soul have to suffer for the broken body?*

Whatever we do, in life or death, that helps others is a good deed. We should help others as much as we can during life, and if in death we can help them further, then we should do that as well. There is a tradition when saints die that they are not cremated, but rather their bodies are floated down Ganga. The reason for this is so that the fish and other animals can gain nourishment from their bodies. The lives of saints are lived for all creatures, and even in death they want every cell to be useful.

The soul certainly does not have to suffer through donating organs, and in fact is benefited. Our souls progress and benefit through every good deed we perform, whether in life or in death.

Question & Answer:
Prayer

Prayer is calling back home.
Prayer is, in essence, coming home,
for it brings us into connection with our deeper selves.
It is the way we speak to God,
and its beauty and poetry and devotion should match that in our hearts.
Prayer is the broom that sweeps out our hearts,
so the home we offer to God is an immaculate
and pure one.
Prayer is a time when our mouths, our minds and our hearts are
filled with the glory of God,
when we simultaneously speak,
think and feel our love for Him.
Prayer is the blanket that wraps itself around our souls
and keeps us warm and cozy.
Prayer is the water that quenches the thirst
of a man lost in the desert.
It is the stars that glisten in the dark of night,
giving light to all those who may need it.
It is the sun that shines in the middle of winter,
coaxing the flowers to open their petals.
It is medicine to the sick, food to the hungry,
and shelter to the homeless.

1. When and why should one offer prayer? Is there a specific time of day for it?

Prayer should be done anytime and all the time; anywhere and everywhere; for any reason and for all reasons. When we speak to God, that is called prayer. Therefore, prayer should be a minute to minute, moment to moment, integral part of our lives. Prayer makes us God-conscious; it brings us into divine connection. It takes our focus away from the material world and into the spiritual world. '

There are, of course, days which are seen as particularly auspicious for offering prayers, certain holidays which have special significance. Additionally, there are three times each day when it's particularly important to pray. The first is when we get up. We dedicate our day to God, saying, "God, this day is Yours. Guide my actions, speak through my voice, make my hands Your tools." Then, at the end of the day, we should offer the day to God. Whatever we have done – good or bad – we should lay at His holy feet. Our successes are due only to His grace, and only He can take care of our weaknesses. Also, before each meal, we should offer our food to Him so that it becomes *prasad*, nourishing our being with not only calories and vitamins but also with His divine light.

However, although certain times and certain days are especially important, the goal is to make every day a holy day. We should start every day with prayer, fill every day with prayer, and end every day with prayer.

2. Should prayer include **mantra, japa, puja, archana, yagna** *or* **havan?** *If so, why?*

Mantras and *japa* help us to concentrate. We live in a world that is overflowing with sensory pleasures and stimulation. Our lives are over-busy with work, errands, chores, etc. Therefore, it is very difficult to simply still the mind. Mantras and *japa* and special *pujas* serve as bridges between this world and the divine realm. They offer us a way to transverse the water which may seem impassable.

It is said that a mantra has three essential components: we must simultaneously picture the mantra, hear the mantra and taste the mantra. It is an experience of the entire being. A mantra is not only the experience of the hand or of the tongue. It must fill our beings.

Mantras and *japa* also purify our minds and hearts. After practicing them for awhile, they become automatic. Typically our unconscious thoughts are filled with trivial matters – conversations we have had or expect to have, groceries we must buy, what we will cook for dinner, or even a persistent commercial jingle. However, by practicing mantras and *japa*, these other thoughts get pushed aside by the automatic power of God's name. Soon, the mantra and *japa* will become as unconscious and automatic as the other thoughts. It is like if you hear a song on the radio over and over, during your drive to work, that song will play in your head all day long. Similarly, if you do your mantra or *japa* as much as possible, it will eventually become automatic. Your mind will no longer be filled with trivial thoughts and worries. Every free moment of thought will be filled with God.

Also, just like a mother cannot ignore her child who cries out, "Mom, mom, mom, mom!" so will God be always present with His devotees who chant His holy name.

However, these things are means to the end of God-realization. They are the means, not the end themselves. Once we develop that close, intimate bond with God, mantras and *japa* become less necessary. Imagine that you love someone with all your heart. You don't need to take a *mala* and recite her name over and over again with the beads of the *mala* in order to remember her. Your heart automatically remembers. Similarly, once we have that deep love for God, we don't need to continue doing *japa* to bring us into contact with Him. We will be in contact all the time. Our lives will become our *japa*.

3. Should one chant shlokas *during prayer? Does the mantra given by a Guru have any significance? If so, why?*

There are so many different *shlokas* and prayers; it is impossible for me to say – in a general sense – which ones we should practice. This is a reason we have the tradition of gurus. After much thought and meditation, the Guru will tell the disciple which mantra to recite. However, until you have a *sadguru*, you can take any name of God, whatever form attracts you most. All of His names are holy; all of the mantras praising Him bring you to His feet.

A mantra given by a *sadguru* has special power and significance. A guru transmits not only the words of a mantra, but the tradition and the *sadhana* of so many enlightened ones. He is giving you not only his wisdom and *tapasya* but also the wisdom and *tapasya* of his *sadguru* and his guru's guru. So, a mantra from a guru carries with it the guru's light, the guru's understanding, and the guru's love.

However, I always say that what matters is your faith, your *shraddha*. That is your real mantra. The words themselves are not nearly as significant as the heart that recites them. So, when we recite our complex Sanskrit *shlokas*, let us make sure we are doing so out of *shraddha* and piety rather than out of ritual and habit.

4. *Should prayer include* namasmarana (*remembering the name of God*), namalekhana (*writing the name of God) or chanting His name on beads?*

All of these are useful. They bring us out of glamour-consciousness and into God-consciousness. They focus our mind on something divine. However, they must be done in the right spirit. It is not enough to spend your days writing God's name in a notebook. His name must be on our lips, in our hearts, and in our thoughts, not only in our notebooks. The ultimate goal, as it says so beautifully in one of our prayers, is to "have His name on our lips and have His work in our hands." That is the goal. If we spend our days writing His name, or if our hands only have *malas* in them, then what are we doing for the world? What is the fruit of this *sadhana*?

5. *Should one recite* Gita, Vachanamrut, *and the* Hanuman Chalisa *regularly each day? If so, how many times per day?*

It is important to recite our scriptures and important prayers like the *Hanuman Chalisa* and other *shlokas*. We must recite these as much as possible, so that they become deeply ingrained into our beings. We must recite them so much that we live and breathe them, so that they become as much a part of our consciousness as the names of our family, as the job we do at work, as the things that normally fill our minds.

However, the key is not in how many times we recite them, or in how many verses we recite, etc. The key to salvation is in how much we live them. In the *Gita*, Lord Krishna says, *"Bhagwad Gita Kinchidadhita."* It means that if we absorb even a small bit of the nectar of the *Gita* and implement it in our daily lives, then we will truly be transformed. If we take even one *shloka* of the *Gita*, one divine word of Lord Krishna and actually live it in our daily lives, then we will see the true, divine magic!

6. Should one sing hymns in praise of one's deity or tell the story of the Deity's life?

Katha is important for the same reason that reading the scriptures is important. *Katha* gives us inspiration and understanding and bring us into the lap of God. But, we must remember that *Katha* is not a social event. *Katha* is about God's word and God's message. That is why we should attend, not just to see our friends.

7. How much time during the day should one devote to prayer?

We should devote at least fifteen minutes in the morning and fifteen minutes at night. But, as I said, our entire lives should be devoted to God. Ideally, there should not be a distinction between "prayer" time and "work" time; even the work becomes prayer. But, in this world I know that is difficult. So, at least fifteen minutes twice a day should be done.

8. What should one do if one cannot offer prayer at the appointed time while traveling?

We should not ignore our spiritual lives when our bodies are traveling. Our prayers should be offered as soon as we can. Do not worry about the time change or a delay or anything like that. God never sleeps. He is always awake and always for you. You do not have to worry about waking Him up when you reach your travel destination.

9. Can prayer redeem sins?

Yes, definitely. However, prayer should not simply be used as an antidote for sin. We should not think that we can sin as much as we want and then we can just pray it away. That is not how it works. The prayer purifies us so that we no longer commit sins. It makes us pure and holy. In the *Gita* it says, "*Kshipram Bhagwati Dharmatma*" and "*Api Chetsu Duracharo.*" This means that a person who surrenders to God, who comes to God's holy feet, becomes instantly pure and holy. Even a criminal who has committed heinous crimes is instantly purified when he truly surrenders to God.

10. If a person offers prayers in the morning but does not observe the moral code of conduct during the rest of the day, will he or she benefit from the morning prayers?

All prayer is fruitful. But, they will also suffer the consequences of their dishonest behavior. One does not cancel out the other. The real goal of prayer is to make every thought, every action, every word honest, pure, and loving. Prayer is the broom which sweeps out our hearts. So, when we pray we should ask God to make us more divine and more holy. Then, we won't have to worry about dishonest deeds.

11. What should one bear in mind during prayer?

Prayer has no side effects, no warnings and no precautions. We should offer ourselves fully to the Lord with no fear and no hesitation. That is true surrender. God is all-loving, all-embracing. It is only our own ignorance that we should fear. God is the shelter from everything harmful. He is the refuge and the salvation.

12. What kinds of prayer bear fruit? What kinds do not?

All prayers are fruitful. No prayers are ignored by God. However, it is not for the fruits that we should pray. The real fruit of prayer is connection to the divine, and that comes with any prayer at any time.

13. What about people who offer prayers out of fear of God?

On the one hand, it is good that they are praying. That is the main thing. However, God should never be feared. He is infinitely forgiving, boundlessly loving and always ready to take us into His arms. It is the temptations of the material world that should be feared. It is those that steer us in the wrong direction and bring us frustration and anguish.

14. Does God heed our prayers? How does one know if God has heard the prayer?

God definitely listens. But, we must realize there is a difference between hearing our prayers and gratifying our every whim. God listens to everything we say, to everything we think, to everything we feel. However, that does not mean that He will always give us what we ask for. God knows what we need; He knows what is best for us, both in the present and for our future growth. So many times we think we know what we want, we think we know what will make us happy. But, only God really knows.

Further, what happens in our lives is a product of many past *karmas* in addition to our goals of today. So, there are many factors in whether or not our prayers are "answered," but we must never confuse an unanswered prayer with thinking that God has not heard us.

How to know if God has heard us? We must establish a divine connection, a deep and strong relationship with God. We must have antennae in our hearts that are tuned to only one station: God. Then, we will know that not only has He heard our prayers, but also that He is speaking back to us. When we speak to God it is prayer. When He speaks back to us it is meditation.

15. Is there any difference between prayer and thoughtful moral action? If so, what is the difference?

Yes, there is a difference, but there should not be. All of our thoughts and all of our observances should be prayer. Typically our thoughts are about relatively mundane things – our selfish desires, our expectations, our plans. Prayer is typically purer, more devotional. The goal, however, is to have every thought be focused on God, to have every thought be pure and holy.

16. What about when sincere prayer does not bear fruit?

As I mentioned, there are so many factors that are woven together into the fabric of our lives. Our prayers are only one of those factors. *Karma* plays a crucial role in what befalls us, whether it's success or failure, prosperity or poverty. That is why we must not only be good, but we must also *do* good! The more good we do in our lives, the more our prayers will be fruitful.

17. Can prayer which is not supported by action bear fruit?

They say, "God helps those who help themselves." In other words, do as much as you can, and then lay the fruits of your work in God's hands. I always say, "Do your best and leave the rest to God."

Question & Answer:
Purity

[Note: The following questions were put forth based around the five types of purity defined by Adi Shankarcharya: Shareer shaucha *(purity of the body),* Manaha shaucha *(purity of the mind),* Karma shaucha *(purity of deeds),* Vaak shaucha *(purity of speech), and* Sheel shaucha *(moral and ethical purity).]*

1. *Shareer Shaucha* – Purity of the Body

Is it absolutely essential that we have a ceremonial bath or go through a process of ablution every time we visit a toilet after we have already had a proper early morning bath?

All of the rituals of physical cleanliness are based around the concept that the body is a temple. Our body is the vehicle through which we realize God, through which we fulfill our divine (and mundane) obligations on Earth. It is the body which sits in meditation. It is the body which bows in the temple. It is the body which prepares and offers food or other offerings to the Divine in *puja.* For this reason, just as one would keep the temple clean, one should also keep the body clean. By emphasizing physical purity, our scriptures are not merely urging us to douse ourselves with water. Rather, the emphasis on physical purity is a reminder that the body must remain pure and that we should not defile it through food, drink, drugs or actions. We would never bring meat, alcohol or drugs into a *mandir.* We would never commit adulterous acts in a *mandir* or lie or cheat in a *mandir.* Thus, by reminding us that our body is a temple, it is a constant reminder that wherever we go and whatever we do, we are taking this temple with us. Hence, we must always act, speak, eat and drink like we would in a *mandir*.

The emphasis and importance should not be merely on the letter of the law regarding bathing practices, but rather should be on living within the body as though it were a temple.

2. *Manaha Shaucha* – Purity of the Mind

Our mind is like a powerful horse and cannot be kept easily under control. How can one keep a tight rein on it so as to keep its movement under strict control?

The mind is, by nature, restless. However, what fuels the restlessness are our desires, our ego, our attachments and our aversions. If you keep a log of all the non-productive thoughts which come to your mind, you will find that in general they fall into the categories of either desires and expectations or aversions – things we want to obtain or events we want to take place, and things we want to avoid at all costs. The remainder of unproductive thoughts are filled by our ego and our attachments. So, one of the best ways to still the mind is to expect less, accept more. The fewer desires, expectations and aversions we have, the less fuel there will be for the fire of our mind. If we can just accept whatever comes as God's blessing, then our minds will neither be filled with cravings nor disappointments nor fear nor aversion.

Meditation is the best way to control one's mind. Meditation teaches us to take the reins of our minds and our lives into our own hands. By first focusing the mind on one target (a mantra, the breath, the flame of a candle, an image of the Divine), slowly all the unnecessary and distracting thoughts dissipate, and the whole mind is focused upon one target. Then, slowly, with the grace of the Divine, the watcher and the watched merge. Slowly there is no object and no subject. Rather, there is nothing but stillness.

3. *Karma shaucha* – Purity of Deeds

What should we do in order to maintain **karma shuddhi** *– purity in our deeds and worldly activities?*

There are two ways to ensure that our actions are completely pure and that they free us rather than trap us. First, we must devote our actions to others. Anything which is done for someone else, for the greater good, for all of humanity will purify us. Our *yagna* ceremonies remind us to keep purity, God and divinity in the center and that our actions should simply be offerings to that divinity. At the end of each mantra in the *yagna*, the priest says, *"Idam namamah."* It means, "Not for me, but for You." If our lives can be dedicated to the Divine, dedicated to humanity, dedicated to others, then our actions will surely be pure. This doesn't mean we shouldn't make money or have a good job or become prosperous. Rather, it means that our motivation in success should not be, "How much money can I accumulate for myself and my two children?" or, "How high can I reach so I am the top?" Rather, our motivation should be, "How can I best use my skills to serve the world? How can I fulfil my duty to the best of my capacity?"

The second way to ensure that our actions and lives stay pure and don't bind us is to offer everything to God. There is a beautiful mantra which can be chanted every evening before sleep. It is as follows:

> *Kaayena vaachaa manasendriyairvaa*
> *Buddhyaatmanaa vaa prakriteh swabhaavaat*
> *Karomi yadyat sakalam parasmai*
> *Naaraayanaayeti samarpayaami*

This means, "Oh Lord, whatever I have done, whatever actions I have performed through my speech, through my mind (anything I've thought), through my intellect (anything I've planned, achieved or understood), through my hands or body or through any of my senses – therefore anything at all I have performed, perceived or thought – it is all due to Your divine grace and I lay it all humbly at Your holy feet."

In this way, by offering everything to the Divine, we remember that really He is the Doer and we are just the vehicle. In this way, by offering our lives as a tool in His hands, and remembering that we must simply let His will work through us, our actions become pure.

4. *Vaak shaucha* – Purity of Speech

The written word is mightier than the sword. Purity of language and good speech are important. Would you call it a breach of **vaani**, *speech* **shuddhi** *(purity), if one has resorted to the use of bad or impolite language inadvertently or unknowingly?*

In the *Bhagavad Gita*, Bhagawan Krishna says that the *tapas* of speech is that speech which is truthful, kind and beneficial. So this is the gauge by which to measure ourselves. If our words fulfil all criteria then they are "right speech." If, however, one of the criteria is not fulfilled (e.g. it is kind but not true or true but not kind), then it should usually not be spoken. Sometimes we think that simply because something is true, it is correct speech. However, there are many hurtful things which may be true but are neither kind nor beneficial. Telling someone, for example, that they are ugly or stupid or fat may be true, but it serves only to hurt the listener. Alternatively, lying to someone just to be kind is also not *tapas* of speech. We must speak the truth, but in a way that serves the greater good, not just our own selves or our egos. Impolite language or profanities are due simply to losing control over ourselves.

One of the best ways to purify our speech and to gain control over our tongue is through the practice of silence. The instinct and impulse to speak, to make our voices heard (literally and figuratively) are innate. Even young babies who cannot articulate their words are eager to babble, and they do so incessantly.

To speak makes us feel that we are alive, that we are someone, that we are not forgotten. Many times people speak without even having anything to say. If you listen carefully you'll hear how much people speak needlessly, giving running commentaries on their own actions, vocalizing every thought and sensation, rehearsing conversations which have not yet taken place and replaying those which have already occurred.

There are so many times in life when we wish we could take back our words. We lie in bed at night hearing and re-hearing everything we said that day which we wish we had not. Yet, a word once spoken is an arrow that has already been let loose from the bow. It can neither be returned to the bow nor caught mid-flight.

The practice of daily silence gets us into the habit of thinking before we speak, of remembering that – although we may have a thought – we have a choice whether to speak it out loud.

When we have a habit of practicing silence we become the master over our speech rather than its slave. Our words become our powerful and loyal servants to be used when, how and where we deem fit.

5. *Sheel shaucha* – Moral and Ethical Purity

Please explain what moral or ethical purity really means. What rules must one obey for maintaining the highest standard of sheel shaucha?

Moral and ethical purity is when our thoughts, our values and our actions are all in alignment. If my ethical beliefs say that honesty is an important virtue, then I am only living a pure life if I speak and act honestly, in accordance with my ethics and morals. Typically, our ethics are proper. Yet when it comes to our actions, we tend to permit our desires, our egos, our attachments and our fears to step in the way of our values and ethics. Then, we rationalize it all to ourselves by adjusting our belief system to match the actions we've just performed or want to perform. This is where impurity arises in our actions and morality. In order to remain pure we must ensure that our thoughts, actions and values are all in alignment with each other and also with our spiritual injunctions.

Moral and ethical purity is to live by the "ten commandments": *ahimsa* (non-violence), *satyam* (truthfulness in word, thought and deed), *asteya* (non-stealing of others' possessions or time), *brahmacharya* (restraint and willpower over one's sensual desires), *aparigraha* (non-hoarding), *suacha* (purity), *santosha* (contentment), *tapas* (austerity), *swadhayay* (self-study and scriptural study), and *Ishwar pranidhana* (surrender to the Divine). If we live by these tenets then our thoughts, words and actions will all be in alignment with each other and in alignment with purity, *dharma* and integrity.

6. Please enlighten us about the ways and means of ensuring physical as well as mental chastity or purity.

Suacha means "cleanliness and purity," but it does not simply imply that one must bathe each day and keep one's fingernails clean. Rather, it pertains to a deeper level of purity – purity on the inside, purity of thought and action. We must purify our thoughts through *japa*, meditation and the practice of positive thinking. We must purify our lives by ensuring that our actions are models of integrity, *dharma* and righteousness. *Suacha* also pertains to that which we allow to enter our bodies and minds – what food we take through our mouths and also what food we take through our ears and eyes. True *suacha* means refraining from putting anything impure into our being. This includes everything ranging from drugs and cigarettes to negative gossip to violent music lyrics to pornography. Practicing *suacha* is like taking perfect care of your brand new car. If you had a $100,000 new Mercedes, you would only put the most expensive, purest, best quality gasoline in the tank. You would never fill it up with cheap, bad quality gas and you certainly would never dump mud into the engine! Yet, our divine selves are more valuable than the most valuable car, and we continually fill them with low-quality, impure junk! True purity is to treat our bodies, our minds, our hearts and our lives as divine temples in which God resides.

Question & Answer:
Caste System

1. All His creation is one and the same to God, and yet Hindus appear to be losing their direction by remaining so divided in terms of castes. How can we bring about unity?

The caste system as it is seen in India today was originally simply a division of labor based on personal talents, tendencies and abilities. It was never supposed to divide people. Rather, it was supposed to unite people so that everyone was simultaneously working to the best of his or her ability for the greater service of all. In the scriptures, when the system of dividing society into four groups was explained, the word used is *"varna."* *Varna* means "class," not "caste." Caste is actually *"jati,"* and it is an incorrect translation of the word *"varna."* When the Portuguese colonized parts of India, they mistakenly translated *"varna vyavasthaa"* as "caste system," and the mistake has stayed since then.

The *varna* system was based on a person's characteristics, temperament and innate nature. The Vedas describe one's nature as being a mixture of the three *gunas* – *tamas, rajas* and *sattva*. Depending on the relative proportions of each of these *gunas*, one would be classified as a *Brahmin, Kshetriya, Vaishya* or *Shudra*. For example, a *Brahmin*, who performs much of the intellectual, creative and spiritual work within a community, has a high proportion of *sattva* and low proportion of *tamas* and *rajas*. A *Kshetriya*, who is inclined toward political, administrative and military work, has a high proportion of *rajas*, a medium proportion of *sattva* and a low proportion of *tamas*. A *Vaishya*, who performs the tasks of a businessman, employer and skilled laborer, also has a high proportion of *rajas* but has relatively equal proportions of *sattva* and *tamas*, both of which are lower than *rajas*. Last, a *shudra*, who performs the unskilled labor in society, has a high proportion of *tamas,* a low proportion of *sattva* and a medium proportion of *rajas.*

These *gunas* are not inherited. They are based on one's inherent nature and one's *karma.* Therefore one's *varna* was not supposed to be based on heredity, and in the past it was not. It is only in relatively modern times that the strict, rigid, heredity-based "caste" system has come into existence. There are many examples in the scriptures and in history of people transcending the "class" or *varna* into which they were born. Everyone was free to choose an occupation according to his/her *guna* and *karma.*

Further, according to the scriptures, there is no hierarchy at all inherent in the *varna* system. All parts are of equal importance and equal worth. A good example is to imagine the human body. The brain which thinks, plans and guides represents the *Brahmin* caste. The hands and arms which fight, protect and work represent the *kshetriya* caste. The stomach which serves as the source of energy and "transactions" represents the *vaishya* caste, and the legs/feet which do the necessary running around in the service of the rest of the body represent the *shudra* caste. No one can say the brain is better than the legs or that hands are superior to feet. Each is equally important for the overall functioning of the body system. They just serve different roles.

The way to unite people now is education. We must bring awareness that all people are equal and that there are no small or big people or superior or inferior people. Spiritual leaders and other teachers can teach the truth of the scriptures and help eradicate this prejudice.

Look at Bhagwan Ram and Bhagwan Krishna. Both show the example of taking their food from even people of the lowest caste and going to the homes of the lower caste people. It is devotion, purity and commitment which make us great or small, not our caste.

2. Caste-based social organisations are formed strictly on the basis of caste by Indians living in foreign countries. Do you think this is a necessary tre· ' *'n the 21st Century? Should such organisations be allowed to continue?*

We should overcome these things. Living abroad, Indian Hindus should be focused on being Indian Hindus rather than being concerned with being a part of their particular caste. Being Indian should be our identity living abroad. In that way, we can be united.

Organizations can certainly exist within the Indian Hindu community, but they should be based on language and culture rather than caste.

3. The caste system is at the root of the differences in the social levels among Hindus. Many reformers struggled during their lifetimes to rid society of this system. Yet, this persists today. What do you think could be done to eradicate this evil?

The problems still exist, but these great souls have also had an effect. The effect is there. Change is there. People are changing. However, more has to be done. We must keep working to eradicate this problem.

4. "What caste do you belong to?" is the first question many Indians ask whenever they meet. Would you consider this kind of questioning appropriate these days?

This is not a good question. Originally, as I mentioned, caste was just a division of labor, a division of jobs. So, really it would be more proper and more in keeping with the true meaning of "caste" if we ask each other, "What is your job?"

Nowadays, caste doesn't bare any relation to jobs. *Brahmins* who are supposed to be the teachers and priests are running shoe companies. *Vaishyas* are taking care of temples and being teachers. *Kshetriyas* are rarely serving as soldiers anywhere. Everyone is doing everyone else's job now. So, the question bares no connection to its original meaning and is used only to give us a way of judging others and putting them into a box of "superior" or "inferior." Therefore it should not be used. These prejudices are simply bringing disease to our community.

A good rebuttal is simply to say, "I am Indian," "I am Hindu," "I am Gujarati," or simply, "I am a child of God." If you really want to answer the question in its true meaning, then you can say, "I am a businessman," "I am a teacher," or, "I am a doctor."

5. Do you think a day will dawn when all Hindus together will say: "We are all one and united"? What should be done by social, political and religious reformers in order to achieve this?

I am very positive and optimistic. I do think that the day will come when we are all united. Bhagwan Ram built bridges between men and men, animals and men, animals and animals. He even built bridges to the demons! We should take this example and the communities should start building bridges between different castes and different communities.

Our problem is our ego. That is the only thing inhibiting our unity. Look at the "I." Wherever it is, it always stands capital, whether at the beginning of a sentence, the middle of a sentence, or the end of a sentence. "I" is always capital, and "I" represents our ego. This capital "I" is a border, a boundary, and a wall between us. Our egos stand in the way of our unity, whether it is our personal egos, or egos about the superiority of our particular caste or society. The key is to bend our egos. We must bend the "I" and turn it from vertical to horizontal. When the "I" becomes horizontal, then it can serve as a bridge between people, families, communities and nations.

The spiritual leaders can teach people to build bridges and to unite. We have travelled across the globe, through the USA, Canada, the Caribbean, Europe, Russia, Africa, South East Asia and the Pacific, spreading the message of *Vasudhaiva Kutumbhakam* – the World is One Family. We have seen that everyone wants to unite. Everyone wants to be together. Everyone wants to be in peace. I am confident that this message and mission will blossom and flourish, and that people across the world of all religions (not only Hindus) will join together as one united family.

Question and Answer:
Karma

1. In the Bhagavad Gita *Lord Krishna tells Arjuna to perform his duties without any attachment to the fruits of his labour. How can one put this advice in practice if one has to perform worldly tasks and not expect any returns?*

Universally Applicable:
What makes the messages given by Bhagwan Krishna to Arjuna so divine and so universal is the fact that they apply to every situation in life – worldly and transcendent. The messages are just as applicable to life in the boardroom as to life on the battlefield. In fact, the *Bhagavad Gita* serves as the essential scripture of modern life for the very fact that its teachings are timeless and universally relevant.

Whatever You Do Will Come Back to You:
Every *karma* has a return, every seed will grow into a plant or tree, every boomerang will come back to the sender. If you flip the switch, the light will go on. If you plant an apple seed, you will get an apple tree (provided that you water it and care for it properly). As Isaac Newton discovered, this is the law of nature. His discovery gives us one of science and nature's most fundamental laws: for every action there is an equal and opposite reaction. This reaction will be there independently of our expectations or attachments. Just as the sun will rise every morning whether we expect it to or not, similarly our actions will bear fruits whether we expect the fruits or not. So, the bottom line is not that there will not be fruit of the *karma*. There definitely *will* be fruit of our *karma*. There definitely *will* be returns of our actions. The bottom line is that we should not become attached to them!

Do Your Best and Leave the Rest:
What is crucial is that we do not become attached to what that fruit is or what those returns are. Bhagwan Krishna's instruction to Arjuna on the battlefield was not that his actions wouldn't bear fruit but that he should not have expectations or attachments regarding what that fruit will be. The motto we should all take from the *Gita* is, "Do your best and leave the rest." We must perform our actions to the best of our ability, with full knowledge that they will bear fruit. What fruit they will bear and when that fruit will be borne is out of our hands.

Expectation is the Mother of Frustration:
The reason that Bhagwan Krishna gave this message is that expectations and attachments are the cause of our unrest and unhappiness. Even positive, fruitful results are rarely up to our highest expectation, and thus expectation nearly always leads to frustration and depression. The solution is to decrease our expectations and do our best without clinging to a desired result.

2. Everyone has some target to achieve and all our activities are aimed at achieving a dream. It is human nature to have some expectation of the fruits of our labour. Yet, are we not committing some breach of this sermon? What is the use of "performing" without any hopes of return?

Hope Versus Expectation:
Yes, it is human nature to have dreams and goals. There is nothing wrong with wanting a particular result or working toward a goal. In fact, it is this which motivates us to act. The dictate of Krishna is very subtle.

He does not mean that we should not work toward a goal or wish for a particular result. Even on the battleground of Kurukshetra, even after having the *Bhagavad Gita* sung to him by the lips of Lord Krishna, Arjuna still naturally fought the war in order to win. He fired each arrow hoping and expecting that it would pierce the target. His actions were thoughtful, careful, focused and goal-oriented. Yet, he was not attached to the end result.

Maintain Emotional Stability:
This is the beautiful and complex subtlety of Krishna's teachings. We must do our best, working toward a goal with focus, attention, care and effort. Yet, our emotional stability and our inner peace must not be affected by the results. We study hard in school and it is natural and correct that our goal is to achieve high marks. If we did not hope to get high marks, there would be no impetus to study! However, is our emotional state contingent upon whether we get an A or a C? Are we ecstatic with an A and bereft with a C? Are we unable to sleep for weeks prior to receiving the results because we are so filled with tension of the result? That's the difference that Krishna is trying to teach us.

These teachings are so crucial today when people are committing suicide and having to take prescription medicines to fight their depression. The more attached we are to a particular result, the more likely we are to be discouraged and dejected if that result does not manifest. That is why we must take the message of non-attachment to heart.

3. Does one have to reap the 'returns of his deeds' even when he performs them without hoping for benefits or returns of his activities?

There are two answers to this question – one answer on the worldly plane and the other answer on the transcendent plane. On the worldly plane, the answer is yes, and on the transcendent plane, the answer is no. Let me explain. Even if one truly becomes non-attached to the fruits of one's labor and if one truly acts only and purely out of duty and *dharma*, one still is living here on Earth and will receive the results of one's actions. For example, you are walking down the road and see an elderly gentleman trying to cross the street. He is handicapped. From a completely pure, unselfish heart you rush to assist him to cross the street. You are not expecting any reward, nor even a word of thanks. Simply due to a spirit of love and *seva* you act out of what you feel to be your duty.

However, unbeknownst to you, the elderly gentleman happens to be a millionaire, even though he is very simply dressed and walking alone. One week after your pure-hearted gesture, you find a check in your mailbox for a large sum of money with a note that says, "Thank you for lending a hand to an old man."

You performed the action with no expectation and no attachment. Your motives were pure, selfless and *dharmic*. Yet, still the action bore fruit. A reward was received. So, that is why I say that on the worldly plane, actions bear fruits – sometimes pleasant and sometimes unpleasant – even if we perform them without attachment or expectation.

However, on a *karmic* level, on a spiritual level, when we speak about the soul having to take birth and rebirth in human form until all *karmas* are washed away, then no. By performing actions selflessly with no attachment to the fruits we are freed of the bondage of *karma*. We do not have to return in a next life to reap the fruits of *karma* we perform which is dutiful, *dharmic* and performed without attachment.

4. Is it wrong to remain hopeful of benefits when one knows that the results of every activity have to be borne in any case?

Indifference is *Not* the Answer:
It is important to realize that Krishna is not telling us to become indifferent or apathetic. This is a really crucial difference. He is not advising us that we should not care about the results. He is simply saying that we should not become affected, internally and deeply, by the results.

As I discussed above, there is a difference between hope and expectation or attachment. There is nothing wrong in hoping for something. Whenever we act, we naturally hope for a particular result. The distinction lies in how frustrated or distraught we become when that particular result does not manifest. If you can hope for a raise from the boss without losing your peace and joy when that raise is not granted, then there's nothing wrong with hoping. However, human nature is to cling to what we feel to be the "desired result." When the result is different we become shattered, broken and depressed.

5. Will you please advise us as to what areas of activities a human can undertake without hoping for any fruits or benefits?

How **We Do, Not** *What* **We Do:**
The key is not in choosing a particular area. The key is not in *what* we do, but rather in *how* we do it. Of course, it is much easier to work in a spirit of duty, *dharma* and selflessness when we are performing deeds that benefit others, when we are serving others rather than ourselves. Thus, performing *seva* is one of the best ways to cultivate the spirit of selflessness and non-attachment.

However, the situation is not black-and-white. There are people who may be able to work in business without any attachment or expectation, who may become millionaires due to their skill, intelligence and destiny, but who get up and go to the office every day simply out of a feeling of duty rather than a feeling of greed. On the other hand, there may be people performing *seva* who are performing deeds that seem to be selfless while their hearts are full of ego, pride and expectation of praise or reward.

6. Take the illustration of a "temple priest" or a Narrator of Holy books (a Kathakar). What kind of fruits of their activities of this nature do they hope to reap? Can these two perform their holy activities without thinking of or expecting any results?

People working in the spiritual field have chosen their life's path due to a wish to serve others, to bring others closer to God. The "fruits" which they probably hope to reap are success in touching, teaching and transforming people, success in bringing peace to the troubled. These goals are clearly very noble and beautiful. However, even for those working in the spiritual field, we still must be unattached. We may perform a *puja* or *yagna* in order to cure a patient of cancer. The goal is noble. However, we must remember that the Divine Doctor and Divine Decider is God, and hence we must neither become full of pride if the patient is cured nor full of despair if the cancer is fatal. Similarly, as spiritual teachers we may guide people and show them the path of righteousness, but we must

154

not be attached to whether they follow our guidance or not.

*7. The Almighty Lord is the one who offers the fruit of every karma. If this is the final truth, then how can **Karma** be regarded as the source of **Moksha** or total emancipation'?*

The Inescapable Law of *Karma*:
The Lord is truly Almighty and can, of course, do anything. It would be overly simplistic for us to say that the law of *karma* overrides the omnipotence of the Lord. However, what we know is that the Lord has created the world in such a way that the Law of *Karma* is binding and inescapable. Certain things may mitigate the effects (e.g. prayer, *sadhana*, a powerful Guru, bathing in the Ganga), but God has made the power of *karma* absolute.

Mitigating the Effects of *Karma*'s Fruit – the Power of the Guru:
For example, due to past actions (*karmas*) the fruit may be that in our thirtieth year of life we will be hit by a car and paralyzed from the waist down for the rest of our lives. However, if prior to this we have been living an exemplary life, if we have a sincere and pious spiritual practice, if we are under the shelter of a divine Guru, the fruit of that *karma* may be mitigated so that rather than being hit by a car and paralyzed, we instead stub our toe and have a black-and-blue mark for one week. It is God's Will to reward our good actions, our prayers and our devotion to the Guru with mitigated *karma*. He could, of course, absolve us completely of the *karmic* fruits but He does not. It is He who has created the Laws and hence even the *karmic* fruits are being given by Him.

*8. Every act aims at some sort of result which we call the fruit, and yet, one is never certain of the results as of his own expectations. In such a situation, how can a man carry out his activities with no fruits in sight at all? And for how long'? Can we not call all such **karma** as having been undertaken with the desire to obtain its fruits or return ?*

As I explained before, there will *always* be fruit to activities. This is the law of nature. Whatever we do *will*, in some way or another, come back to us. If we perform good, selfless actions, these will definitely, in some way and at some time, come back to us. Similarly, if we perform selfish, injurious acts, we will definitely suffer in the future. So, the message is not that that there are "no fruits in sight at all." The message is that we should leave the fruits in God's hands. Our job is just to do our best. It is His job to take care of the rest.

9. What is Karma Yoga? Can we deem all Karmas performed without expectations of their "fruits" as performing a Karma Yoga? When can such a Karmayogi attain Godliness?

Karma Yoga = Union With God Through Action:

Yoga means "union." It is, ultimately, union of the Self with the Divine. Hence, *karma yoga* is action performed which unites us to God, action which brings us closer to Him, action which purifies us. *Karma yoga* is not simply action performed without expectation of fruit. If I randomly stab a man with no attachment to whether I get caught and go to jail or not, that is not *karma yoga*. The action must be one which is also pure, holy, *dharmic* and dutiful. These are the two essential components of *karma yoga*. First, the action itself must be *dharmic*, dutiful and something which is in the service of the world. Second, I must not be attached to the fruits of my labor, but rather I must do it just for the sake of fulfilling my duty.

10. In today's world, a team leader gets his teammates to perform various tasks. Can the team leader and team really carry on such activities and devote themselves whole-heartedly to the performances without expectation of any results? Is this possible?

As I mentioned before, the issue is not that we should not expect results. Results are always there. The issue is that we should not expect a particular result! A team leader should inspire his teammates to work to the best of their ability, with full sincerity and dedication and then to have faith that God will take care of the rest. Sometimes, we may do our best, but – due to the complex web of *karma* into which our lives and the lives of all others are woven – we may not receive the reward we want. Our actions may not bear the desired fruit, even though we have worked sincerely and assiduously. However, that is part of the divine drama called "human life." Sometimes we will succeed and sometimes we will fail. Sometimes we will win and sometimes we will lose. However, our purpose here on Earth has nothing to do with winning, losing, succeeding or failing. Our purpose is to realize our Divine Nature and unite with God. This can only be achieved when we see everything we do as our divine duty and perform it with devotion, sincerity, integrity and skill without being emotionally attached to what the end result will be.

So, the team leader must instill the attributes of integrity, honesty, tenacity and dedication in his teammates. He must encourage them to perform up to their highest potential. But, he must not focus all energy and attention on what the end result will be.

11. Lord Krishna tells Arjuna in the Bhagavad Gita, "Remain focused to yoga and do thy deeds." Will you enlighten us on this?

This *shloka* –"*Yogah Karmasu Kaushalam*"– means that performing your work with excellence and sincerity is yoga. It is a very important passage because it teaches us that yoga is not merely about postures or breathing exercises. Yoga is about how we live and how we work. Whatever your duty is, if you perform it with utmost sincerity to the best of your ability and with excellence, that is yoga. When we remember that yoga means union, particularly union of the self with the Divine, we can extrapolate the message that one way to become progress on the spiritual path and become united with God is through performing every act with sincerity and excellence.

The Mantra For Everyone:
The best and simplest way to avoid the binding chains of *karma* is to surrender everything we do and everything we receive (the action and the reaction) to God. There is a beautiful prayer that says:

Kaayena vaachaa manasendriyairvaa
Buddhyaatmanaa vaa prakriteh swabhaavaat
Karomi yadyat sakalam parasmai
Naaraayanaayeti samarpayaami

This means, "Oh Lord, whatever I have done, whatever actions I have performed through my mouth (anything I've spoken or eaten), through my mind (anything I've thought), through my intellect (anything I've planned, achieved or understood), through my hands or body or through any of my senses – therefore anything at all I have performed, perceived or thought – it is all due to Your divine grace and I lay it all humbly at Your holy feet." If we can chant this prayer each evening before we go to sleep, and truly live its meaning, then we will be free from the bondage of the fruits of whatever *karmas* we have performed.

ARTICLES

Question and Answer:
Bhagavad Gita

1. What is your favorite holy scripture?

There is a true galaxy of holy scriptures, each one its own solar system of stars and suns. Each contains an unparalleled wealth of wisdom and inspiration from our *rishis*. These scriptures are the lamps that shine brightly on the path of righteousness and truth, guiding our way in the dark of night.

However, if I had to choose one, I would say it is the *Shrimad Bhagavad Gita*. As Pujya Paramhansa Yoganandaji said, "The *Bhagavad Gita* is the most beloved scripture of India, a scripture of scriptures. It is the Hindu's *Holy Testament*, the one book that all masters depend upon as a supreme source of scriptural authority." The *Gita* provides wisdom and upliftment, comfort and solace to people of all ages, from all walks of life, from all corners of the Earth.

"*Bhagavad Gita*" literally means "Song of the Spirit, Song of the Soul, Song of God." Like any truly divine song, the language of the original lyrics and the religion of the original singer are irrelevant. For once it has been written and sung, the song itself becomes alive, bursting forth across oceans and mountain ranges, breaking all barriers of caste, creed, and nationality. Such is the power of a divine song. However, as the original "singer" of the *Gita* is Lord Krishna Himself, this is the holiest and most sacred of all the songs of God. Its power to transform, heal, and uplift is as limitless as the Singer.

It has been said that the *Upanishads* are the cows, Lord Krishna is the cowherd, Arjuna is the calf, and the *Gita* is the milk. But, it is not just any milk. This milk is nectar that flowed from the Gods with the power to heal the sick, comfort the lonely, guide the lost, uplift the fallen and bring peace to the troubled. The milk is gentle and pure enough for a baby, but strong enough for a warrior.

2. *How and when were you introduced to this holy scripture?*

I was introduced to this incredible work by my Spiritual Master when I was eight years old. The *Gita* was his favorite text and he used to carry it everywhere with him. He said it was the most important piece of wisdom for everyone, regardless of education, caste, or spiritual aspirations. When he initiated me, he gave me my own copy – a small, simple version in the original Sanskrit. I learned Sanskrit through the Gita, through memorizing its entirety. In that way, Lord Krishna's message and His language came alive for me simultaneously.

3. *How much time do you devote each day to the* Gita*?*

Now, approximately an hour each day. But at the beginning, in my early years, it was my life. Every minute of my day was spent in either meditation, *japa*, or contemplation on God and the *Gita*. While I may only spend an hour each day studying the *Bhagavad Gita*, I spend all twenty-four hours living the *Gita*.

4. *What is the* Bhagavad Gita*'s impact on your life ?*

The *Gita* has made me अस्त (*ast*), व्यस्त (*vyast*), मस्त (*mast*) and स्वस्थ (*swasth*). What do I mean? First, I became *ast*, emerged in God. I was like the sugar that – when mixed in water – loses itself and becomes one with the water. The sugar was so solid and separate when it sat on the spoon. But, in the vastness of the water, the structure of the sugar simply dissolves.

The *Gita* became the blanket that wrapped itself around me in the cold and dark of night. I was alone in the forest, and became completely immersed in Lord Krishna; His words spoke to me through the *Gita*, through my mantra, and through His own voice. They comforted me, taught me, and guided me.

Then, as I studied the message and the wisdom of the *Gita* more, I learned how to be *vyast*. *Vyast* – in essence – means "doing is be-ing, and being is doing." This is Lord Krishna's message. So many people today assume that a spiritual path is one of idleness, one of silent contemplation high on a mountain top. But, Lord Krishna teaches otherwise. We should be the hands that do God's work – this is *Karma Yoga*. We should not only be divine, but we should *do* divine. "Serve, serve, serve, do your duty on Earth." But, again, *vyast* is a different kind of "doing" than most people do. It is "be-ing" while "doing." What does this mean? It means having your work be prayer, be meditation. All the time your hands are doing, your mind should be being. Have His name be on your lips and in your heart, and have His work be on your hands.

From *ast* and *vyast*, I became *mast* – ever happy, ever joyful, ever blissful. When you are immersed in Him and His work is flowing through you, what else can you be?

When you are *ast*, *vyast*, and *mast*, you automatically are *swastha* – completely healthy, and in perfect balance. But *swastha* does not imply only perfect physical health; rather, it is a full health of body, mind, soul and spirit. Every pain, every ache, every discomfort becomes *prasad* as you lay it in His lap. His love and His presence dissolve all that hurts both within and without. Your body and your soul become in perfect harmony.

5. *How do you convey the message of the* Gita *to your devotees?*

The *Bhagavad Gita* is not abstruse. It is intricate and deep, but nei-ther complicated nor difficult. Its messages are clear. Through the story of Arjuna and the battle, Lord Krishna gives us lessons for our lives. The real Kurukshetra is within us. Each of us is Arjuna, struggling with right and wrong, temptation, fear and frustration. Our bodies are our chariots, being driven all too frequently by our senses as the horses. The mind, ego, desires, lust and greed are the evil Kauravas with whom we must do righteous battle, from whom we must not shy away in fear and trepidation. If, instead of letting our chariots be driven by our senses, we give the reins to Lord Krishna, we will surely be victorious.

Additionally, the central message of the *Gita* is to perform your duties diligently and piously, but without any expectation for what the result will be. You must till the soil, plant the seeds, water and tend the seedling, and take care of the tree without any thought of how much fruit the tree will bear. You must be God's gardener, carefully tending the garden but never becoming attached to what will blossom, what will flower, what will give fruit or what will wither and die. Expectation is the mother of frustration, but acceptance is the mother of peace and joy.

Lord Krishna says, "Stand up! Do divine! Be divine! Don't expect, but accept!" Life is about the journey, not about the destination. If the reins of your life-chariot are in His hands, you will be ever happy, ever peaceful. This is the lesson of ultimate surrender that I convey to my devotees. Put all your assets in the Divine Insurance Company, and you will always be taken care of .

6. *How relevant is this message for today's life?*

The message of the *Gita* is as relevant for people living in the West today as it was for the people of India more than 5000 years ago. It is as relevant for Hindus as for people of all other religions. It teaches Hindus how to be better Hindus, but it also teaches Muslims to be better Muslims, Christians to be better Christians, and Jews to be better Jews. For, if something is really "truth," it must be universal. Truth is not limited to a religious framework. If it is truth, it must pertain to all. Such is the profound truth of Lord Krishna's words.

Like Mother Ganga, like the rays of the sun, the *Bhagavad Gita* does not discriminate. Mother Gangaji does not bring water to only Hindus' farms. The sun does not shine only on Hindus' flowers. Similarly, the *Gita* does not provide light and inspiration to only Hindus' minds and souls.

7. *Is the* **Bhagavad Gita** *useful for people in the West?*

Definitely. Aldous Huxley said, "The *Gita* is one of the clearest and most comprehensive summaries of the Perennial Philosophy ever to have been made. Hence its enduring value, not only for Indians, but for all mankind."

Perhaps people in the West actually need this wisdom even more. People in the West seem to hold even more tenaciously to their agendas, their expectations, and their desires. The message in much of the West is, "If you work hard, you will succeed, you will become prosperous." So, people don't work for the sake of being God's hands. They work to reap the benefits, and when the benefits don't come or don't come quickly enough, they are frustrated.

Hence, it seems people in the West greatly need both the message and the comfort of the *Gita.* Mahatma Gandhiji said, "When disappointment stares me in the face and all alone I see not one ray of light, I go back to the *Bhagavad Gita*...I immediately begin to smile in the midst of overwhelming tragedies, and my life has been full of external tragedies. If they have left no visible, no indelible scar on me, I owe it all to the teachings of *Bhagavad Gita.*" The lives of people today seem colored by indelible scars. I hope they will all turn to the *Gita* as the remover of pain and the bestower of light. I hope we can all sit together in the lap of the Mother.

8. *All the time you are moving from city to city, from country to country. You are so busy with all of your spiritual and charitable activities. Do you find time to read the scriptures of other religions as well?*

Definitely. I have read the major scriptures of most religions. I feel that the truth is one, although the paths are many. Therefore, each path, each religion has great value for me. I have read *Shri Guru Granth Sahib*, the holy book of Sikhism, the *Koran*, and the *Bible*, as well as numerous other religious works from other religions.

9. *Do you compare these works?*

No. Every book gives an important message; in fact, the messages are the same, although the languages are different. Each work teaches the message of, "Love all, hate none; heal all, hurt none."

If you don't fully understand something (like another religion), you should never criticize it. Instead of criticizing the principles of others, our energies should be spent on following the guiding principles of our own religion. That is what will lead to health, happiness, peace and prosperity.

10. *How can the* **Bhagavad Gita** *be useful in achieving salvation and Self-realization?*

The *Gita* provides the guiding principles for both peace in this life as well as for ultimate salvation. When I was in Japan, I saw a sign that said, "Follow the rules, and enjoy your stay." While it is simple and trite, it is also true. The rules for our lives are laid out in the scriptures: do divine, be divine, serve without expectation, love all, and surrender to God. When we follow these rules, our lives become infused with joy and love and peace. It is when we ignore these commandments or amend them to suit our own agendas that we bring pain and turmoil into our lives. The *Gita* is a complete yet concise listing of all the teachings necessary to achieve Self-realization in this life as well as eternal salvation and liberation.

11. *Does the* **Bhagavad Gita** *answer the youth as well?*

Of course. The trials and tribulations of youth are not so different from those of adults: Who am I? What do I believe? What do I want out of life? What is my purpose here? Are these not questions that continue to plague us throughout our lives? Childhood and adolescence are simply times in which the intensity of the questions and the agony caused by not knowing the answers are at their peak. Sure, the logistic concerns of youth differ from the logistic concerns of old age; however, at the core, we are all searching for truth, peace and happiness. The *Gita* provides this. Additionally, because it was sung by Lord Krishna Himself, the *Gita* has the miraculous ability to give the reader exactly the answer and meaning he/she was searching for. So, if you open it today in the midst of a crisis at work, you will come upon a passage that will speak something different to you than when you open it a year from now, looking for comfort after the death of a parent. Similarly, youth will find a different jewel in the treasure chest than adults will. But, it is still a jewel from the ultimate treasure chest.

12. *In today's changing world, is there something in the* **Gita** *for all of humanity?*

Definitely. The truth is there for all to see. The sun does not disappear behind a cloud simply because a Christian or a Muslim goes outside. The *Bhagavad Gita* shows us the way to live with God, to live with each other and to live with Mother Earth in peace and harmony. This wisdom and insight is as changing as the River Ganga – it is able to address the concerns of each generation, yet it is as stable and everlasting as the Himalayas themselves.

Question and Answer:
Politics and Religion

1. Should politics and politicians be influenced by religion?

First of all, it is important to distinguish between religion and spirituality. Religion, in its best form, is something that uplifts, inspires and guides people, bringing meaning to their lives. When I speak about religion in these questions, I will be using that definition.

I think it is fine for religion (spirituality) to enter into politics, because what are the basic tenets of religion? Honesty. Integrity. Selflessness. Piety. Purity. All of these tenets are ones which are very beneficial in every sphere and can certainly help keep politicians on the right path. However, when religion becomes dogmatic, exclusive, and close-minded, then of course it is detrimental to any public arena and should be kept out.

In general then, it is okay for religion (in its best and purest sense) to enter into politics but politics should definitely not enter into religion!

2. Can politicians govern effectively while following the dictums of religion?

If they are truly religious and not merely following a dogma, then yes. In fact, religion will help them to govern more effectively because it will give them a sense of deeper meaning and higher purpose. Religion, at its best, reminds us that we are merely tools in God's hands and that whatever we are achieving is due only to His grace. If they follow the true tenets of their religion, whatever it is, they will be honest, righteous, hardworking and selfless in their service of the needy.

3. What are the principles politicians should bear in mind in their

166

endeavour to govern wisely?

Politicians must remember that they are public servants, not public masters. Too many politicians these days think that they are masters and they forget that they are servants. They must always remember that they have been appointed or elected to uphold a sacred tradition – that of caring for others. The people have put their faith in the politicians out of true belief that these politicians will make the best, wisest and most beneficial choices. The politicians must remember that they are not entitled to be post-holders, nor are they inherently better or more deserving than others. If they can keep their ego and selfish motives at bay, they will govern wisely.

4. What principles and factors do you believe governing politicians should keep in mind when they create and pass laws which directly affect civilian life?

Mahatma Gandhiji said beautifully, "There is more than enough for everyone's need, but there is never enough for any man's greed." In our world, in our societies, we have enough resources to take care of all citizens. It is simply a matter of management, dispersal and priorities. The politicians should never let themselves off lightly by assuming that there is nothing they can do or that bad situations are irreparable. They must have the courage, the initiative and the forbearance to change things for the better. After all, that is why they were elected!

5. How should the common person, of whichever religious denomination, perform his or her duty to the Nation?

Selflessly. If every person put the needs of the nation above his/her personal desires, we would have very few problems. If there is one motto, one mantra, that can be given to all people it is: put your own desires last. Think first for others and then yourself. Rather than asking yourself, "How will I benefit?" ask yourself, "How many others will benefit?"

6. Corruption is sin. It is unholy. Is it acceptable to appoint such corrupt politicians to positions of power and authority?

Absolutely it is wrong. Corruption has no place in any sphere of society and it should be extinguished wherever it is found. However, we must also work to clean up the systems themselves, as I think that frequently politicians may be influenced by a corrupt system. If the system were completely clean, honest and systematic, then even if they had a tendency toward corruption, it could not bear fruit. On the other hand, if the system is one in which dishonesty can blossom, then even those who are mostly honest may find themselves succumbing to *adharmic* temptation.

7. Should spiritual leaders seek to influence politics or get involved in the matters of governing and politics?

Spiritual leaders should seek to influence politicians only in order to make sure they are walking honest, righteous, egoless paths. Spiritual leaders, themselves, must have no other agenda than the service of the greater good of the nation. Therefore, if they have an ability to help bring back a politician who has gone astray into realms of corruption or deceit, then they certainly should do so. But they should do nothing for their own personal benefit.

8. Should the government meddle into the affairs of the religious institutions? Should the government take over the control and administration of a religious mission or institute?

The government should not get involved with the affairs of religious institutions as long as these institutions are not violating the human rights of any of their followers and are not breaking any laws. Obviously, if an institution, under the guise of a religious institution, is cheating people or otherwise harming them (physically or emotionally), that must not be allowed, nor should religious institutions be exempt from the laws of the state. Other than these areas, the government should not intervene. People should be free to worship in whatever way they deem appropriate, so long as it does not injure any other living creature or violate any law.

Stories

To Teach Your Mind, Touch Your Heart, and Uplift Your Spirit

The Time for A Spiritual Life is Now

There was once a disciple of a Guru who was living a divine life of sadhana and seva in his Guru's ashram. One day, he went to his Guru and said, "Guruji, I want to live a spiritual life. I want to live in the service of God. I want to go beyond the binding chains of this mundane, materialistic world. But, I feel that I am not quite ready. My desires for a family, for wealth and enjoyment are still too strong. Grant me some time to fulfill these wishes and then I will return to your holy feet."

So the Guru said, "No problem, my child. Go. Get married, have a family and earn wealth. In ten years, I will come back for you. My blessings are with you."

With the blessings of his Guru, the man went out and quickly found a beautiful girl to marry. They had three beautiful children, and the man become financially successful.

After ten years, there was a knock on the door of their home. The man's wife opened it to see a haggard-looking beggar standing on the doorstep. The beggar asked to see her husband. At first she started scolding the beggar, thinking that he was just there to beg for money. But, the husband realized that the beggar was his Guru so he lovingly invited him inside.

"I have come to take you away from this world of illusions now that you have fulfilled your desire of having a wife, family and earnings. Come with me, my son, let me show you the way to God."

But, the man looked at his Guru pitifully and said, "Dear beloved Guru, you are right. You have given me my ten years ever so generously and

172

with your blessings I have prospered. But, my children are very young and my wife would not be able to handle the burden of all of them alone. Allow me to stay another ten years until the children are old enough to care for themselves."

A true Guru will guide you to the path, show you the light and help when help is requested, but will never force a disciple – against the disciple's will – to follow any particular path. Thus, the man's Guru compassionately agreed, saying, "So be it, my son. Stay another ten years until you feel that your mission is fulfilled."

Ten years later, the Guru returned to the home and again gave his disciple the call, "My child, I am here to take you away from this world of illusion. Your children are now grown. You have given twenty years to married life. Come now and embark on your spiritual journey."

However, the man fell at his Guru's feet and cried. He said, "My Divine Guru! Yes, it is true that ten more years have slipped by, but you see that now my children are just finishing their education and they are just getting ready to marry. I cannot leave this householder world until I marry off my children and get them settled professionally. My youngest is fifteen, so if you could ever so graciously give me only ten more years, then all of my responsibilities will be complete."

"So be it, my child," the Guru said. "But remember that your true path is a spiritual path. Remember to keep your aim on God. Fulfill your duties but do not become too attached."

Ten years later, the Guru returned to the house to find a large bull-dog out front guarding the house. Immediately he recognized his disciple in the dog and saw – with his divine vision – that the man had passed away in an accident several years prior but, due to his intense protectiveness over his family and wealth, had reincarnated as a guard dog. The Guru put his hand on the dog's head and said, "My child, now that you have regressed from a human to a dog due to your attachments to worldly things, are you finally ready to come with me?"

The dog licked the hand of his Guru lovingly and said, "My beloved

DROPS OF NECTAR

Guruji. You are right that it is my own attachment which has driven me to take birth as a dog, but you see my children have many enemies who are envious of their wealth and power. These enemies are very dangerous to my children and I must stay here to protect them. However, I am sure that within a few years everything will sort itself out and they will be fine. Give me just seven more years to protect them, then I am yours."

The Guru left and returned seven years later.

This time, there was no dog out front and the home was filled with grandchildren running around. The Guru closed his eyes and saw with his divine vision that his disciple had taken birth in the form of a cobra, wedged into the wall near the family safe to guard the money. He called the grandchildren of the house: "My children," he said. "In the wall to the right of your safe, there is a cobra curled up in a small nook. Go there and bring the cobra to me. Do not kill it. It will not harm you, I promise. But, just break its back with a stick and then bring it to me." The children were incredulous, but went to the wall where the old man had directed them. Incredibly, they saw that a cobra was curled up in the wall. Following the Guru's orders, they broke the cobra's back and carried it outside to the Guru. The Guru thanked the children, threw the cobra over his neck and left.

As he walked away carrying the cobra over his neck, the Guru spoke to the injured and aching cobra, "My child, I am sorry for hurting you, but there was no other way. Thirty seven years and three births ago you left to taste the material world of sensual pleasures. But the ways of Maya are so alluring and so subtle that they trap us instantly. You have wasted these lifetimes in the futile pursuit of material success and in attachment to people who also are only actors in the Cosmic Drama. My child, all here is Maya - Cosmic Illusion. It lures us into its trap, convincing us that it is real, permanent, everlasting and significant. But, in reality, the only thing which is real is Him, and the only true purpose of life is to get close to Him. These attachments merely divert our attention and focus away from the true purpose of life. I had no choice but to come to your rescue as I saw you sinking deeper and deeper *into the deep clutches of* Maya."

*   *   *

So frequently in life we think, "Just one more year," and then I will simplify my life, minimizing luxuries. "Just one more year," and I will cut back on my time at the office to allow me to spend more time engaged in spiritual pursuits. "Just one more year," and I will dedicate more time to meditation, *seva* and *sadhana*. "Just one more year," and I will delve into the divine depths of spirituality. "Just one more year," and then I will cut down on indulging in sensual pleasures. It goes on and on. But, that "one more year" never comes. We continue to put off valuable life-changes until "tomorrow," and unfortunately, "tomorrow" never comes. Each day we again say, "From tomorrow I will begin."

Our intentions are good. We want to be more spiritual. We want to devote more time to spiritual pursuits. We want to spend less, need less and serve more. We want to be the master over our lust, anger and greed rather than vice versa. Yet, we are deluded, deceived and blinded by the power of *Maya*. Thus, we continue to find excuses for why we must work fifty or sixty-hour work-weeks, why we still have no time for meditation, why we can't squeeze a visit to holy places into our year's planning, and why we must continue to satiate our insatiable sensual urges. Then, we feel guilty for our lack of will power, and we again vow that "from tomorrow I will start."

This lack of will power is frequently misconstrued as a lack of strength. It is not that. It is not actually weakness. Rather the lack of will power to implement the changes we know we should undertake is due to the gripping, seizing, clutching power of *Maya* who wraps us so tightly in her soft, sweet-smelling, hypnotizing veil that we cannot see to the Truth that lies beyond. The veil of *Maya* intoxicates us in the allure of more and more – more and more wealth, more and more possessions, and more and more sensual enjoyments. She casts her spell upon us and we follow, blindly, like the circus animal promised a reward for his jump through the hoop.

When we read spiritual literature, when we listen to the holy ones, when we spend a few moments in meditation and prayer, that veil is temporarily lifted and we can see where we need to go, just as the man was able, whenever his Guru was present, to realize that ultimately he needed to leave the world and follow the Guru. However, the moment his Guru departed, the curtain of *Maya* dropped down again and the next act in the drama of his life unfolded as though there had been no intermission.

We are the same. We see where we need to go. We see what we need to do. We pledge over and over to implement the changes "next year" or "tomorrow." Yet, the changes rarely come, for we continually get carried out on the waves of *Maya* back into the tossing, turning, cresting, falling, tumultuous ocean of *samsara*.

What to do then? Are we, as ever-so-suggestible humans, destined to a life lived in the clutches of *Maya*? Are we destined to a life of only fleeting glimpses of the Truth? Are we to be forever imprisoned by her blinding and suffocating grip? No. We can break free. We can live in truth. In fact, the very nature of our existence, the very purpose of our human birth is to realize our ultimate divinity, to re-unite with that which is Divine, to break the chains of *Maya*. Anything less is a disservice to He who brought us into existence.

But how? The only way to break free from the veil of illusion that Maya wraps around our minds is to surrender to God and beg Him to show us the true light and to give us the strength to walk the path of light. Our personal, human willpower is, inherently, significantly weaker than the power of *Maya*. Alone, we cannot hope to break her chains. We cannot hope for Divine Realization or Illumination or even for a truly meaningful human existence. It is only by surrendering ourselves to God, by aligning ourselves with His ultimate and divine power that we can have the strength to walk the right path.

By relying solely on our own human will-power, we will forever fail. The power of *Maya* is too great. However, when we rely on the Divine power, we will forever succeed. When we rely on that power within us which is One with Him, we will neither fail nor fall. When we pray to Him – with a pure, devout, pious heart – for strength, the strength is given instantaneously. True, deep prayer melts away the chains of *Maya*, chains which fall to the wayside, powerless to bind us.

Yet, we must also remember that although God gives us the strength to break free from *Maya* and to both see and walk the divine path, we also have to put in the effort. It is not simply that we can say, "Okay, God. You give me the strength. I will do nothing." For then, when our resolve fails and we slip back into our old, familiar ways, rather than blaming ourselves we blame God. We say, "Well God didn't give me the strength," or "God did not help me." It is a dual effort, a joint effort. God gives the strength, but we must do the work. A famous saying is that "God helps those who help themselves." This is absolutely true. We must pray to God for strength, but simultaneously vow to utilize all the strength He gives us.

Thus, the only way to break free from the blinding veil of Maya is a two-fold practice. First, we must surrender to God and ardently pray for Him to take our lives in His hands, guiding us and giving us strength. Second, we must make *and stick to* concrete vows of how we are going to be better people. Rather than saying, "I will find time to meditate," we must say, "I will not leave for work without sitting in meditation and I will not sleep at night without doing my nightly introspection." Rather than saying, "I will try to visit holy places whenever I can," we must say, "I will take a spiritual holiday this year." Rather than saying, "I will try to cut back on my expenses so that my financial needs are less," we must say, "I will not buy another jacket or pair of shoes [or anything] until the ones that I have are broken, torn or no longer fit me." Rather than saying, "I will try to overcome my anger, lust and greed," we must commit to having daily appointments with God in which we introspect on all the times we allowed ourselves to be overpowered by these emotions, and we must pray for strength *daily* to remain calm, peaceful and *sattvic* in our lives.

If we wait for the right time, that time will never come. The time for a spiritual life is now.

The Lasting Danger of Anger

There was once a young boy with a terrible temper. He used to speak harshly and get angry many times a day, at the slightest provocation. His wise father told him that every time he got angry he had to hammer a nail into the wood fence in the backyard. The first day the boy hammered forty-five nails into the fence – practically his entire day was spent in the backyard. The next day, with his arm sore from hammering, he tried to get angry less. He hammered only twenty-five nails into the fence the second day. By the end of a few weeks, the boy proudly went to his dad and told him that he had not gotten angry at all that day.

So, the boy's father told him that now he could start removing the nails from the fence. There were two ways that nails could be removed: either if the boy could go an entire day without getting mad, or if the boy apologized sincerely to someone whom he had hurt through his anger.

So, the boy began to apologize to people whom he had wounded and he tried hard not to get angry. Slowly, the nails began to get pulled out of the fence. One day, the boy proudly went to his dad and told him that all the nails were out of the fence. He told his dad that his anger was "a thing of the past."

His dad then led the boy by the hand to the fence and showed him how the fence was now riddled with holes. It was no longer the sturdy, strong fence it once had been. It was now weakened and damaged. Every time the wind blew strongly the fence swayed in the wind, for it was so full of holes that the breeze caused the fence to move.

"Do you see that?" the father asked the boy. "For you, anger is a thing

---

of the past. Yet, this fence will never recover. Every time you get angry at someone, it is like driving a nail into them. You may later remove the nail, but the hole is still there. The effect of your anger cannot be removed."

*   *   *   *

In life sometimes, it is easy to get angry, easy to yell, easy to hit those we love. We assuage our own consciences by saying, "He made me mad," or, "She made me hit her." But, whose hand is it really that hits? Whose mouth is it really that speaks harsh words?

We think, "It's no big deal. I said sorry." Or we say, "Oh, but that was yesterday. Today I've been nice." For us, it may be that easy. But remember the fence is still sitting there with a hole in it, even though you have moved on. If you hammer enough nails into someone, eventually they will be forever weakened, forever damaged. You can stab someone with a knife and then pull out the knife, but the blood will continue to pour. "Sorry" does not stop the blood of wounds. It may pave the way to recovery, but the wound is still there.

The goal in life should be to be like water – a stone falls in and only causes a ripple for a moment. The "hole" in the water caused even by a large boulder does not last for more than a few seconds. When we get hit – verbally, physically or emotionally – we should be like the water. We should be able to just let the ripples flow and, within a few moments, it should look as though nothing happened.

However, unfortunately it is very difficult to be like the ocean. Very few people in the world are able to accomplish this task, for it is a task of great *sadhana* and *vairagya* (non-attachment). It is much more common that people are like fences – the holes you hammer into them stay with them for a lifetime. Children, especially, are like the wood fence. No matter how much they grow in life, no matter how wise they become or how old and strong they become, those holes are still there.

We must remember that our loved ones are like wood. Therefore, we must try to be very, very careful before we hammer holes into anyone, before we stab knives into anyone's heart. If there are too many holes, the fence will fall.

Judgment: Who is the Saint & Who is the Sinner?

There is a wonderful story told of two monks who had renounced the world and taken vows of celibacy and simplicity. One monk was older and the other was relatively young. They were wandering in the forest one day and came upon a rushing river. On the edge of the river stood a beautiful young woman. Her face was marked by anxiety as she explained to the two monks that she needed to get across, but the river was rushing too fast and she was afraid. She humbly asked if one of the monks would be good enough to carry her across. The older monk immediately picked her up gallantly and carried her to the other side while the younger monk walked by his side. Upon reaching the other shore, the monk placed the woman safely on the ground, and they bid her farewell.

One week later, the two monks were sitting under a tree for their morning meditations when the younger monk suddenly exclaimed, "Okay, I've been keeping this inside for the last week but I cannot keep it inside anymore. I cannot believe the way you picked up that young, beautiful woman and carried her body so close to yours! After taking vows of celibacy before God, after promising to forsake the touch of a woman, how could you wrap your arms around her body and carry her tightly in your arms? I have had such respect, even reverence for you for so many years, and now I feel so betrayed. You are not a true monk! You are not a true celibate. I must find another companion with whom I can tread a path of purity."

The elder monk listened with a faint smile growing across his face. "My brother," he said when the younger monk had finished his tirade. "I carried that young woman in my arms for approximately two minutes and left her by the side of the river, after setting her down safely. She *has not been with me since. You, on the other hand, have carried her in your heart for the last week. You have slept with her, eaten with her, breathed with her and even meditated with her because you cannot get her out of your mind. She is living permanently in your heart. It is your own heart you must seek to purify, not the actions of your traveling companions."*

*   *   *

How many precious minutes of each day do we waste by judging others? Too many, I think. We barely even realize how much we do it. We analyze and judge each other's actions, words, and even each other's articles of clothing or choice of perfume. We assume, naturally, that if we were in their shoes we would do nearly everything better. But, like in the case of the two monks, it is really our own hearts which need to be bettered, not the actions of another.

This constant judging and condemning of others pollutes our own hearts, wastes our precious time, creates boundaries and barriers between us, and steals our peace. We are so busy re-hashing everything other people did during the day, of which we did not approve, that we cannot fall asleep at night.

Our constant judging of others is not only detrimental to our interpersonal relationships but it also wrecks havoc on our own mental health. The more we become focused on others and their perceived faults, the farther we stray from our own path. To judge others makes us feel superior, confident, worthy. We value ourselves in comparison to others. Putting others down makes us feel higher in comparison. However, this is not the way to succeed in any arena of life.

We may feel temporarily good when we put others down. Our egos get a natural "high" when we criticize and condemn the other. Yet, we are actually sinking lower and lower on our own quest for true peace.

Searching for the Key

Once a woman was standing outside in the street searching and search-
ing for something under the bright street lamp. A wise man walked by
and asked her, "Mother, what are you searching for?"

She replied, "I have lost my key and I am looking for it." The man
helped her search for quite sometime, all to no avail. Finally, he asked,
"Mother, where exactly did you lose your key?" She replied, "I dropped
it inside the house and now I cannot find it."

The wise man queried, "But Mother, if you lost your key inside, then
why are you searching outside for it?"

The woman answered, "Inside it is dark and I cannot see. Here, with
the light of this lamp, I can see easily and search for my key."

The wise man counseled her, "Mother, go back inside. It may be dark
and difficult to see, but your key is inside. Light a candle and search
inside. You will never find your key out here."

*   *   *

We laugh at the silliness of the old woman who looked for her key
outside even though it had been lost inside. Yet, we do the same
thing in our lives. We look outside for our happiness, for our fulfillment and for our joy. We look to possessions to fulfill us. We
think that if we have the newest model car, a new CD or a new
pair of shoes that we will be happy. When we feel depressed or
stressed, what do we do? We go shopping or we go on a holiday
to the beach.

Yet, we all know that happiness and peace are not there. We are

---

never truly happier or more peaceful the day after buying something new than we were before. In fact, we frequently forget that we even bought it! The new coat, pair of shoes or CD gets put in a closet or store room and we forget about it.

For this old woman the key was, perhaps, the key to a dresser or a safe or a door. For us, it is the key to peace. We search and search outside for that key when really we have lost it inside. We look in the shopping malls, in retreats, in courses, in possessions, and in other people. But the key is in none of these places. The key is within us.

The reason that these external things don't bring happiness is that although we may have a new coat, it is still being worn by the same person. We may have new shoes, but they are covering the same feet. We may be driving a new car, but the driver is the same. We may be in Hawaii or Tahiti or on a cruise ship – but *we* are still there.

Our pain comes from within, not from without. If the dissatisfaction and the pain come from within, then how can the satisfaction and joy come from without? They cannot. The sooner we realize that the true answer lies within – in our hearts, in our relationship to God, and in our inner selves – the quicker we will find that answer. It is a rare person, though, who pauses to look inward for answers. Most of us are so busy searching shopping malls, vacation catalogues and our relationships with other people for the answers.

Why do we look outside? Because it is lighter. It is easier. It is easier to see things and other people than our own selves. So we search these things and these other people for the keys to our happiness. But, although the light is there, the key is not.

We must go inward, even though it seems dark and even though it seems that we may never find anything. We must have faith and start searching. Meditation, prayer, faith in God, a spiritual practice, a Guru, introspection, silence – these are all things that light the way for us to look inward, to find that key.

STORIES

Our candle may be dim at first, it might be hard to see. But slowly that candle will get brighter and brighter, and we will eventually find the key which we lost. However, the longer we search outside, the longer our key will remain lost.

I pray that you all may turn inward. I don't mean that you should ignore your family and friends or not buy gifts for your children. Rather, as you enjoy the time with your family and as you enjoy the gifts you receive, please remember that nowhere – other than within your own heart – lies the true answer to your happiness. Love your family without expectation. Enjoy the material gifts without expectation. Enjoy the vacation without expectation. When we expect these external things, people and places to bring us the ultimate bliss in life, that is when we will be disappointed. When we love and appreciate them as they are, but turn inward and to God for the true bliss, that is when we will be satisfied both externally and internally.

Sacred Drops of Blood

There was once a very great sanyasi who possessed the ability to transform people by his mere words. The sound of his voice carried listeners into the stillest, most peaceful meditation. But, he wanted to do more for the world. His vision was to help all of humanity, to be of service to all those he met, and to heal the world on a massive scale.

He prayed to God to give him the ability to save people's lives. "You cannot save everyone; you cannot be of service to everyone. Just keep speaking, keep chanting, keep writing, keep praying. In this way you will really heal," God said to him.

But the saint was not persuaded. "Please, God, let me be of direct service to all. Let me save people's lives."

The sanyasi had performed so much tapasya and was so pure in his desire to help, that God granted him the boon of being able to save the life of anyone who came to him. He had simply to take a drop of his blood and place it on the patient's upper lip. Any ailment would be cured; any suffering would immediately be alleviated. The saint was exuberant; his dream had been fulfilled. Now he felt that he would really be able to save the world and to cure those who came to him.

The first day four people came. For each person, he simply pricked the tip of his finger with a needle and the blood came out. One small drop had such miraculous healing powers. That night, the selfless saint had a beaming smile on his face for those whom he had cured.

The next day, forty people came, having heard of his miraculous powers. For each he squeezed a small drop of blood from his finger and blessed them as he placed it on their upper lip. Each was instantly cured. Paralysis, leprosy, depression, anxiety – all disappeared with the simple drop of the sanyasi's blood.   As word spread throughout the land, more and more people flocked to his healing magic. The sanyasi was in bliss – here he was using his simple God-given blood to cure so many. He dispensed these drops freely, with no hesitation, no discrimination, and no vacation. "I am in your service," he would say.

Soon, thousands were flooding the simple ashram in which he lived; they were overflowing in the streets. The saint was dispensing the equivalent of cups of blood each day. But, he did not even notice. Such was his dedication and devotion to those whom he was curing. He sat, in meditative bliss, as he squeezed first his fingertip, then the veins in his arm to dispense blood to those in need.

It was not long before the sanyasi had to squeeze harder in order to coax the blood from his body. Soon, a mere needle prick was not a large enough opening; he needed small knives to pierce the prominent veins of his forearms and legs. From there, the blood flowed freely again, and all were relieved. However, soon, even those veins were no longer coursing with high volumes of healing nectar. They, too, were becoming drier and drier.

As his blood volume dropped each day, the sanyasi became weaker. The color drained from his once vibrant face. Darkness drew circles around his eyes. His voice, which previously had boomed, singing forth the divine glories of God, was now not much more than a whisper. But, the sanyasi was not worried. Those who loved him urged him to take rest, to take at least a break from giving blood, to let himself recuperate.

Although he listened with his ears and appreciated the concern, he could not stop pumping blood from his body. He would say, "I am in the service of the world...These people have come from so far...They have been waiting for so long...This man is an important minister, but he's suffering from pneumonia...I feel no pain. I feel no weakness. I feel only the joy of giving myself to others." Those who loved him could do nothing, other than watch the scores of people continue to pour in, pleading for "just one drop."

DROPS OF NECTAR

Soon, even the once succulent veins of his forearms would give no more blood. Even the largest, most abundant veins of his body held on self-ishly to their sparse quantity of this life-giving fluid. But, the sanyasi *was not deterred. "This is only a challenge. Only more* tapasya *to do," he would say. He ordered his servants to build a device which would squeeze harder than human hands were able to, a vice-like apparatus into which he could place a limb and have it milked completely of the blood inside.*

Throughout this, the people kept coming. As word spread – in frantic whispers – that the saint was ill, that the blood was running dry, the people flocked even more frantically. They pushed and trampled one another in an effort to get "just one drop." People, who perhaps had been postponing a visit until a later date, dropped everything and came running. "Please Maharajji," they would plead. "Please, just one drop. We have come from Madras, we have come from Nepal, we have come from London. My daughter has this horrible affliction on her face. My husband lost his arm in a car wreck. My son refuses to get married. Please Maharajji, please just one drop. Just one drop and then we'll go away so you can take rest." For each who came, the saint smiled as he placed a drop of blood on their upper lip.

The ocean of his blood soon became an arid desert. Where once his veins had flowed like copious rivers, they were now limp and desiccated.

His devotees pleaded with him to stop; their tears of concern poured onto his holy feet. But, all he could see were needy, ailing people stretch-ing out to the horizon, each one crying pitifully, "Please, Maharajji, just one drop."

When those who had flocked for blood realized that the sanyasi *could give no more, they were undeterred. "We will work the pumping ma-chine," they screamed. And they stormed toward the saint, who sat peacefully, although nearly lifeless, draped only in his simple* dhoti. *But, the pumping machine was not powerful enough to pump water from a desert. So, they tied him up, the ropes cutting deep into his parched skin. And as some pulled the ropes tighter and tighter, others cut into his veins with knives (no longer small ones, but now the type used for butchering animals). "There must be another drop left. There must be!" they cried furiously.*

As his beloved devotees watched, the last drop of life blood was cut from their great sanyasi, who had once overflowed with life, vigor, and dynamism. Now he hung, lifeless, still in the ropes which had tied him, completely desiccated. However, they noticed, there was a smile on his limp and pallid face.

*   *   *

"Just five minutes," we plead. "Just step foot in my house to bless it…just take one meal at my home." It may not be physical blood we demand, but both our desperation and the effects on the saints is the same. "But, I've waited five years. But I've come from America. Please, Maharajji, just five minutes….but Maharajji, my daughter said she won't get married unless you are there…but, I can not go into surgery unless you come to the hospital…but it would mean so much to us if you could just come to our home for ten minutes…"

When we go to visit a saint, rarely do we ask when he last took his meal or what his usual time for rest is. "It's only five minutes," we convince ourselves. "Just one drop, one drop of blood…" When we are blessed enough to have a saint at our home, rarely do we say to him, "Go to sleep. You must be tired. You have sat with people [or worked] all day long." Rather, we think, "But, it's only once a year he comes," or, "But this is the first time we've ever had him alone."

"Just one drop…just one drop and then we'll let you take rest."

Sure, it is only five minutes, or one hour, or one night – *for us.* But, we do not have the vision to see the streams of people, flooding out to the horizon, who will beg for "just five minutes," after we have had ours. Rarely even do we lift our eyes to look.

"But," you may ask, "if the saint healed so many with his blood, why does it matter that he died? His purpose on Earth and his desire were to heal people. So, why does it matter that he lost his physical body in the meantime?"

The answer is that a doctor could have healed most of the physical ailments that came to him. Those suffering from emotional/psychological problems could probably have been helped had they put into practice that which he taught in his lectures. He did not need to give his actual blood to so many. But, it is easier to get the "instant cure," easier to let him place the blood on us than to make the trip to the doctor and take the medicine he prescribes, or to implement the necessary diet of less fat, less sugar, no meat, etc.

It is easier to be cured by someone than to cure ourselves. Somehow, when a saint speaks in public, giving instructions and messages publicly, we think that it pertains to everyone but us. "But I need to speak to him personally," we decide. "My problem is different." Rarely do we take a saint's "no" as "no." We know that if we plead harder, beg more desperately that they will give in, because they truly are in the service of humanity.

But, do we want to milk the blood from their bodies? Do we really want to be healed at their expense? Is that what love really is? We must realize that each of our demands, that each five minutes, each compulsory visit to a home, each drop of blood, is only one of thousands that he is selflessly giving to others. We must be careful to let him nourish himself such that his blood continues to flow. We must make a sincere effort to keep the life alive in these saints who would give their lives to us, without hesitation and without discrimination.

Our Endless, Insatiable Desires

Once, many years ago, before the severe violence in Jammu-Kashmir, we traveled to Kashmir to spend a few days meditating on the beautiful and heavenly Dal Lake. However, we enjoyed ourselves so much that we actually stayed one month instead of a few days. Each week we would postpone our departure from that heavenly, pristine, glorious environment.

Finally, after one month we knew we needed to leave so we went to bid farewell and give payment to the kind boatman who had taken us out onto the lake each day. When one of the devotees offered payment, the simple boatman refused. He said, "I thank you for the money, but more than the money I want one special blessing from Swamiji. Could I please speak to Swamiji and ask his blessing?"

When the boatman came to see me, he fell in prostrations on the ground and finally looked up, tears in his eyes, and said words I will never forget. He said, "Swamiji, I don't know what horrible karma I must have performed to be stuck here on in this lake for my whole life. I beg you to please give me the blessing that I may go one day and see Bombay."

I was amazed! We had come from all over India (and many devotees were from Bombay, Calcutta, Delhi, etc.) and we had fallen in love with the serene, divine atmosphere in Kashmir. The devotees from Bombay would have given anything to be able to stay forever on the lakeside. Tourists travel from every corner of the Earth to visit Kashmir. When there is not war going on in the area, it is known as the greatest natural paradise on Earth.

Yet, this man who had taken birth here, who lives every day in the midst of the most beautiful lake, dreams of nothing but Bombay! Those in

Bombay are crying to take a holiday to Kashmir, and those in Kashmir are crying to go to Bombay.

*   *   *

One of the greatest plagues of human beings is our insatiable desires. We truly never feel satisfied. We never feel that we have had "enough." We are always looking for more and more. This pertains to almost every area of our lives. Obesity, diabetes and heart disease are sky-rocketing because we always want "just one more" *ladoo, gulab jamun* or piece of chocolate cake. Our bank accounts are getting fuller but our lives are getting emptier. We are always striving to close "just one more deal" or to take on "just one more project," thereby sacrificing the precious time that we could otherwise spend on spiritual pursuits, with our families, or engaged in service for others.

It is through surrendering to God that we become desireless. Through being desireless we attain peace and joy. We think, mistakenly, that it is by fulfilling our desires that we will attain joy. However, it is the opposite. Fulfillment of desire leads to temporary happiness *not* because the object of desire was attained, but simply because the desire temporarily disappeared! If I am craving a new car and I get a new car, then my desire for a new car has gone away. It is not the new car itself that gives me the joy, but rather it is the fact that I am now free of the desire for a new car. The diminishment of desire is what brings joy to us. But the way to diminish our desires is not to rush around and try to fulfill them. There are always more. They are like weeds in the garden of our mind. No matter how many we pluck, there will always be more. For a short while we are satisfied, but then the fire of desire begins burning again. We can only become free of desires by accepting God into our lives and taking whatever comes as His *Prasad*.

Have Faith in the Divine GPS

Once there were three men sitting under a tree in a garden and they started talking about God. One man said, "I don't believe that God is perfect. In fact, there are so many things which even an ordinary reasonable man would be able to plan better than God. For example, look over there." The man drew his friends' attention to the pumpkin patch where hundreds of pumpkins were growing large and round. "God has put these huge, heavy pumpkins on the end of tiny, thin vines which always collapse under the weight of their enormous fruit."

One of the other men joined in, "Yes, you're right," he said. "Look there at the mango trees – huge, strong, sturdy trees. And their fruit? A tiny four-ounce mango! What kind of backwards planning is this? Put the heavy fruit on the thin weak vine and put the light fruit on the tall strong tree? I agree that God definitely is far from perfect."

However, the third man was unpersuaded. "What you both are saying certainly is compelling. You are right that it might have made more sense to put the heavy fruit on the strong tree and the light fruit on the thin vine, but still I believe that there must be a bigger, better Divine plan. I still believe that God knows exactly what He's doing and that His planning is perfect, even if we don't understand it."

The two friends chided the third for his simplicity and blind faith. "Can't you see with your own eyes how stupid it is? Even an idiot would know better!"

Wounded by the other men's criticism, yet secure in His faith, the third man stood up and went to rest under a nearby tree, separate from his two critical friends. All three drifted off into a deep afternoon slumber in the shade of the mango trees.

With the afternoon clouds, a strong wind rose up and whipped through the trees. Branches swayed in the heavy wind, causing ripe mangoes to fall to the ground. The sleeping skeptics awoke, startled by mangoes falling on them.

One of them exclaimed, "Our friend the believer was right! It is certainly a good thing that only mangoes hang from these branches. The weight of a falling mango was enough to startle me from sleep and bruise my cheek. Had it been heavy pumpkins falling onto us we would have become pumpkin pie! It is very good those heavy pumpkins grow so close to the ground!"

*   *   *

Frequently in life, we doubt God's path. "Is this really the way?" we wonder. We become skeptical of the Divine plan. We lose heart and faith. God's ways are frequently mysterious; we fail to see the full picture until it is unveiled for us. However, the enigmatic nature of His plan should not cause us to lose faith or to impose our own will.

These days in the West all the new cars have GPS navigation systems where the computer in the car gives directions on how to reach your destination. As you sit in the car you just enter the address of where you are going, and throughout the journey a pleasant woman's voice guides you, "Take a left turn in 200 meters." However, after you've entered the destination address, before her guided instructions begin, you must press the "Accept" button on the screen. If the button is not pushed, the guided route will not begin and you will be left to your own device to reach the destination.

GPS stands for "Global Positioning System," but I also think it stands for "God's Perfect System." He knows the way to the destination of our life, to the fulfillment of our unique, special and divine mission. He has designed the map. He has laid the roads. He has created the mountains, rivers, highways and train crossings. He knows every turn, every corner, every one-way street. He never loses His way.

STORIES

If we don't push "Accept" on the GPS system in the car, our journey will be filled with tension and worry. At each intersection we will have to gauge whether it is best to continue ahead or to turn left or right. We will have to stop and ask directions from passers-by who may not be any more acquainted with the roads than we are. We may eventually reach the destination, if we are focused, efficient and lucky, but we will likely be late and the journey will have been tense.

Alternatively, if we simply press "Accept," we will be guided gently and correctly at every step. We will know where to turn, where to continue straight and where to stop. Our minds will be free to contemplate God, to think pleasant and peaceful thoughts, and to converse with others in the car. The journey will be peaceful, smooth and enjoyable.

Similarly in our lives, if we accept God's will, if we allow Him to guide us along the path, our lives will be filled with inspiration rather than perspiration, and we will certainly reach the destination in the shortest amount of time.

We must continue to "Accept" the guidance given by God's Perfect System whether we are familiar with the route He is taking us or not. Let us always remember that He is the creator, He is the planner, He is the driver and He is the guide.

How to Walk the Path of Life

When I was very young, not long after I came to Parmarth Niketan, a very old, revered saint came to Rishikesh to give his divine satsang at Parmarth Niketan.

However, rather than staying in the comforts of the ashram, he used to stay in a small hut on the banks of Ganga a little bit away from the center of the ashrams.

I was given the special seva of going to pick him up each morning and bring him to the ashram. As we walked through the busy marketplace, I would try to push everyone and everything out of his way so that this revered saint could walk comfortably and unimpeded to the ashram. I asked everyone along the way, "Side please. Please give us the way to walk." I would gently push all of the wandering cows out of his path. I moved standing bicycles and fruit carts out of the way so he could pass.

Finally, as we reached the gate of the ashram, I was feeling very glad that I had been able to bring him so safely and smoothly to the ashram, and that I had been able to clear such a nice path for him to walk.

This saint, however, looked at me lovingly and said, "Beta, kis kis ko hatate rahoge? Aur kab tak hatate rahoge?" ("My child, how many people and cows can you push out of the way? For how long can you move other people and things out of your path? That is not the way.") "Apna rasta banate jao. Apna rasta banake nikalte jao." ("Do not try to move others; rather find your way between the others and around them. Make your own path, but do not worry about moving others. Find your own way in the midst of the chaos.")

*   *   *

In our lives we frequently get frustrated and broken by feeling that others are blocking our way and thwarting our path. We blame their presence and their actions for our own failure. We tell ourselves that we would have been able to succeed if only they had let us, if only they had moved out of the way for us. We try to push people and obstacles aside to clear a way for ourselves in life.

However, obstacles never stop coming. People who are jealous never stop trying to block our path. For how long can we try to move them aside? How many obstacles, how many enemies can we try to push away? The answer is to simply find our own way, around and between them. If they are blocking the path on the right, we walk on the left. If they are blocking the path on the left, we walk on the right.

We must be more concerned about finding our own way than focusing on moving all of those whom we think are blocking our path. For those who are pure in mind, thought and deed, there will always be a path in which to walk. The path may be narrow at times and it may seem that obstacles and enemies line both sides., but we must humbly and sincerely make our own way on the path of life. We must just keep walking the path of our *dharma*, the path of righteousness, and the path of honesty, purity and piety without worrying about those who try to block our way.

So much of our precious time, energy and focus are wasted in the futile task of trying to remove obstacles and people from our path. It is not necessary. Find your own path around the obstacles. Find your own path around the enemies. Do not try to push them aside or push them down or fight them for the right of way. Rather, carefully examine the situation and see where the path is clear. Then, choose that path and continue on your way.

The more attention we give to those who are trying to sabotage us and thwart our progress, the less time and energy we have to walk the right path. In that way then the enemies win, for they have stolen our peace of mind, our tranquility, our joy and our time. Instead of trying to fight them out of the way, we must remain humble, pure and single-minded on the goal. If we can see our destination clearly, then we will always be able to find a path in which to walk.

So, keep the destination firm in your mind. Stay focused on the goal and *nikalte chale, nikalte chale jao* [move around the obstacles and continue on the path].

The Importance of the Bhagavad Gita in Our Lives

There once was an elderly couple living in the mountains. They were of simple means, yet were extremely devoted and pious. The man would sit every morning at the small temple in their home and read passages from the Bhagavad Gita. *The couple's grandson, who was completely enamored with his grandfather, lived with them. The young boy would emulate everything his grandfather did.*

One day, the boy came, sat down in his grandfather's lap, and said, "Grandfather, I see you read the Bhagavad Gita *every morning and I see the way your eyes fill with tears. I have heard you tell so many people that the* Gita *has changed your life. So, I have also started to try to read the* Gita, *but I do not understand it. If I do understand a small passage of it, in just a few short hours I have already forgotten what I read." The old man simply said, "Do not worry, my child, if you understand it or not. Just keep reading it." So, the boy did as he was instructed. However, a few weeks later he again came, sat on his grandfather's lap and admitted, "Grandpa, I have done what you said, but still I do not understand the* Gita, *and I forget so quickly. It seems like such a waste of time. Why is it so important to keep reading if I am not benefiting?"*

At this, the Grandfather handed the young boy an empty basket that was used for carrying coal. He said to his grandson, "Take this coal basket down to the river and bring me a basket of water." The boy did as his grandfather instructed, but inevitably he returned with an empty basket. All the water had leaked out of the many holes before the boy had reached home. Again the grandfather sent the boy to the river, telling him, "Bring it faster next time, before it leaks out." So the boy ran quickly from the river to the home, holding the basket as water poured out. Again, the basket was empty long before arriving at his grandparents' house. He told his grandfather that carrying water in a basket was impossible and instead he would require a bucket or pail. But the grandfather was firm. "I don't want a bucket of water," he said. "I want a basket of water. You'll have to try harder next time."

This continued for five or six rounds from the river to the house. Each time the boy would arrive, breathless from his sprint, the basket would be empty. Finally the boy dropped to his knees and said, "Grandfather, it is useless." Sitting down, the grandfather took the boy and basket in his lap and smiled. "You think it is useless, my child?" he asked. "Have a look at the basket." The boy turned his attention from the lack of water to the actual basket, and he noticed that where the basket had once been black and dirty from all the coal was now clean and beautiful. The trips to the river, attempting to carry back the water, had washed the basket clean.

"Just as you may not have succeeded in carrying the water to me," the grandfather said, "your act of trying has served to transform the dirty, old basket into a clean, beautiful basket. Similarly, you may not succeed in understanding or remembering everything in the Gita, but the act of reading it cleans you from the inside out! When Lord Krishna enters our lives, we too become new and transformed."

*   *   *

The Bhagavad Gita literally means "Song of God, Song of the Soul, Song of the Spirit." It is not a scripture reserved for Hindus, but rather is universal. Regardless of your religion or culture, the Gita has the power to transform, to heal, and to uplift, and will bring greater insight and awareness to one's life.

The Bhagavad Gita is a journey from depression and despondency to devotion. The great warrior Arjuna was despondent and dismayed as he surveyed the battlefield of Kurukshetra. Suddenly, Arjuna laid down his arms and told Krishna that he could not fight. "I see in the opposing army my cousins, my uncles, my revered teachers. It would be better to renounce the kingdom than to fight with those who are so close to me," he bemoaned. Thus, to pull Arjuna from his despondency and to remind him of his *dharma*, Lord Krishna put forth the *Bhagavad Gita*.

Lord Krishna took Arjuna on the journey from despondency to devotion – devotion to God and devotion to his own *dharma*. That is the divine gift of the *Gita*: to carry us from a state of despair to a state of joy.

The teachings of the *Gita* are not applicable merely to life on a battlefield, when war with our relatives is imminent. Rather, the true battlefield is within us. Through the story of Arjuna and the war of Kurukshetra, Bhagwan Shri Krishna gives each of us lessons for our lives. The real Kurukshetra is within us. Each of us is Arjuna, struggling with right and wrong, temptation, fear and frustration. Our bodies are our chariots, being driven all too frequently by our senses as the horses. The mind, ego, desires, lust and greed are the evil Kauravas with whom we must do righteous battle, from whom we must not shy away in fear. If we give the reins of our lives to God (as Arjuna made Krishna his Divine charioteer), we will surely be victorious.

If we, too want to transform our lives from despair and depression to devotion and delight, we merely have to allow ourselves to be bathed in the *Bhagavad Gita*'s divine and healing powers.

The Saint & The Scorpion – What is Our Dharma?

Once there was a sadhu (a renunciant) living on the banks of a river, performing his sadhana with great piety and determination.

One day as the holy man went for his bath in the river, he noticed a scorpion struggling in the water. Scorpions, by nature, cannot swim and the sadhu knew that if he did not save the scorpion, it would drown. Therefore, carefully picking up the scorpion, the saint lifted it out of the waters and was just about to set it down gently on the land when the scorpion stung his finger. In pain, the sadhu instinctively flung his hand, and the scorpion went flying back into the river.

As soon as the sadhu regained his composure from the sting, he again lifted the drowning scorpion out of the water. Again, before he could set the scorpion safely on land, the creature stung him. Again, as the sadhu shook his hand in response to the pain, the scorpion fell back in the water. This exchange went on for several minutes as the holy man continued to try to save the life of the drowning scorpion and the scorpion continued to sting his savior's hand before reaching the freedom of the river bank.

A man, who had been out hunting in the forest, noticed this interaction between the holy man and the scorpion. He watched as the saint carefully and gingerly lifted the creature out of the water, only to fling it back in as his hand convulsed in pain from each fresh sting. Finally, the hunter said to the sadhu, "Revered Swamiji, forgive me for my frankness, but it is clear that the scorpion is simply going to continue to sting you each and every time you try to carry it to safety. Why don't you give up and just let the evil creature drown?"

The holy man replied, "My dear child, the scorpion is not stinging me out of malice or evil intent. It is simply his nature to sting. Just as it is water's nature to make me wet, so it is the scorpion's nature to sting in order to protect himself. He doesn't realize that I am carrying him to safety. That is a level of conscious comprehension greater than what his brain can achieve. But, just as it is the scorpion's nature to sting, so it is my nature to save. Just as he is not leaving his nature, why should I leave my nature? My dharma *is to help any creature of any kind, human or animal. Why should I let a small scorpion rob me of the divine nature which I have cultivated through years of* sadhana?*"*

*   *   *

In our lives we encounter people who harm us, who insult us, who plot against us, and whose actions seem calculated simply to thwart the successful achievement of our goals. Sometimes these are obvious acts, such as a co-worker who continually steals our ideas or speaks badly of us to our boss. Sometimes these acts are more subtle – a friend, relative or colleague who unexpectedly betrays us or whom we find has been surreptitiously speaking negatively about us behind our back. We often wonder, "How could he/she hurt me like that? How could they do this to me?" Then, our hearts become filled with anger and pain, and our minds start plotting vengeance.

Slowly we find that our own actions, words and thoughts become driven by anger and pain. We find ourselves engaged in thoughts of revenge. Before we realize it, we are injuring ourselves more than the other person injured us by his words or actions by allowing the negative emotions into our hearts. Sure, someone may have insulted us, plotted against us or interfered with a well-deserved achievement at work, but we injure ourselves more deeply and more gravely by allowing our hearts and minds to turn dark.

Our *dharma* is to be kind, pure, honest, giving, sharing, and caring. Others, due to ignorance, due to lack of understanding (much like the scorpion who doesn't understand the *sadhu*'s gentle intention) or due to the way in which their own *karmic* drama must unfold, may act with malice, deceit, selfishness and indifference. But we must not let their actions or their ignorance deprive us of fulfilling *our dharma*. We must not allow ourselves to be lowered by their ignorance, their habits or their greed. The darkness in their heart should not be allowed to penetrate into the lightness of our hearts.

Sometimes people ask, "But Swamiji, how long should we continue to tolerate, to forgive, to love in the face of other people's aggression, jealousy, hatred and malice?" The answer is forever. It is not our job to hand out punishment to others based on their negative actions. That is God's job and the law of *karma*'s job. They will get their punishment. They will face the same misery they are bringing to you. Do not worry. But, it is not our job to give that to them. It is God's job and – with the exacting law and science of *karma* – evildoers will receive punishment. But not by our hands. If we allow ourselves to injure them, insult them, plot against them and hurt them, then we are simply accruing more and more negative *karma* for ourselves.

If the *sadhu* had allowed the scorpion to suffer and drown in the river, he would have forsaken his own divine path in life. Sure, we can say that the scorpion deserved to die for what he had done to the *sadhu*. We can say that the *sadhu* had tried and tried to save the scorpion but the scorpion would not let him. We can give a list of explanations to excuse the *sadhu* for not rescuing the scorpion. But, to pardon bad behavior is not the goal. To excuse ourselves for failing to fulfill our duties is not the goal. The goal is to live up to our full, divine potential as conscious, holy beings.

So, let us pledge to always remember what our *dharma* is – to live lives of purity, piety, peace, selflessness, integrity and love – and let us never allow anyone to divert us from that goal.

The Pain of A Broken Connection

A man once went to see a doctor complaining of aches and pains all over his body. "Doctor, my whole body hurts," he moaned. The doctor asked him to show exactly where the pain was.

The man explained, "When I touch my shoulder, it hurts. When I touch my back it hurts. When I touch my legs, they hurt."

The doctor did a thorough examination and told the man, "Sir, there is nothing wrong with your body. Your finger is broken. That is why it hurts wherever you touch. Get your finger plastered, rest it for a couple of weeks, and all of your pains will disappear."

*   *   *

In life so frequently it is our own perspective that causes us pain. As we go through life "feeling" the world with our fingers, if our finger is broken naturally we will experience pain everywhere. But, we make the mistake of blaming the external world for our ailments: "My job is over-taxing, my husband is too demanding, my wife nags, my children are disobedient, my in-laws don't understand me, etc. etc." But if you look throughout the world, you will be able to find someone who has the same type of job but is calm, or someone who has the same type of spouse but is happy, or someone who has the same type of children but is patient, or someone who has the same type of in-laws but is grateful.

What is it that allows two people to experience the same external situation but respond in two different ways? Our own perspective. Our own perception. The key, then, is not to try to change every situation in our life, but rather to change the glasses through which we see the world. Sure, if we have a fixable situation at the office or at home, we should definitely do our best to improve it. But, what I have seen is that if someone has the nature to be dissatisfied, or the nature to be stressed, or the nature to be pained, that person's nature is not going to change simply by changing the external situation.

A massage for the back, shoulder or legs or a chiropractic or acupuncture treatment would not have helped the man in our example because it was his finger that was broken. He could spend hundreds of dollars to ease the pain in his body, but unless he put his broken finger in a splint, he would continue to experience pain every time his finger touched the various parts of his body. Similarly, we run around through life trying to "fix" our jobs or marriages or family life, but frequently the problem is in our own perspective. If we spend the same amount of energy "fixing" our perspective as we spend trying to "fix" our spouse or children, everything would be fine.

This is not to say that pains and troubles don't really exist in our day-to-day life. Of course they do. The man in our example may also have a stiff back or sore shoulders. But the excruciating pain he experienced was due not to the minor aches and pains in his body, but due to the severely broken finger with which he was touching them. Similarly, our jobs and our families are taxing. They demand a lot of us. However, the unbearable pain many of us experience is due not to the demands and commands from without, but due to the demands and commands from within ourselves.

In the *Bhagavad Gita,* it is said that we are our best friend and also our own worst enemy, depending upon how we live our lives.

Let us all take some time to examine what our own personal "broken finger" is. What is it within ourselves that causes us to experience pain in the world? What irrational fear, what unfulfillable desire, what selfish motive, what ego-driven need has broken the finger with which we feel the world or has colored the glasses with which we see? We spend so much time examining others, but very little time examining our own selves.

STORIES

The Source of all joy and peace lies within us. The key to finding and tapping into that Source must come from within. Let us find the key within ourselves and unleash the Ocean of Divine Bliss in our lives.

The Power of Love

I heard a beautiful story of a college professor in New York who gave his business-economy students the assignment of going into a slum and finding ten children each to interview. Then, the university students had to prepare reports on each of the ten children they had interviewed. The final item of the assignment was for the students to rate each child's chance of success in the world.

So, the students all completed their assignments. With twenty students in the class, the professor ended up with 200 papers on 200 different children living in a slum area. Every single report ended with the last question, "What are this child's chances of success in the world?" Each had the same answer: "This child has no chance."

Twenty or thirty years later, another professor at the same college came upon these 200 old reports in the economy department's filing cabinets. He thought it would be interesting to see whether all 200 children had really turned out to be victims of their impoverished, crime-ridden upbringings.

Amazingly, over 90% of the children who had "no chance" had turned out to be successful doctors, lawyers or professionals. The professor was astonished and went to each one to ask what had helped him or her become a success. Every single respondent (now they were middle aged) said, "Well, there was this one teacher I had who changed my life and gave me the ability to succeed."

The professor finally found this one teacher who had changed the lives of all the children. When he found her, she was past ninety and very frail. He asked her how she had possibly taken these impoverished children who had no chance of success in the world and turned more than 90% of them into successful professionals. The old woman looked at the professor smiled and said, "I just loved those children."

*　　　　*　　　　*

The power of love is enough to give hope to the hopeless, enough to turn failures into successes, enough to make lives worth living.

The teacher had not done any special program, nor had she taught the children any special skills. None of them recalled a particular lesson, activity or project. Rather, the simple fact that she loved them and believed in them was enough to change their lives.

We all have this power to transform not only ourselves, but others as well. Yet, do we use it? Do we take the divine gift of love in our hearts and use it as much as possible, to help as many as we can?

The message of Bhagwan Shri Krishna is, "Love, Love and Love all." From the moment He was six days old, He had enemies. So many demons and *asuras* came to kill Him. But what did He do? Did He fight them with anger? Did He hate them? Did He send them forever to Hell? No. He granted them all liberation.

Wherever Bhagwan Krishna went – whether it was to palaces, to the simple hut of Viduraji, to the gardens of Vrindavan – He brought only His divine love. His divine love changed not only the lives of all those who met Him during His physical presence on Earth, but the ever-present love He continues to shower upon us changes all who open their hearts to it.

Let us take to heart His divine message of :

"Love All, Hate None. Heal All, Hurt None."

God has given us a special ability to touch others with our smiles, to change a life with a simple warm embrace, to bring meaning to the lives of others by our love. We must use this divine gift and never let it go in vain.

Flowers blossom under the warm rays of the sun, and the flowers of our lives – our children, our families, and all those around us – will blossom only under the warm rays of our love.

If we learn how to love others, really and truly, not for who we want them to be, but rather for who they are, for the perfect souls that God has created, then we have learned one of the greatest lessons of life.

Shake It Off & Step Up

There is a story of a farmer who had an old mule. One day the mule fell into the farmer's empty, dry well. As the mule cried for help, the farmer assessed the situation. Although the mule had served the farmer faithfully for many years, the farmer decided that neither the mule nor the well was worth the trouble. So, he decided that instead of bothering to lift the heavy mule from the well, he would simply bury him in there. The farmer called his friend and together they began to shovel dirt into the open well.

When the first shovelful of dirt hit the mule he panicked. "What is this?" he thought. When the second shovelful hit him, he began to cry. "How could the farmer do this to me?" he wondered. When the third shovelful hit him, he realized the plan. However, the mule decided that he would not allow himself to be buried alive. As each shovelful hit fell upon his back, he rallied himself to "shake it off and step up." As shovelful after shovelful of dirt hit him on his back, and as he felt dejected and pained, he continued to chant to himself, "shake it off and step up." This he did, shovelful after shovelful, until – as the dirt reached the top of the well – the mule triumphantly walked out of what would have been his tomb.

If the farmer had not decided to kill the mule, the mule would never have survived. Ironically, it was the dirt which was meant to end the mule's life that actually ended up saving him, simply due to the way in which the mule handled the situation.

*   *   *

In life, sometimes we feel as though the world is "throwing blows at us." We feel shattered and broken. We feel as though we are being "buried alive." Perhaps someone is actually trying to injure us; or perhaps we are simply stuck in a difficult situation. Either way, we have two choices. We can either succumb to the onslaught and allow ourselves to be buried, or we can "shake it off and step up." The latter is surely a more difficult path. It requires resolution, the will to survive, fortitude and faith. But, in the end, it is the path that will lead to our triumph. If we continue to "shake off" whatever hits us in life, and we continue to "step up" and rise above any situation, then we too will always be victorious and our lives will be successful and joyful.

Service of Others
is the Best Medicine

There is a beautiful story of a princess who was suffering from an un-diagnosable illness. She lay in bed, listless, unable to walk or to exert herself at all. She had lost all her appetite and her parents feared she would soon perish. Her father, the King, called in all the top doctors and medical specialists, but none could either diagnose or cure the young princess. They gave her allopathic, homeopathic, and ayurvedic medicines. They gave her pills, compresses, powders, massages and mineral baths. Nothing made even a dent in the princess's condition. She continued to lay, limp and mute, on her bed, staring blankly at the ceiling above her.

Finally, in desperation, the King called a revered holy man, a saint who was worshipped throughout the kingdom as having divine knowledge and powers. As soon as the sage saw the princess, he understood ex-actly what was wrong. "Pick her up and place her in the carriage," he ordered. The King refused. "How can you take this weak, fragile being outside in the carriage?"

Yet, the saint insisted. "If you do not follow my orders, your daughter may not recover. Wrap her warmly if you like and place her in the carriage. We will travel alone." The King had no choice; his options were exhausted and none had borne any fruit. He could only pray that the holy man knew what he was doing.

So the princess was wrapped in the warmest shawls and gingerly placed – supported by numerous feather pillows – in the King's carriage. The holy man got in beside her and instructed the driver where to go. He explained to the princess as they traveled, "I have a few urgent jobs to take care of on our way. You can accompany me." They soon stopped in a poor area on the outskirts of the Kingdom. The sage stepped down from the carriage, carrying large sacks filled with clothing and food. He walked house to house, delivering bags of rice, lentils, and wheat to the impoverished villagers.

Soon, he returned to the carriage to find – as he had expected – the princess sitting up straight in her seat, peering eagerly over the side of the carriage. They drove a little way, and again the sage stopped the carriage in another poor, rural village outside the wealthy kingdom. "I need your help in this village. There is too much for me to carry," he told the princess. She barely needed the help of his hand to get down from the carriage.

The sage carried the heavy bag and gave the princess the task of handing the food items and wool sweaters to the grateful villagers. At the first house, she walked slowly, delicately, and meekly put her hand in the large sack to take out the bags of rice and lentils.

However, by the third house she was striding confidently down the path, and by the fifth house she was picking up the young children to hold them in her arms. As they walked back to the carriage, she insisted on helping the saint carry the sacks of food, and she did not need any assistance to get back up into the carriage. Her cheeks were rosy; there was a beautiful, radiant smile on her face and a glow in her eyes.

Upon returning to the kingdom, three short hours after leaving, the princess nearly jumped out of the carriage and skipped up the steps to the castle! The King was amazed! How had the saint cured his daughter so completely in such a short amount of time?

The saint explained, "Your daughter was suffering from a lack of meaning in life. She was suffering from the disease of being spoiled and having every whim gratified. She was ill from a life being lived in vain. A journey to the poorest of the poor, a few hours of giving rather than taking, the experience of service and selflessness are the only possible cures."

STORIES

Thereafter, the princess traveled twice each week with the saint, back into the poor villages, distributing food, clothing and other necessary supplies. She used her position as princess to help improve the living conditions of all those who lived in poverty. She dedicated herself to helping all those in need.

And she never suffered from a day of listlessness again.

*　　　　　*　　　　　*

Every day people in the West go out, go to work, earn money and become more prosperous. Yet, at the end of the day, when they return home, they are not happy. What is the true secret to internal peace and everlasting joy? I always tell people, *"Be God-conscious, not glamour-conscious."* Have Him in the center of your lives and you will find peace, happiness, meaning and joy.

However, it is difficult frequently to know *how* to implement the teachings of God in daily life. Yes, we should go to temple. Yes, we must chant His name (any name which appeals to us – whether it is Krishna, Rama, Jesus, Allah, Adonai, or anything else). Yes, we must read from His holy words. Yes, we must pray to Him and offer our lives to Him.

However, what else can we do, so many people ask, to really become aware of God – full of God-consciousness – in our daily lives? *We can serve His people!* Through service of the poorest of the poor we come closest to God. It is easy to see the divine in holy people, easy to serve those who look pious, proper and beautiful. But, the spiritual challenge is to see the divine in all, to serve all – from the highest King to the sickest leper – as though they are manifestations of God.

Through this selfless service, we not only benefit those whom we are serving, but we also benefit ourselves immeasurably. Our hearts fill with joy, with peace and with love. Our lives become full of meaning.

Who is Handicapped?

Across the world there is a wonderful organization called the Special Olympics. This foundation sponsors "Olympics" for people who are physically and/or mentally handicapped. These people who may be suffering from anything ranging from partial paralysis to brain damage to what is just referred to as "retardation." Participating in these events not only trains the athletes to perform up to their highest potential, but it also infuses them with a sense of success, competence, and achievement.

Recently, I heard a beautiful story about a race taking place in the Special Olympics. The athletes were lined up at the mark. The official yelled, "Ready, set, go!" and the athletes took off, all running as fast as their legs would carry them, with looks of determination, dedication and drive on their faces. All except one, that is. A young boy had tripped, immediately after starting, and had fallen into the dirt. He looked forlorn as he watched his peers race off without him.

Then suddenly, a young girl who was running turned her head to see what had happened to the boy. As soon as she realized he fell, she turned around and ran back toward him. One by one, each of the athletes turned around to go back and look after the fallen boy. Soon all the runners were gathered around the young boy; they helped him to his feet as one girl brushed the dirt off his pants. Then, all the athletes held hands as they walked together, slowly, toward the finish line.

*   *   *

These are the people we refer to as "handicapped" or "retarded" or, euphemistically, "mentally and physically challenged." Yet, would we who have full use of all our limbs, whose brains function at their highest capacity, ever turn around in the middle of a race, giving up our long sought-after hope of winning and go back to look after someone who was down? Would we ever sacrifice getting to the top, being the best, winning it all, just to lend encouragement to another? Rarely.

We spend our lives pushing to be higher and higher, better and better. We want to be the best, to be the top, to be number one. But at what stake? What do we give up in the process? They say, *"The mark of a true man is not how tall he stands, but how frequently he bends down to help those in need."* How frequently are we willing to bend?

The goal of life is not the accumulation of more and more possessions, or more and more degrees. The point of life is to move toward God, to realize our oneness with Him. The point of life is to fill every moment with compassion, with love, with prayer and with service.

Of course we must go to work and we must do our best in every possible arena. Of course we must attempt to succeed; we must live up to our fullest potential. But, too frequently, we become narrow-minded in what we see as our "potential." Is our potential merely financial, or academic, or professional? Might we have another potential – a divine, compassionate, pious, devoted potential that is just waiting to blossom?

Let us vow to live up to every potential – not just those that confront us obviously in our daily life, but also those which may be hidden below the surface. The athletes may have thought (and the audience may have thought as well) that their success and achievement would be marked by how quickly they could run the one hundred yards. However, the deep potential of these athletes was even greater than completing a "quick sprint." They chose compassion over competition; they chose unity over individual success; they chose to really show us what it means to be divine souls.

Let us take a lesson from these athletes, who are far less "handicapped" than most of the people in the world. Let us learn that each race in life may have two different paths for success; let us learn that compassion, love and unity are much more everlasting achievements than a blue ribbon.

Let us vow to turn our heads around frequently and see whether, perhaps, there is someone who needs our help.

STORIES

Raise Yourself, Don't Erase Others

Once, a wonderful spiritual master gave a demonstration in front of a large class. He drew a horizontal line on the chalkboard and asked the class the following question: "Is there anyone in the room who can make this line appear shorter without erasing it?" The students thought and thought. They concluded that the only possible way to reduce the size of the line would be to erase part of it from either side. Thus, they told Swamiji, "No, there is no way to reduce the size of the line without erasing any of it."

Swamiji then proceeded to draw another, much longer, horizontal line on the board, a few inches above the previously drawn line. "Now," he asked. "Hasn't the first line become shorter in comparison to the new, longer line? Doesn't it appear quite short?" Everyone agreed that the line now appeared much shorter. "One does not have to erase a piece of the first line in order to make it appear shorter. One simply has to draw a longer line near it, and it will automatically seem shorter."

*　　　　*　　　　*

In life, in the rush to get ahead, in the rush to prove ourselves and make a name for ourselves, we frequently resort to criticizing, condemning and bad-mouthing others. In order to make ourselves look better, we put other people down. So many times we tell examples of the shortcomings of our colleagues so that we – in comparison – will appear better, or we criticize those with whom we are in competition.

However, this is not the way to get ahead or make a name for ourselves. Let us not try to diminish others in order to look good ourselves. That is like erasing the line to make it shorter, simply so we will look bigger in comparison. The way to get ahead in life should not be at the cost of others. Instead of bringing others down, let us raise ourselves up. Instead of cutting others, let us learn how to grow. Let us become long lines ourselves, rather than erasing others. If we focus on becoming as "long" as we can, then we will naturally shine above others.

It is very difficult in life to accept our own responsibility, our own mistakes. It is much easier for us to condemn others, criticize others, judge others and blame others. We rarely realize how frequently our own actions contribute to a negative situation. It is so much easier to simply blame others. This is like erasing others in order to look long ourselves.

A woman once went to the doctor. She told the doctor, "My husband talks all night long in his sleep. You must give me some medicine for him to make him stop talking in his sleep." The doctor gave the woman a prescription for medicine and told her, "If you take this medicine every day, your husband will stop talking in his sleep."

But the woman was shocked, "Why must I take the medicine, doctor? It is my husband who has the problem. I am not sick. My husband is the sick one who talks in his sleep. It is for him you must prescribe medicine."

The doctor explained to her as follows: "Ma'am, your husband talks in his sleep because you don't let him talk during the day time. Every time he tries to say something you correct him, belittle him or tell him to be quiet. So, he has no choice other than to talk in the night. The medicine will make you be quiet during the day so your husband can say what's on his mind. Then he won't have to talk in his sleep anymore!"

Whenever we are in a difficult situation, a frustrating situation or a challenging situation, let us examine what we can do to solve the problem. Let us examine what role our own actions may have played in bringing about the current circumstances. Let us work *with* others to get ahead, rather than work *against* others. Let us cooperate instead of compete.

Indian culture teaches us *"milaanaa* not *mitaanaa"* and *"journa* not *tourna*" ("Bring together, don't cut. Unite, don't break."). But, don't break what? Don't break others' minds, hearts and spirits with our selfishness. When we push ourselves ahead at the expense of others, we naturally hurt them in the process. We break their spirit, their enthusiasm and their self-esteem. Heights of success must not be attained through lowering others. Rather, we must climb higher and higher to fulfill our own divine potential, to live our own divine *Dharma*.

When Bhagwan Rama sent Angadaji to Ravana in Lanka in order to bring Sitaji back, he told Angadji, "*Kaaj Hamaara taasu hita hoi*" ("Fulfill your mission in rescuing Sita, but do not hurt Ravana in the process. Just try to make him understand that he should peacefully return her."). This is the Divine way: do your duty, do your best, fulfill your obligations, but don't hurt anyone in the process, either physically or emotionally.

We must dedicate our lives to growing as much as we can, to learning as much as we can, to serving as much as we can and to getting closer and closer to the ultimate goal of Union with the Almighty. We must not let competition, jealousy, complexes or petty complaints stand in the way of our great Mission.

Footprints

I heard a story once of a man who was a great devotee of God. Always throughout his life, God was his companion. He loved God more than anything else in all the world. When the man was very old, he lay in his bed one afternoon and had a dream. In this dream, he could see his entire life stretched out before him, as though it was the coastline along the ocean. He could look back and see his footprints – deep impressions in the wet sand – marking the path he had walked in this life. As he looked back further and further, he could see that, in fact, there was not one, but two sets of footprints, side by side, along the edge of the ocean. He knew the other footprints were those of God, for he had felt God's presence beside him throughout his life.

But, then he saw something that woke him immediately from his dream; his heart beat fast and he could not hold back the tears. "God!" he cried out. "I just had a dream, and in this dream I could see the whole path of my life; I could see the footprints I left along the way. And beside my footprints, there were Yours, for You walked with me, and..." Now the man was full of tears and could barely speak. "God, sometimes there was only one set of footprints, and when I looked, I could see that those were the times I was really fallen, really broken, when I needed You most. How, God, how could You leave me when I needed You most? I thought You promised You'd be with me forever. Why did Your footprints disappear at the times I really needed You?"

Softly, gently, God laid a hand on the man's head and wiped away the tears. "My child, I promised to always be with you, and I have never left you for a second, not even while you slept. Those times when you see only one set of footprints, those darkest moments of your life, it was those times that I carried you in My arms."

There are times we feel abandoned by God, times we doubt His presence in our lives. It is easy to have faith when all is going well, easy to believe in a plan when that plan brings us joy and fulfillment. It is much more difficult to believe in the inherent goodness of the Planner when the plan causes agony. Do we all not, on some level, feel that when our lives are tough, that we have been left by God? But, it is those times that our faith will carry us through. It is truly those times in which we are being carried by God. Perhaps, as we get so much closer to him, as we move from walking beside Him to being in His arms, we actually feel His presence less, so we doubt it. Perhaps as the boundaries and borders between Him and us dissolve, and we simply become His children, perhaps that is when we truly lose ourselves in Him. As the otherness is gone, perhaps we feel less aware of the presence.

Love, Success & Wealth

A young woman heard a knock on her door one day. When she went to open it, she found an old man on her door step. "Come in, come in," she said. The man asked, "Is your husband home?" The woman explained that her husband was not home, but she invited the man inside anyway.

He refused, however. "I am here with my two friends," pointing to two elderly men waiting in the front yard. "However, we will wait outside until your husband returns."

That evening as soon as the husband came home, his wife told him what had happened. "Quick, quick, call them inside," the husband exclaimed. "We cannot leave old men standing in the cold outside."

So, the woman went outside and beckoned the men in. One of them rose and said, "Ma'am, all three of us cannot actually come in. You see, I am Love, and with me are Success and Wealth. Only one of us can enter your home. Please, go and ask your husband which of us he would like in the home." So, the woman went and after relaying the story to her husband, said, "I think we should invite Success in. Then, you will get the promotion you've been waiting for and we will become more prosperous."

However, the husband thought and said, "But, Honey, I only want the promotion so we can be rich. If we invite Wealth into our home, then it won't matter if I get the promotion, because we will already be rich. I think Wealth is a better choice."

Their daughter then quietly spoke, "Mom, Dad, let us bring Love into the home. If we have Love with us, then we won't care so much about

Success or Wealth. We will be rich on the inside."

Her parents thought for a moment and finally acquiesced to their daughter's wish. So, the woman went outside and, addressing the man who had introduced himself as Love, said, "Okay, we have decided. You can come inside." S o, Love took a step forward and began to walk toward the house. As he passed through the doorway, the woman noticed the other two men following. "Wait!" she exclaimed. "We have chosen Love. You said that only one could come inside."

Love then paused and explained gently, "If you had chosen either Success or Wealth, he would have had to enter alone. However, wherever Love goes, Success and Wealth always follow."

*   *   *

If you ask most parents what their concerns are regarding their children, you'll hear, "I want him to get into a good university. I want her to get a good job and be successful." Time and energy are therefore expended in pushing the child academically, encouraging the child to excel, punishing or reprimanding the child for anything less than a superb performance. Yet, a degree from a top university, a well-paying job, a lucrative career – these are not the true marks of "success" in life.

True success comes when we are fulfilled, joyful, peaceful and prosperous – both internally and externally. So, fill your homes with love – love for God, love for each other, love for the community, love for all of humanity. Then, through that love, through that divine connection, all else will automatically follow. It is when we focus only on Success or Wealth that we find ourselves rich but not fulfilled, successful but not content.

Breaking Through Our Own Shell

There was once a man who noticed a beautifully woven cocoon on a tree outside his home. He carefully watched the cocoon every day in order to catch the first glimpse of the beautiful butterfly he knew would emerge. Finally, one day he saw a tiny hole in the cocoon which grew quickly as the hours passed. He sat watching the butterfly break her way out of the cocoon. However, suddenly he noticed that it seemed the butterfly had stopped making progress. The hole did not get any larger and the butterfly seemed to be stuck. The cocoon was bouncing up and down on the branch as the butterfly tried to squeeze herself, unsuccessfully, through the hole she had created.

The man watched in dismay as it seemed his butterfly would not be able to emerge. Finally, he went inside, took a small pair of scissors, and carefully cut the cocoon, allowing the butterfly to emerge easily. However, the butterfly immediately dropped to the ground instead of soaring gracefully into the sky as he imagined she would.

The man noticed that the butterfly's stomach was swollen and distended but her wings were small and shriveled, explaining her inability to fly. He assumed that after some time, the stomach would shrink and the wings would expand, and she would fly in her fullest glory. However, this was never to be.

The man didn't know that it was the very act of forcing her body through the tiny hole in the cocoon which would push all the fluid from her stomach into her wings. Without that external pressure, the stomach would always be swollen and the wings would always be shriveled.

*　　　　*　　　　*

In life, too frequently, we avoid the challenges, looking for the easy way out. We look for people who will "cut our cocoons," so that we never have to work and push our way through anything. However, little do we realize that it is going through those times of difficulty which prepare us for the road ahead. The obstacles in our path are God's way of making us able to fly. With every bit of pushing and struggling, our wings become fuller and fuller.

So frequently, people come to me and say, *"Oh, why has God given me so much strife? Why has He put so many obstacles in my path? Why is He punishing me?"* We must realize these are not punishments. Sure, *karma* plays a large role in what we receive in this lifetime, but even the things that seem like "bad" *karma* are actually opportunities for growth. Even an extra small hole to squeeze through is actually an opportunity for our wings to expand to great lengths.

So, let us learn to take our challenges for what they are, rather than looking around for a "different" hole, or for someone with a pair of scissors. These things may help us quickly through the cocoon, but we will be unable to fly in life.

God's Helping Hand

There was once a man who was a great devotee of God. He always believed that God would take care of him, regardless of the circumstances.

One day a great flood came to the town in which he lived. All the neighbors began evacuating their homes. However, this man was not worried. "God will take care of me," he assured himself.

Soon, the flood waters began to rise and water filled the first floor of the man's home. "No problem," he thought, and he moved to the second floor. At this time a boat came by, and the men in the boat shouted to him through the window, "Climb in, we'll save you."

"No," the man replied calmly. "That's all right. God will save me."

The men in the boat urged him to evacuate his home. "The waters are rising and rising," they cried. But, the man was undisturbed and sent them away, firm in his conviction that God would come through for him.

However, the rain continued and the waters rose and rose. The second and then third floor of his house filled with water. "No problem," he thought as he moved onto his rooftop. Sitting on the rooftop, wrapped in a rainjacket, the man saw a helicopter fly overhead. From the helicopter, a life preserver dropped down into the man's lap. "Grab on," the pilot yelled. "I'll save you."

But, the man would not grab on. "God will save me," he yelled back. "I don't need your life preserver." So, eventually, the helicopter flew away.

STORIES

The flood rose and soon the man drowned.

When he entered Heaven, he said to God, "What happened? How could you let me drown? I thought you said you'd always save me. I had such faith in you."

God looked at the man sadly and said, "I sent you a boat; I sent you a helicopter. What else could I do?"

*   *   *

How many times in life do we avoid taking advantage of the situations which present themselves, instead holding tenaciously to our belief in *karma*, or fate, or divine will/intervention? God will not always come to you draped in a saffron *dhoti*, flute in hand and whisk you away from unfortunate situations in His chariot. He is more subtle, less obvious. He sends us the life preserver, but it is our choice whether to recognize it as "God-sent" and grab on, or to cling to the belief that something better and easier will come along shortly.

Karma does not mean that we have no choice or free will. It means we are handed a certain set of circumstances due to past lives, *sanskaras*, and many other factors. However, what we do with that set of circumstances is only partly determined by "fate"; the rest is determined by our own free will. For example, let's say that due to past *karmas*, in this birth we are given a cow. The cow is due to our past *karma* and our fate. We cannot change it and get a goat or a dog instead. Yet, what we do with the cow is up to us. If we drink its milk and use its manure in our fields, then we will have radiant health and rich, fertile crops. But, if we eat the manure and spill the milk on the ground, our health will suffer and our crops will be weak and unproductive.

So many times we blame God for the situations in our lives, or we simply concede that it "must be our *karma*." Yet, sickness and failing crops are not our "*karma*"; rather they are due to our own bad choices that we made with the cow that we were given.

We must realize that everything comes from God, that everything is due to His will, yet simultaneously we must understand that He has given us the power of discrimination and reasoning to make the right choices. It was the man's *karma* to have a flood destroy his home. It was God's kindness and compassion that sent the boat and helicopter, but it was the man's own ignorance and obstinacy that led him to drown.

So, when a flood comes in our lives, no problem. Perhaps that was meant to happen. But, when boats and helicopters come to save us, we must recognize them for what they are – God-sent.

Heaven & Hell –
Life is What You Make it

I have heard the story of a land called Hell. In this land, the people are emaciated and famished. Yet, they are surrounded by bowls and bowls and platters and platters of luscious food. Why, then, are they ravished with hunger? Because, in this land called Hell, their arms cannot bend and thus they cannot carry even one morsel of food from the plates to their mouths. Their hands grasp fresh breads, ripe fruits, spoonfuls of hot stews. But, in this land of Hell, their bodies can not receive the nourishment of this, for it cannot reach their mouths. Their stick straight arms wave wildly in the air, desperately trying to figure out a way to carry the delicious food to their mouths.

The people in Hell cry out day and night. They futilely try to force their arms to bend. But the arms are rock-solid straight. They try to eat directly with their mouths, but this is forbidden and they are beaten for it. So, they wither away for eternity in this land of never-ending frustration, deprivation, and starvation.

I have also heard the story of a land called Heaven. In this land as well, the people have only stick-straight arms. They, too, are surrounded by platters and bowls of scrumptious food which they cannot carry to their mouths. Yet, in Heaven, everyone is plump, well-fed, satisfied and joyful. Why is this? If you look carefully you will notice that, rather than obstinately trying to bend their own unbendable arms, they have simply learned to feed each other.

*　　　　*　　　　*

This is truly the only difference between Heaven and Hell. Do we stubbornly fight the will of God? Do we wrestle unsuccessfully each day with situations that cannot be changed? Do we flail around, wildly and desperately, trying to change the unchangeable? Do we ignore our loved ones, our friends, our colleagues who could help us immeasurably? Do we insist on suffering in silence, never asking for a helping hand from those near us? Do we watch others suffering and withhold our own help because we are so caught up in our own distress? If so, then we are living in Hell.

Or, do we assess the situation, look around and see how the situation can be improved? Do we graciously offer our hands and our help to others? Do we accept others' help when we are in distress? Do we take joy in "feeding others"? Do we spend time nourishing each other's bodies, minds and hearts? Do we let ourselves be fed with love? Do we allow others to nourish us, rather than thinking, "I can do it myself?" If so, then we are living in Heaven.

Too often in the world I see people who are living in the Hell of their own isolation, in the Hell of their own frustration, in the Hell of their own determination to change the very nature of the world in which they live.

Families and friends gather together, frequently after many months of separation. Too frequently, though, I hear people say, "Oh, I dread this time of year. I dread it when the whole family comes together," and then they continue on in a litany of complaints about this relative, that in-law, this friend. I have seen innumerable situations in which family members and friends could so easily put an end to another's pain. Yet, they won't. They don't want to be the one to offer, "Here, let me feed you."

Or, in the opposite, but similar situation, I see so many people suffering who could be helped by their families and friends. Yet, they won't ask for help. They won't let others help them. They say, "I can do it myself." Their pride and ego will not allow them to say, "Will you feed me, please?" However, this is not the way it should be. When we gather with our loved ones, we must realize that it is they who can feed us when we are hungry, it is they who can alleviate our suffering, it is their love which will turn our lives from Hell to Heaven.

STORIES

We must be willing to see the situation as it stands. If our arms are unbendable, we must accept that they are unbendable and then look for other ways to solve the problem. If we keep trying to change the unchangeable – in ourselves, in others or in the world – we will forever be frustrated and hungry, not only in the body but also in the heart and soul.

So if you see someone suffering, be the first to offer your help. Put aside any grudges or complaints or judgments. Simply offer your hand in assistance. And, if you are in distress, ask for help. These are your closest family and friends. Put aside your ego and pride. See how they can help you and ask for that. Then, as you feed them and as they feed you, your lives will change from Hell to Heaven.

Real Education

Once there was a boat, sailing in the middle of the ocean. On this boat were a philosopher, a scientist, a mathematician, and the boatman. The philosopher turned to the boatman and asked, "Do you know the nuances of Vedanta? Do you know the theories of Plato and Aristotle?" "No," replied the boatman. "I have never studied those things. I only know to take God's name in the morning when I wake up and at night before I sleep, and to try to keep Him with me all day long." The philosopher looked at him with disdain. "Well, then at least 30% of your life has been in vain."

Next, the scientist asked the boatman, "Do you know Einstein's Theory of Relativity? Do you know Newton's laws?" The boatman looked out at the reflection of the moon on the water. The light seemed to dance playfully off of the waves, touching first here, then there. He gently shook his head in response to the scientist's question. "No," he said. "I am not learned in that way. I have only learned to be kind, to give more than I receive, and to be humble and pious." "Well," the scientist exclaimed. "At least 40% of your life has been in vain."

The mathematician then turned to the boatman. "You must at least know calculus? You must know how to compute advanced equations?" The boatman closed his eyes and entered a meditative trance. "No," he said softly, a smile creeping across his sun-weathered face. "I do not know those things." "Then, your life has been at least 50% in vain!" The mathematician retorted.

The four sat in silence for awhile, when suddenly the waves began to rise up furiously; the sky turned dark, obscuring the blanket of stars. The boat – thin and wooden – began to rock back and forth, up and *down, with each thrust of the waves. The boatman fought diligently, using every muscle in his body, every skill he had to regain control over his boat. But the storm was winning the fight, and with each surge of the waves, the boatman became more and more convinced that the boat could not withstand this beating. As a wave lifted the boat high into the air, the boatman asked his passengers, "Do you know how to swim?" "NO!" they all cried at once. The wave dropped the boat, upside down, back in the raging water. The boatman watched sadly as the scientist, the philosopher and the mathematician drowned. "Well," he whispered, "I think 100% of your lives have been in vain."*

*   *   *

In this life, there are so many things to learn, so many things people say are important. Education is, of course, quite important. A doctor cannot operate if she doesn't know where the organs are, or how to sew a wound back up again. A scientist cannot perform experiments unless he knows which chemicals to use, and how much of each. An architect cannot design buildings without knowing what foundations and supports are necessary.

However, in the big picture, these are not the lessons or the education that truly liberate us. It is not this knowledge that saves us from drowning in the ocean. Only the knowledge of God can do that. Only love for Him, devotion to Him, and a life-vest inflated by Him can protect us in the raging sea of this world. For, many times in life, we feel like we are drowning. Many times we feel like we have swallowed so much water we can't breathe. It may seem as though our legs cannot possibly tread water for another minute.

At times like this we tend to turn to what we already know – more education, the acquisition of more possessions, the fulfillment of more sense pleasures. However, perhaps it is these that have caused our boat to capsize in the first place. Perhaps the ominous waves of the ocean are actually made up of our insatiable desires, of our purely academic educations, of our disregard for the Supreme Power behind and within everything.

Instead of making ourselves heavier and heavier, in which case we will surely drown, we must turn to the light, ever-present life vest around our bodies. It is knowledge of God, of how to truly live that will save us. The boatman knew how to see the stars; he knew how to watch God play in the light; he knew how to remain calm and serene even when challenged and insulted. He knew how to really swim.

Just Do Your Duty &
The Rest Will Follow

There was once a horrible drought. Year after year not a drop of rain fell on the arid ground. Crops died, and, as the land became parched, farmers gave up even planting their seeds. As the time of planting and tilling the ground came for the fourth rainless year in a row, the farmers of the region had given up hope and they sat listless, passing their time with playing cards and other distractions.

However, one lone farmer continued patiently to plant his seeds and sow and till his land. The other farmers poked fun at him and derided him as he continued daily to take care of his fruitless, barren land.

When they asked him the reason behind his senseless tenacity, he said, "I am a farmer and it is my dharma to plant and till my land. My dharma does not change simply due to whether the clouds rain or not. My dharma is my dharma and I must follow it regardless of how fruitful or fruitless it appears to be." The other farmers laughed at his wasteful effort, and went back to their homes to continue bemoaning the rainless sky and their fruitless land.

However, a passing rain cloud happened to be overhead when the faithful farmer was giving his answer to the others. The cloud heard the farmer's beautiful words and realized, "He's right. It is his dharma to plant the seeds and to till the land, and it is my dharma to release this water which I am holding in my cloud onto the ground." At that moment, inspired by the farmer's message, the cloud released all the water it was holding onto the farmer's land. This rain cloud then continued to spread the message of upholding one's dharma to the other rain clouds, and they too – upon realizing it was their dharma to rain – began to let go of the moisture in their midst. Soon, rain was pouring *down upon the land, and the farmer's harvest was bountiful.*

*   *   *

In life, we tend to expect results from our actions. If we do something well, we want to be rewarded. If we work, we want to be paid (whether financially or in some other way). We want to work only so long as the work reaps rewards. If the fruits cease to come, we decide the work is not "meant to be," and we abandon it.

However, that is not the message which Lord Krishna gives to Arjuna in the *Gita*. The message is that we must do our duty regardless of the fruits. We must live according to our *dharma* regardless of whether it appears to be "successful." We must perform our duties for the simple fact that they are our duties.

Lord Krishna tells Arjuna to stand up and fight, and says that, even if he dies in the battle, he must still do his *dharma*. The Lord tells Arjuna that it is divine to die on the battlefield of life (meaning engaged in performing your duty). He explains that either way, Arjuna will "win." If the Pandavas win the battle, then they will obliterate the evil influence of the Kauravas and inherit the kingdom. If, on the other hand, the Kauravas win the battle and the Pandavas are killed, then they will go straight to the Lord's eternal abode, for they died in the service of *Dharma*.

Usually in life, we know what our duties are. We know our responsibilities. We can see the "right" thing to do. This is especially true if we take time to meditate, reflect and contemplate. Yet, too frequently we walk away from doing the "right" thing or from performing our duty due to the uncertainty of the result. We don't want to waste our time or look like a fool. We neglect our responsibilities by saying, "It doesn't matter anyway." We shun our duties with words like, "Well, no one else is doing it, so why should I?"

This is not the way to live. We must realize that there is an enormous, infinite cosmic plan at work and we must all perform our allotted tasks to the best of our ability. Whether we actually succeed or fail in the venture should not be the biggest concern. True success

238

comes not in a financial "win," but rather in the humble, tenacious, dedicated performance of our tasks.

Interestingly enough, when we act with righteousness and integrity, we find that others will follow. It is not that we are taken advantage of, as we frequently fear. Rather, if we set the divine example, others will follow. Just as the rain cloud followed the example of the tenacious farmer, so will those in our lives follow our own examples. If we act with honesty, we receive honesty. If we act with dedication and love, so we will receive dedication and love. If we fulfill our *dharma*, so will those around us learn to do the same.

Yet, even if we are the only ones acting piously, acting honestly, acting with devotion, it should not matter. Our lives, our happiness, and our *karma* are individual entities. They are not dependent upon the response from others.

Therefore, we must all learn to stand up, have courage and keep performing our duties, regardless of whether it looks like success or failure will result. Through the fulfillment of our *dharma* we will achieve the greatest success in life – bliss, peace and enlightenment.

The Leaky Bucket

In the very olden times, there was once a great king. This king had many, many servants to take care of every task. One particular servant was responsible for bringing water from the well to the King's table. However, it was a long journey from the castle to the well from which fresh, clean and pure water could be obtained. As this was the time before cars and other convenient machines, the servant carried two buckets - one attached to each end of a long stick - to transport water back to the castle. One of the buckets was new - it shone in the sunlight and it was perfect in every way. The other bucket was older and it had a small hole on one side that caused water to leak from it onto the ground along the road back to the castle.

Thus, whenever the servant arrived back at the castle, although he had filled two buckets of water, he had only one and a half to present to the king. This caused the leaky bucket great distress. Twice a day when the servant picked up the buckets to go to the well, the older one would look longingly at the new one and bemoan, "Oh, why can't I be as shiny and flawless as the other?" The leaky bucket would cast envious looks at the new bucket as not a single drop fell from its new, glistening metal.

The leaky bucket tried every possible way of shifting its weight, of rotating its sides to minimize the leakage, but all to no avail. It could retain no more than half a bucket of water through the long walk back to the castle.

One day, the leaking bucket was distraught and cried out to the servant, "Why don't you just throw me away? I'm of no use to you. I can do barely half the work of your new bucket. You have to walk such a long *way back and forth to the well, and I leak out half of the water you fill me with. The king is such a good, noble, divine king. I want to serve him as well as your new bucket. But I can't; I can't even give him a full bucket of water."*

The servant was very wise (sometimes wisdom lies hidden in places where we don't expect it). He said to the bucket, "Look down. Look below you on the path to the castle, the path upon which you leak your water." The bucket at first was too ashamed to look and see drops of precious water scattered on the ground. When it finally looked, however, it noticed a thick row of beautiful flowers - so many lush, blossoming varieties - lining the path with vibrancy and beauty.

"Every day I pick these flowers to decorate the king's table and his room," the servant said. "When I noticed that you were leaking, I planted seeds all along the path on your side of the road. Then, twice a day you come and water them. Now, they have grown and blossomed into the king's favorite centerpiece. He says their fragrance calms his mind and brings peace to his heart. So, see, you are not useless at all. Rather, you are serving two purposes - both to bring water and also to bring beautiful flowers to the king's castle."

*   *   *

So many times in life we condemn ourselves for our failures, we compare ourselves unfavorably to others, we grieve over our own shortcomings, wishing that we could be different, more like someone else or some pre-conceived ideal. And as we do this, we blind ourselves to our real assets, to the flowers we are watering each day, to the real gifts we can give to the king.

God has given everyone a unique, special set of gifts, and it is up to us to make the most of these. Some of us will be able to carry water without spilling a drop. Our gift to the world will be a full bucket of water. Others of us will be able to give only half a bucket of water, but we will line the world's paths with beautiful flowers and sweet fragrance. Let us never underestimate our potential or the significance of our own gifts. Let none of us ever feel just like a "leaky bucket."

God, You're My Number 1

There once lived a king, but he was not just any king. He was one of those kings who was so important, so powerful that history books will talk about him forever. This king ruled an area bigger than the land now called America. His territory extended from sea to sea, across mountain ranges, jungles, and deserts. No one knew how many subjects he had, as there were too many to count. People used to say that if you put all his money together in one place, it would fill the oceans.

This king was the most powerful man the world had ever seen. Anything he commanded happened instantly. One time in the middle of winter, the king was craving mangoes. But, it was winter, and the trees only give mangoes in the summer. However, this king was so powerful that when the mango trees heard he wanted their fruit, they began to produce huge, beautiful mangoes. The snow was washed off, and the king had sweet mango in December.

Being such a powerful king of such a large region, he had to travel quite a bit. Travel in those days was not as easy as it is today. There were no trains or airplanes. The king traveled by carriage, or rather with a whole army of carriages. Because travel was so slow and difficult, he was frequently gone for long periods of time.

One time, he had been away for many months, visiting the farthest reaches of his kingdom, ensuring that everyone was happy and taken care of. For, even though he was so rich and very powerful and had more subjects and money than one could count, he had a very pure heart and was very dedicated to all of his subjects. When he was about to return home, he sent letters to all of his queens (in those days kings had many, many queens). In the letters he asked if there was anything they would like, any special gift he could bring them from far away. Of course, he always returned with carriages collapsing under the weight of so many gifts for his family, but he wanted to know if they had any special requests.

Each queen sent a list back to the king. "Bring me silk sarees, lined with gold...bring me diamonds, fresh out of the Earth....bring me pearls from the depths of the sea...." However, while all of the other queens sent long lists, one queen sent only a piece of paper with "1" written on it. The king was baffled. He turned to his chief minister and said, "This queen is stupid. I knew when I married her that she was stupid. Everyone else sent a list of gifts they want. This queen writes only '1' on the paper. What is '1'?"

The chief minister was very wise; he was a true man of God, and he could see people's hearts. He laid his hand on the king's shoulder. "No, no," he said. "The '1' means 'only you.' She is saying that she only wants you. Everyone else wants jewels and sarees and silks. When this queen writes '1,' she is saying that you are her number one, that you are all she wants. If you are there, with her, everything is there. In your presence, she wants nothing, needs nothing. And if you are not there, nothing can fill the hole left by your absence - not sarees, not diamonds, not jewels. If you are not there, for whom will she wear the sarees? For whom will she wear the silks, the diamonds? What is the point of all these things if you are not there? Where you are, everything is. So, she wants you to bring yourself to her, and nothing else."

The king was silent. "Oh," he whispered, trembling, for now he understood. His whole life people had wanted him for what he had, for what he could do for them, for what he could bring to them. He could bring wealth, he could bring possessions, he could bring health (for he had all the best doctors), he could bring grace and blessings (in those days, people believed that kings carried divine powers). But, no one had ever wanted only him, just for him. No one had ever wanted only his presence, even if it carried none of the other gifts.

Immediately, he sent his servants to fill the orders on the lists sent by *the other queens; he sent his messengers to deliver those orders. He however went to the queen. When he saw her, his eyes locked with hers. Their tears seemed to flow together. Their souls seemed to embrace, although their bodies were still many feet apart. He moved slowly, almost as though floating, toward her. He took her in his arms and held her. "You are the only one who has ever really loved me. The others thought they loved me. But, they loved me for what I brought to them. They loved me for how they felt when they were with me. They loved me for what I symbolized. But you love me only for me."*

And the king stayed there, forever, with the queen. Because of its purity, their love just grew and grew, and it showered everything near them with light and joy. Everything in their presence flourished and blossomed. People talked far and wide about how the flowers in their garden were brighter, bigger, more alive than flowers anywhere else, how the birds all seemed to stay close to the castle. Even in winter when all the other birds flew to warmer ground and the land became silent, the birds at this castle stayed, and sang their blissful songs all year long. Even on cloudy days, there was always a break in the clouds big enough to ensure that the sun could shine on this castle.

And the king became even more rich and even more powerful - although if you asked him, he would not have even noticed; he was too busy serving his subjects, serving God, and loving his queen. Their love and light was so strong that it radiated to the farthest reaches of the kingdom, bringing joy and peace to all the creatures of the land, from sea to sea, across mountain ranges and deserts, and through the jungles.

*   *   *

So many times we become completely convinced that having this or doing that or going there will bring us happiness. "If only I had more of this," we say. Children are famous for this, but perhaps they are actually only more vocal. We watch TV, we see movies, we see advertisements. The message in all of these is, "Buy this, and then you will be happy." Sure the "happiness" takes different forms: some products bring happiness through beauty, others bring it through success, others bring it through the right foods. But, the message is the same: own this and you will be happy.

God is kind; God is giving. We are His children. So, naturally, He will frequently give us what we ask for.

But, when we ask for these things, aren't we saying to God, "I don't really need You, I only need this possession. Your only purpose is to bring me the possession"? If, however, we have God in our lives, we have everything. Do you think that when the King himself goes to the queen's palace, all his messengers and servants, all his possessions don't come with him? Of course they do. Everything goes with the king. Where the king is, everything is.

God is the Supreme King. The King of our lives. Where He is, everything is. Let us not lose sight of what it is we really need to be happy.

It's The Little Things In Life

Once there was a saint who lived in the Himalayan forests. He lived in an ashram deep in a beautiful jungle where he spent his time in meditation and looking after the ashram.

Once a traveler came upon the saint and the ashram while trekking through the Himalayas. The young man started talking to the saint about the spiritual life. The young tourist asked him, "What did you do before you became enlightened?"

The saint replied, "I used to chop wood and carry water from the well."

The man then asked, "What do you do now that you have become enlightened?" The answer was simple. The saint replied, "I chop wood and carry water from the well."

The young man was puzzled. He said, "There seems to be no difference then. What was the point in going through all those years of sadhana in order to attain enlightenment if you still spend your days doing chores and menial tasks?"

The Master replied, "The difference is in me. The difference is not in my acts, it is in me. Because I have changed, all my acts have changed. Their significance has changed. The prose has become poetry, the stones have become sermons, and matter has completely disappeared. Now there is only God and nothing else. Life now is liberation to me, it is nirvana."

*   *   *

So many people complain, "My job is not spiritual," or, "How can I live a spiritual life while I have to care for children and a family?" The answer to a spiritual life is not in *what* you're doing, but in *how* you're doing it. How attached are you to the details of what you're doing or how focused is your mind on God? Have stones become sermons? A spiritual life is not about renouncing work or renouncing chores or renouncing tasks that we may see as "beneath us." Rather, a spiritual life is about turning these tasks into *tapasya*, turning jobs into joy, turning stress into *sadhana*. This is a spiritual life.

People tend to think: first I'll complete my householder years (the years, typically from the age of twenty-five to fifty, which in traditional society are dedicated to having a career and family) and then I'll turn myself to God. Yes, in our culture, one dedicates one's life after retirement to God, to simplicity, to *seva*, to spirituality. But, you don't have to wait until you've retired in order to attain that glorious state. You can attain it while living *in* the world. It's all a matter of the mind. Are you counting cars in front of you before you reach the tollbooth on the highway, or are you counting the names of the Lord in your mind? Are you reciting lists of things to be done when you get home from the office, or are you reciting God's holy name? Is your tongue speaking angry remarks at your family, your co-workers and your neighbors, or are you speaking only pure, calm, peaceful words?

Attaining enlightenment does not mean being out of the world or away from tasks. It means being *in* the world, but not *of* the world. It means *doing* tasks, but not *being* the tasks.

Let us try, today as we complete our daily routine, to ask ourselves, "How would this routine be different if I were enlightened? How would my attitude change? How would my actions change?" Let us pray to God for the strength to act accordingly. Then we'll know that we're really living a spiritual life, not merely relegating it to a few moments alone in the *mandir* at the end of the day.

We Are Only His Tools

Several years ago the United Nations was having its 50th Anniversary Golden Jubilee celebration. World leaders – religious, political, and social – were gathered together to commemorate this special anniversary. Numerous renowned people gave speeches on the global significance of the UN, on the importance of fostering inter-ethnic harmony, on how to curtail the insidious trafficking of drugs, on the necessity of preserving and protecting our rapidly diminishing natural resources, and similar subjects.

Each speaker was allotted a short period of time in which to speak. Most were given three minutes; some were given five minutes. Time was watched carefully. Note cards were held up, alerting the speaker that he or she had three minutes left, then two minutes, then one minute.

A divine, elderly, revered Indian saint, clad only in scant white robes, walked slowly, yet purposefully and unwavering to the podium when it was time for his talk. As he spoke, silence descended upon the room. While most speeches were read from notecards, or were the product of careful and deliberate editing, his words seemed to speak themselves. Dadaji was given five minutes to speak. However, as the organizers held up signs that read, "Two minutes left," then, "One minute left," he showed no signs of winding up his talk. The next sign read, "Thirty seconds left," then, "Finished!" Yet, the saint was in such ecstasy, he was so impassioned with the words that were effortlessly flowing from his mouth, that he seemed not to even notice the signs.

At first the organizers were noticeably restless and anxious. After all, there were so many other people to speak, so many other segments of this important function. How to get this saint to step down from the *podium? But as he continued, his words acted like a lullaby. Even the anxious organizers became still and peaceful, mesmerized by the quality of his words and his tone. The hall – filled with an audience of thousands – was as quiet as if it were empty. Dadaji spoke for twenty-five minutes, an unprecedented amount of time.*

When he concluded, the silence of the auditorium broke like thunder into a clamorous standing ovation. No one who was present was unchanged. The saint's words had reached not only minds, not only hearts, but also souls. He was flooded with accolades and tear-streaked faces as he descended from the stage. "Oh Dadaji, your speech was incredible. So inspiring. So uplifting. It was just wonderful." Everyone wanted to praise this elderly yet seemingly ageless Indian saint. After one man took Dadaji's hands and gave particularly effusive praise, the saint looked sweetly into his eyes and replied, "Yes, it was wonderful. I was also listening."

*   *   *

"I was also listening." This should be our mantra. For, it is not we who speak. It is He who speaks, although we like to take the credit. How easy it would have been for Dadaji to have simply replied, "Oh, yes, I know my speech was good. I spent days preparing it," or, "Yes. I'm a very good speaker, aren't I?" However, he is a true man of God. He knows from where his words come. He knows whose words flow through his mouth. Those who are the true inspirations, who are the true teachers of this world, are actually simply channels. They are not the ones who spend lifetimes refining their tenaciously-held beliefs and then impose these upon others. Rather, they simply open up the channels inside them and let God flow into their hearts and through their mouths or pens. We are all here as tools for His work, as expressions of His love. Let us realize that. Let us break the dams within us, so the river of His work and His message can flow ceaselessly through us.

Teachings of the Buddha

There is a beautiful story told of a disciple of Lord Buddha who wanted to publish a book of the teachings of Buddhism. He spent several years compiling the great wisdom of Lord Buddha and placing it in book form. After that, it was time for the task of raising enough money to publish the book. He went door-to-door to his friends and neighbors requesting help in bringing this project to fruition.

After he had collected enough funds, he was about to publish the book when a large cyclone hit a poor area of the country. Immediately, he sent all the funds to the disaster-struck region to help the victims.

Again he had to undertake the task of collecting money to publish this important book. Again, his friends, relatives and colleagues helped him reach the goal. But then an earthquake struck another area of the country, killing thousands, and once again the disciple sent all of his hard-earned funds to the region.

Several years passed during which he tried, with difficulty, to raise the funds a third time. However, people were not ready to keep giving for the same book. Thus, it took him quite some time to raise enough money, but eventually no catastrophe struck and the book was published. On the inside cover of the book, beneath the title "Teachings of Lord Buddha," was written "Third Edition."

*   *   *

So many times in life we read spiritual teachings, we listen to lectures and *katha*, and we say our prayers, but do we actually implement these teachings in our life? The book was a "Third Edition" because the teachings of Buddhism include compassion, non-attachment and service to the poor. Thus, by donating the funds for the book to disaster-struck victims, the disciple was actually teaching and illustrating the words of the Buddha.

He knew that the word of the Buddha was to help those in need. Thus, it is even more illustrative of Buddhism to help the poor than to publish books.

In our lives, too, we must remember not only the words of the teachings, but also the true message of the teachings. We read the books, we listen to the lectures, but do we absorb the message? Sometimes we get so caught up in reading, hearing and reciting these teachings that we forget to live them!

Service to others is the true message, the true teaching, and the true wisdom of spirituality.

God's Wife

A small, impoverished boy was standing barefoot on the New York City streets, looking wistfully in the window of a shoe store. A well-dressed woman saw him and asked him, "Why are you looking so solemnly in this window?" The small boy looked up at her and replied, "I am asking God to please give me a pair of shoes."

The woman took the boy's small hand and led him into the shoe store, where she immediately asked the clerk for a bucket of warm water and ten pairs of socks. Then, placing the boy's dirty feet into the water, she tenderly washed them and put a pair of warm socks on him. After this she told the clerk to bring shoes for the boy.

As they left the store, the boy's small feet now snugly in a pair of new shoes, he clenched the woman's hand and looked up into her eyes. "Are you God's wife?" he asked.

*   *   *

This story is not only a beautiful snippet from life in a big city. Rather, it is a deep lesson about how to live our own lives. Instead of simply saying, "Oh, how sweet," and moving on, let us really take this story to heart.

How easy it is to pass by those less fortunate with a simple sigh of sympathy or with a token "aid," perhaps a coin or two tossed in their direction. These small gestures of empathy and charity make us feel like we are compassionate people who just live in an "unjust" world. However, is the homeless man helped by our sigh of disdain? Does the coin we hand him really make a difference? Are we really being compassionate, or are we just soothing our own consciences?

How much more difficult it is to really stop, take a moment out of our hectic lives and see what is needed. Yet, how much more divine that is. There are always places to be and things to do. If we wait until we are "free" in order to take care of others, the time will never come. Real divinity, real selflessness is giving when it is not necessarily convenient to give. It is giving according to the others' needs, not according to our own agenda and convenience.

The wealthy woman probably had some place else to be on that cold day in New York City. She could have easily walked by the boy, thinking to herself, "Our government really needs to do something about homelessness." She could have looked the other way and continued on with her errands. But she didn't. That is what makes her special.

We tend to give decadently to ourselves and to our own families. We will pile gifts under Christmas trees until there is no room left. We will shower each other with new clothes, toys, and other merchandise on birthdays and anniversaries. No problem. We love each other and so we give gifts. This is fine. However, let us also remember to extend that compassion and that love to others who really need it. Let us vow never to turn a blind eye on someone in need. Let us vow to use what God has given us to really serve His children. Let us live our lives as though we too are "God's wife."

Gold Under Boulders

I heard a beautiful story that happened in an ancient village. One day, the villagers found a large boulder in the middle of their main pathway, and people reacted in many different ways. The busy, rich businessmen and merchants had their servants carry them around it. Others simply turned back and returned in the direction from which they'd come, realizing that to try to pass was futile. Others gathered around the site of the boulder to criticize the King of the area for not taking better care of the roads. They stood by as the boulder obstructed passage on the road, condemning the King and his ministers for their laziness!

Finally, a peasant came by who was carrying a load of vegetables to sell in the market. He needed to pass the boulder, and so he calmly put down his heavy load and tried to push the boulder out of the way. However, the boulder was quite heavy. But, the peasant just kept pushing from different angles and finally the boulder rolled out of the road. As he bent down to pick up his load of vegetables, the peasant noticed something lying in the road where the boulder had been. It was a wallet filled with gold coins and a note from the king. The note said, "This reward is for he who has the commitment to move the boulder from the road."

*   *   *

So frequently in life we see that the "King" has thrown obstacles in our path. Our natural instinct is to bypass them – using our influence or wealth – or to simply turn around and go a different path. Or, we give up the path altogether, seeing the obstacles as insurmountable. Perhaps we find ourselves criticizing life, circumstances, or the great "King" who is making our lives difficult. Yet, for he who has the commitment and dedication to conquer the obstacle, the rewards are great. Not only will the path be clear, but we will also become far richer (whether spiritually, mentally or financially) by having the tenacity to overcome the hurdles in our path.

Life is not always a clear path. If it were, we would learn very little. Rather, to test us, to teach us, to mold us and to make us stronger, God challenges us. He – as the King of kings – places obstacles in our way. And, just like the king in the above story, He watches to see who will have the courage and the commitment to overcome these difficulties.

There is a beautiful saying in our scriptures which says:

> *Prarabhyate na khalu vighna bhayena nicheh*
> *Prarabhya vighna vihata virmanti madhyah*
> *Vighneh Punah punarapi prati-hanya manah*
> *Prarabhya chottam-janah na parityajanti*

This means that there are three types of people in the world. The first type, the lowest on the hierarchy of evolution towards God-realization, contemplate the possibilities of failure before undertaking any task. Then, realizing that some obstacle will inevitably arise, and fearing the difficulties inherent in overcoming the obstacle, they decide not to act. Thus their lives pass in vain, and they perform no good deeds at all, for they are paralyzed by thoughts of hurdles that may arise.

The second type of people begin to perform good deeds but as soon as they encounter any difficulty, they turn back and relinquish the task. These people have good hearts and good intentions and they want to perform worthwhile deeds; however, they are unable to gather up the inner resources necessary to overcome any challenges. Thus, their lives also pass in vain, and although they have innumerable projects that began well, they have not even one that has been completed.

The third, and highest type of people are those who just keep going, no matter what obstacles they find in their path. They are so committed to completing their duties successfully that they steadfastly remove all hurdles from their way. They are entirely focused and centered on the ultimate goal, and they keep God's image in their mind, knowing that He is with them and that He will help them achieve their noble goals. These are the people who succeed, not only professionally in life, but also spiritually and mentally.

STORIES

Needle to Heaven

Once, Shri Gurunanak Devji Maharaj, the founder of Sikhism and a very great saint, was on a pilgrimage. This was approximately 500 years ago, and the saint would travel by foot, freely dispensing wisdom, guidance and blessings to thousands of people. Along his way, a very rich man invited Gurunanak Devji to his home for the night. This home would be more aptly called a palace. There was marble and gold everywhere, expensive horses and carriages, and dozens of sumptuous foods served out of silver dishes. Tokens of the man's success abounded.

A truly great saint is always thinking about how to help us grow spiritually, how to uplift us, how to turn our minds and hearts to God. Gurunanak Devji Maharaj was such a saint. Additionally, a saint will never take anything without repaying the giver in some way. So, when he left the rich man's home, he handed the man a small sewing needle. "Hold on to this for me. I will take it back when I next see you," the saint said to the man.

Later, when the man told his wife what had happened, she was furious. "How could you have taken something that belongs to a saint? What happens if he dies before he sees you again?" It is considered a great sin to keep something belonging to a saint or to be in a saint's debt, so the rich man's wife was very angry. She told her husband, "You can not take the needle with you to Heaven when you die. So, if he dies first, you will never be able to give it back to him. Go now. Return the needle immediately!" So, the man set out after the saint.

When he found Shri Gurunanak Devji, he handed him the needle and said, "Guruji, I cannot bear the thought that if you should die, I would have no way of returning your needle to you. It is not as though I could take it with me when I die and then give it back to you in Heaven. I cannot. So, please take it now."

The saint smiled, took his needle, and looked deep into the rich man's eyes. "You are right. You cannot take this needle with you when you die. But, if you cannot even take this tiny needle, how do you think you will take all your possessions and wealth? That, too, must stay behind when you go. You can not even leave this Earth with a tiny needle, let alone a palace full of wealth."

"Oh my God, you are right." The man became white as a sheet. "All my life I have struggled for things that are as transitory as this body. I have sweat and slaved and forsaken my family in favor of acquiring more and more wealth. Yet, if God takes me tomorrow, I will lose it all in a breath. I have acquired nothing that will last. I have not done good deeds for others; I have not practiced sadhana; I have not served the world."

When he returned home, he immediately sold all his possessions (except the most basic necessities), donated all the millions of rupees to the poor, and devoted the rest of his life to God and the world. And do you know what? As he lay on his death-bed in the small, simple house with his wife and family by his side, he said, "I am far richer today than I was thirty years ago when Shri Gurunanak Devji came to my home."

*   *   *

What can we learn from this wise saint? His message is as apt and valuable today as it was in the rural villages of India centuries ago. We come into this world with nothing but the love of our parents; we leave this world with nothing but the love we have created. All material things we acquire we must leave behind. I have never seen a rich man, a sports star, a movie actress, a businessman, a doctor, a fashion model, or even the president ride to Heaven in a Mercedes, carrying a basket filled with luscious snacks. No, we leave this Earth alone. We cannot take our car, or our favorite clothes, or our finest china – not even one cent. All we can take is the *karma* of this life and the knowledge that we have spent this life in service, that the world is a better place because we lived.

Once a great king who had conquered many lands and attained much wealth was dying. He begged his doctors to find some cure, to somehow salvage his failing health. The doctors sadly explained that there was nothing more they could do, that they could not give him even one extra breath. At this the king asked that, upon his death, his arms should be kept out of his casket instead of inside. When a corpse is placed into a casket, the arms are always laid neatly at the body's side. However, the king wanted his arms, palms up, out of the casket. He said that it was important for people to realize that even though he had conquered entire countries and kingdoms, even though he had obtained vast amounts of riches, even though his wealth and power were unparalleled, he still had to leave this world empty-handed. His bounty of wealth and power could neither prolong his life nor travel with him into the next world.

Every Outstretched Hand is God's

A wealthy man was once walking back to his home on a cold, windy, winter night. On his way home he met a beggar who was clad in nothing but a thin cloth. The beggar beseeched the rich man, "Please, sir, give me your shawl. Otherwise I fear I will not make it through the cold tonight."

The rich man was also a pious man, a devoted man. However, he still had a few blocks to walk to his home and he did not want to suffer during those few blocks without a shawl. Yet, his heart was pulled by the poor man and he knew that he had to help those in need. So, he decided that the best solution was to give half of his shawl to the poor man and to keep the other half. So, he cut the shawl in half, wrapping himself in one half and giving the other to the homeless man.

That night as the wealthy man slept, Lord Krishna came to him in a dream. In the dream, it was winter and Lord Krishna was shivering, wrapped only in half a shawl. "Lord, why are you wearing only half a shawl?" the man asked. Lord Krishna replied, "Because that is all you gave me."

*   *   *

Our scriptures say that God comes in many forms. Frequently, He comes to us in the guise of someone in need – an orphan, a homeless beggar. That is why our scriptures say to look on everyone, whether they be a prostitute, a crippled man, a dirty child or a crook, as Divine. It is easy to see God in His glorious, beautiful form. It is easy to adorn the temple deity with fine clothes and sandlewood tilak and to cook for Him with love. It is easy to sacrifice our own needs while we do the seva of a revered saint. It is much more difficult to extend the same love and selflessness to those in whom we don't see the direct embodiment of the divine.

However, that is the task; that is the divine challenge. Our vision is limited. We see only on the surface. We see only the outer manifestations of what we perceive to be either holiness or lowliness, and we make our judgments based on these faulty perceptions. We give to those whom we deem worthy; we give as much as we decide the other needs. This is our mistake, and this is why we see Lord Krishna wearing only half a shawl!

So, we must learn to cultivate divine vision. We must pray for the sight that shows us God in everyone and in everything. Who would give God only half a shawl? Who would even hesitate before offering God all we have and all we are? No one. In fact, our tradition is based on the very idea that everything we are and everything we do is for God. In *yagna* we say *"Idam namamah"* – "Not for me, but for You." Before we eat, we offer *prasad* to Bhagwan. We will not take food until He has first been served.

As our world is flooded with poverty, with violence, with hunger, with homelessness, and with destitution, let us open not only our two physical eyes, but let us also open our third eye, the divine eye. Let this eye show us God's existence in everyone, and let us serve others and treat others just as though they were Lord Krishna Himself who had come to us for assistance. Then, and only then, can we obliterate the distress in the world.

Loyalty of the Birds

A long time ago, in the times when animals, plants, and man still spoke the same language, there was a large fire that threatened to burn down many acres of forest. Flames whipped through the ground, devouring small shrubs, bushes, flowers and grasslands. All the animals scampered for safety. Squirrels climbed high in the trees, frogs hopped quickly to lily pads in the middle of ponds, deer ran briskly to higher ground, birds flew to safety. As the fire raged, the billowing flames became more and more ominous, engulfing more and more of the forest. The waters of the pond began to boil, and the frogs hopped desperately from lily pad to lily pad.

Soon the rising flames began to envelop even the oldest, sturdiest, densest trees, consuming them from the inside out. Squirrels hopped and monkeys swung from branch to branch, tree to tree, trying feverishly to escape the fury and momentum of the fire.

High in one tree sat two birds, and they neither cried with fear nor attempted to fly to safety. When the forest ranger, clothed in a fire-proof suit and attempting to ensure the safety of as many animals as possible, saw them he became frantic. "Fly away!" he cried. "Go...shoo...fly!" He yelled as loudly as he could, hoping to startle them into flight.

Yet they remained still, unwavering and complacent. The ranger picked up branches and began to throw them into the tree. "Fly away....Go! Go!" he beseeched them, but the birds would not budge.

Finally, the ranger looked up and cried, "The forest is burning. This tree will be nothing but ashes in a few hours. You will die for sure. Why in the world won't you fly away?"

After many moments of silence one of the birds spoke. "We have lived our lives in this tree. She has given us branches on which to build our nests and raise our young. She has given us fruit to eat and worms to feed to our babies. Her leaves capture the moisture each night, and in the morning she has let us suck on them for water. In the summer, she has blocked the sun and provided us with shade. In the winter, she has caught the snow herself, so it would not fall on us. As the wind blows through her leaves, she has sung to us. She has let us fly quickly to her highest branches to escape the tigers or other animals that would eat us. We know she will burn. If there was anything we could do to save her, we would do it. But, as much as we have tried to think of something, we realize we are helpless. There is nothing we can do. However, we will not leave her now.

"Our whole lives, and our parents' lives and our grandparents' lives, she has stood beside us, never flinching, never failing to provide us with anything we could need. How, in this most dire moment, could we abandon her? We may not be able to save her, but we will not let her die alone. That is why we stay. She will die, and we will die, but she will not leave us and we will not leave her."

*   *   *

We are so quick in life to switch loyalties – from one teacher to another, from one spouse to another, from one way of being to another. Our hearts are fickle. We will remain loyal as long as it serves us to do so, as long as we benefit from the loyalty. But, is that really devotion? There is a reason that wedding vows include the phrase, "for richer and for poorer, in sickness and in health."

It is very easy to be attached to someone who is healthy, happy and prosperous. It is more difficult to remain with someone who is sick, depressed and indigent. It is even more difficult to maintain the devotion when it may bring what looks like harm to you. I say "looks like harm" because the loss of your faith actually is more damaging to your soul than any of these other superficial "catastrophes."

Pure, single-minded devotion is one of the most beautiful things on Earth. It is, in fact, the path of *Bhakti*. Yet, how many of us are really able to maintain this? Usually, we love God and have faith in Him when all is wonderful. It is more difficult to believe in a Divine Plan when that Plan causes agony. Know, though, that it is at times of distress that your faith is most important. For, these are really the lessons of life. This is real spirituality. Spirituality is not about being where and with whom you are most comfortable. It is keeping the fire of your loyalty burning regardless of how much water is being poured on the flames.

This is the beauty of the birds. They realized there was nothing they could do to keep the fire away from their tree. So, they calmly and faithfully waited out God's plan. This sort of devotion may be seen as blind; it may be viewed as childish. Yet, those views are from a standpoint which can only see devotion and loyalty as the means to another end. However, they are ends in and of themselves.

Their simple and pure loyalty is going to carry these birds' souls to Heaven more than anything they would be able to accomplish with their remaining years if they had forsaken their "mother" tree.

Buried Treasure

There is a beautiful story of a beggar who lived all of his life under one tree. Each day he would go out into the villages and beg for some dry bread crumbs to sustain his life. Then, he would come back to his tree and eat his bread or whatever scraps the villagers had given him that day. For forty years the beggar lived under the same tree, pleading with the people to give him some food. He'd walk to all the nearby villages, alternating days, begging for his nourishment. Slowly, day by day, he became weaker, and finally one day his body could no longer sustain itself and he passed quietly into death.

When the villagers found him, they decided to bury his ashes under the tree where he lived out his life. As they began to dig in order to place his ashes deep in the ground, they found a treasure chest – a chest full of gold, diamonds and jewels a mere six inches below the ground.

For forty years, the beggar had lived, barely scraping by on his dry bread crumbs, sitting six inches above a treasure chest which would have rendered him as rich as a king. If only it had ever occurred to him to explore the depths of the Earth on which he sat, or to delve deeply into the recesses of his home, he would have discovered this treasure chest. But, he did not. Rather, he sat on the surface, suffering and withering away day after day.

*   *   *

Too frequently in life we are also like this beggar – running here and there searching, begging for that which we need to fulfill our lives. Perhaps we are not begging for food or basic life necessities. More likely we are searching and yearning for peace, happiness or God. We go here, we beg there. We search this place, we search

---

that place. But, that priceless and crucial peace and happiness still elude us.

If only we would sit still for a moment and go deeper within, we would find that treasure chest. We don't even have to dig six inches. Just right within us, sitting in our heart, is God, and through our connection to Him, all of the riches of the world are bestowed upon us.

However, too frequently I see people running in the opposite direction in their fruitless search. They run from this workshop to that workshop, from this new trend to that new trend, all the while being frustrated in their search. Stop for a moment and look within.

The Indian youth, especially, are all incredibly blessed. Your culture, your heritage and your traditions are a true treasure chest of meaning, understanding, wisdom and insight. Through opening this box of jewels you will definitely find the happiness, contentment and peace for which you are searching.

Go back to your roots, back to your heritage, back to the temple. Listen to the stories of your parents and grandparents. Perform *aarti* with deep devotion. Go to have the *satsang* and the *darshan* of visiting saints. Take a trip to India rather than to the beaches or ski slopes. Through this reconnection to your culture and your heritage, you will find the key which will open the treasure chest.

But, never forget that the treasure chest is inside of you, flowing through your veins. It is not some external "thing" to be obtained or found. Rather, the divine joy is residing within you, in your heart, in your breath and in your blood.

Pieces Sent By Others

We offer our appreciation to those who have forwarded
these important pieces to us, and we apologize where
the name of the author is uknown.

Give

You give but little when you give of your possessions.
It is when you give of yourself that you truly give.
For what are your possessions
but things you keep and guard
for fear you may need them tomorrow?
And tomorrow, what shall tomorrow bring
to the over-prudent dog burying bones in the trackless sand
as he follows the pilgrims to the holy city?
And what is fear of need but need itself?
Is not dread of thirst when your well is full,
the thirst that is unquenchable?
There are those who give little of the much they have –
and they give it for recognition,
and their hidden desire makes their gifts unwholesome.
And there are those who have little and give it all.
These are the believers in life and the bounty of life,
and their coffer is never empty.
There are those who give with joy, and that joy is their reward.
And there are those who give with pain,
and that pain is their baptism.
And there are those who give and have not pain in giving,
nor do they seek joy, nor give with mindfulness of virtue;
they give as in yonder valley the myrtle
breathes its fragrance into space.
Through the hand of such as these, God speaks,
and from behind their eyes He smiles upon the earth.
It is well to give when asked,
but it is better to give unasked through understanding.
And to the open-handed the search for one who shall receive
is joy greater than giving.

PIECES SENT BY OTHERS

And is there aught you would withhold?
All you have shall some day be given;
therefore give now, that the season of giving
may be yours and not your inheritors'.
You often say, "I would give, but only to the deserving."
The trees in your orchard say not so,
nor the flocks in your pasture.
They give that they may live, for to withhold is to perish.
Surely he who is worthy to receive his days and his nights is
worthy of all else from you.
And he who has deserved to drink from the ocean of life
deserves to fill his cup from your little stream.
And what desert greater shall there be,
than that which lies in the courage and the confidence,
nay the charity of receiving?
And who are you that men should rend their bosom and unveil
their pride, that you may see their worth naked
and their pride unabashed?
See first that you yourself deserve to be a giver,
and an instrument of giving.
For, in truth it is life that gives into life —
while you, who deem yourself a giver, are but a witness.
And you receivers — and you are all receivers —
assume no weight of gratitude,
lest you lay a yoke upon yourself and upon he who gives;
rather rise together with the giver on his gifts as on wings.

By Khalil Gibran

Reasons to Give Thanks

If you woke up this morning with more health than illness, you are more blessed than the million who will not survive the week.

If you have never experienced the danger of battle, the loneliness of imprisonment, the agony of torture or the pangs of starvation, you are ahead of five hundred million people around the world.

If you attend a temple or church meeting without fear of harassment, arrest or torture of death, you are more blessed that almost three billion people in the world.

If you have food in your refrigerator, clothes on your back, a roof over your head and a place to sleep, you are richer than 75% of this world.

If you have money in the bank, in your wallet, and spare change in a dish someplace, you are among the top 8% of the world's wealthy.

If your parents are still married and alive, you are very rare.

If you can hold someone's hand, hug them or even touch them on the shoulder, you are blessed because you can offer God's healing touch.

If you can read this message, you are more blessed than over two billion people in the world who cannot read anything at all.

Get A Life

Note: *This is a commencement speech made by Anna Quindlen at Villanova University.*

It's a great honor for me to be the third member of my family to receive an honorary doctorate from this great university. It's an honor to follow my great Uncle Jim, who was a gifted physician, and my Uncle Jack, who is a remarkable businessman. Both of them could have told you something important about their professions, about medicine or commerce. I have no specialized field of interest or expertise, which puts me at a disadvantage talking to you today. I'm a novelist. My work is human nature. Real life is all I know.

Don't ever confuse the two, your life and your work. The second is only part of the first. Don't ever forget what a friend once wrote Senator Paul Tsongas when the senator decided not to run for re-election because he had been diagnosed with cancer: "No man ever said on his deathbed I wish I had spent more time at the office." Don't ever forget the words my father sent me on a postcard last year: "If you win the rat race, you're still a rat." Or what John Lennon wrote before he was gunned down in the driveway of the Dakota: "Life is what happens while you are busy making other plans."

You will walk out of here this afternoon with only one thing that no one else has. There will be hundreds of people out there with your same degree; there will be thousands of people doing what you want to do for a living. But you will be the only person alive who has sole custody of your life. Your particular life. Your entire life. Not just your life at a desk, or your life on a bus, or in a car, or at the computer. Not just the life of your mind, but the life of your heart. Not just your bank account, but your soul.

People don't talk about the soul very much anymore. It's so much easier to write a resume than to craft a spirit. But, a resume is a cold comfort on a winter night, or when you're sad, or broke, or lonely, or when you've gotten back the test results and they're not so good.

Here is my resume: I am a good mother to three children. I have tried never to let my profession stand in the way of being a good parent. I no longer consider myself the center of the universe.

I show up. I listen. I try to laugh. I am a good friend to my husband. I have tried to make marriage vows mean what they say. I am a good friend to my friends, and they to me. Without them, there would be nothing to say to you today, because I would be a cardboard cutout. But I call them on the phone, and I meet them for lunch. I would be rotten, or at best mediocre at my job, if those other things were not true. You cannot be really first rate at your work if your work is all you are. So here's what I wanted to tell you today:

Get a life. A real life, not a manic pursuit of the next promotion, the bigger paycheck, the larger house. Do you think you'd care so very much about those things if you blew an aneurysm one afternoon, or found a lump in your breast?

Get a life in which you notice the smell of salt water pushing itself on a breeze over Seaside Heights, a life in which you stop and watch how a red-tailed hawk circles over the water or the way a baby scowls with concentration when she tries to pick up a Cheerio with her thumb and first finger. Get a life in which you are not alone.

Find people you love, and who love you. And remember that love is not leisure, it is work. Pick up the phone. Send an e-mail. Write a letter.

Get a life in which you are generous. And realize that life is the best thing ever, and that you have no business taking it for granted.

PIECES SENT BY OTHERS

Care so deeply about its goodness that you want to spread it around. Take money you would have spent on beers and give it to charity. Work in a soup kitchen. Be a big brother or sister. All of you want to do well. But if you do not do good too, then doing well will never be enough.

It is so easy to waste our lives, our days, our hours, our minutes. It is so easy to take for granted the color of our kids' eyes, the way the melody in a symphony rises and falls and disappears and rises again. It is so easy to exist instead of to live.

I learned to live many years ago. Something really, really bad happened to me, something that changed my life in ways that, if I had had my druthers, it would never have been changed at all. And what I learned from it is what, today, seems to be the hardest lesson of all.

I learned to love the journey, not the destination. I learned that it is not a dress rehearsal, and that today is the only guarantee you get. I learned to look at all the good in the world and try to give some of it back because I believed in it, completely and utterly. And I tried to do that, in part, by telling others what I had learned. By telling them this:

Consider the lilies of the field. Look at the fuzz on a baby's ear. Read in the backyard with the sun on your face. Learn to be happy. And think of life as a terminal illness, because if you do, you will live it with joy and passion as it ought to be lived.

Without the Master

A temple roof cannot stay up without rafters;
So without Nam how can one cross the ocean?
Without a vessel water cannot be kept;
So without a Saint man cannot be saved from doom.
Woe to him who thinks not of God,
Whose mind and heart remain absorbed
in ploughing the field of the senses.

Without a ploughman land cannot be tilled,
Without a thread jewels cannot be strung,
Without a knot the sacred tie cannot be made;
So without a Saint man cannot be saved from doom.

A child cannot be born without father and mother,
Clothes cannot be washed without water,
There can be no horseman without a horse;
So without a Master none can reach the court of the Lord.

Without music there can be no wedding;
Rejected by her husband, a bad woman suffers misery;
So man suffers without a Saint.
Says Kabir, My friend, only one thing attain:
become a gurumukh that you not die again.

By Kabir

Watch & Listen Carefully

The man whispered, "God, speak to me,"
and a meadowlark sang.
But the man did not hear.

So the man yelled, "God, speak to me!"
and the thunder rolled across the sky.
But the man did not listen.

The man looked around and said, "God, let me see you,"
And a star shined brightly.
But the man did not notice.

Then the man shouted, "God, show me a miracle!"
and a life was born.
But the man did not know.

So the man cried out in despair,
"Touch me God, and let me know you are here!"
Whereupon, God reached down and touched the man.

But the man brushed the butterfly away and walked on.

How to Survive a Heart Attack Alone

Let's say you're driving home after a hard day on the job. Suddenly you start experiencing severe pain in your chest that starts to radiate out into your arm and up into your jaw.

What can you do? Without help, the person whose heart stops beating properly and who begins to feel faint has only about ten seconds left before losing consciousness.

However, these victims can help themselves by coughing repeatedly and very vigorously.

A deep breath should be taken before each cough, and the cough must be deep and prolonged, as when producing sputum from deep inside the chest.

A breath and a cough must be repeated about every two seconds without let up until help arrives, or until the heart is felt to be beating normally again.

Deep breaths get oxygen into the lungs, and coughing movements squeeze the heart and keep the blood circulating. The squeezing pressure on the heart also helps it regain normal rhythm. In this way, heart attack victims can get to a phone and, between breaths, call for help.

From: Health Cares Rochester General Hospital

PIECES SENT BY OTHERS

I Am Grateful

For the teenager who is not doing dishes, but is watching TV,
because it means he is at home and not on the streets.

For the taxes that I pay, because it means that I am employed.

For the mess to clean up after a party,
because it means I have been surrounded by friends.

For the clothes that fit a little too snuggly,
because it means I have enough to eat.

For a lawn that needs mowing, windows that need cleaning, and
gutters that need fixing, because it means that I have a home.

For the parking spot I find at the far end of the parking lot,
because it means I am capable of walking and that I have been
blessed with transportation.

For my huge heating bill, because it means that I am warm.

For the lady behind me in church who sings off key,
because it means that I can hear.

For the pile of laundry and ironing I have to do,
because it means I have clothes to wear.

For the weariness and aching muscles at the end of the day,
because it means that I am capable of working hard and that I have
employment.

For the alarm that goes off early in the morning,
because it means that I am alive.

The Tragic Paradox of Our Times

We have taller buildings but shorter tempers,
wider freeways, but narrower viewpoints.
We spend more, but have less. We buy more, but enjoy less.
We have bigger houses and smaller families,
more conveniences, but less time.
We have more degrees but less sense;
more knowledge, but less judgment;
more experts, yet more problems; more medicine, but less health.
We have multiplied our possessions, but reduced our values.
We talk too much, love too seldom, and hate too often.
We've learned how to make a living, but not a life.
We've added years to life, not life to years.
We've been all the way to the moon and back,
but have trouble crossing the street to meet a new neighbor.
We conquered outer space, but not inner space.
We've done larger things, but not better things.
We've cleaned up the air, but polluted the soul.
We've conquered the atom, but not our prejudice.
We build more computers to hold more information,
to produce more copies than ever, but we communicate less and less.
These are the times of fast foods and slow digestion,
big men and small character, steep profits and shallow relationships.
These are the days of two incomes but more divorce,
fancier houses, but broken homes.
These are days of quick trips, disposable diapers,
throw-away morality, one-night stands, overweight bodies,
and pills that do everything from cheer, to quiet, to kill.

Author Unknown

PIECES SENT BY OTHERS

God's Perfection

In Brooklyn, New York, Chush is a school that caters to disabled children. Some children remain in Chush for their entire school career, while others can be main-streamed into conventional schools. At a Chush fund-raising dinner, the father of a Chush child delivered a speech that would never be forgotten by all who attended. After extolling the school and its dedicated staff, he cried out, *"Where is the perfection in my son, Shaya? Everything God does is done with perfection. But my child cannot understand things as other children do. My child cannot remember facts and figures as other children do. Where is God's perfection?"* The audience was shocked by the question, pained by the father's anguish and stilled by the piercing query.

"I believe," the father answered, *"that when God brings a child like this into the world, the perfection that he seeks is in the way people react to this child."* He then told the following story about his son, Shaya:

One afternoon, Shaya and I walked past a park where some boys Shaya knew were playing baseball. Shaya asked, "Do you think they will let me play?" I knew that my son was not at all athletic, and that most boys would not want him on their team. But I understood that if my son were chosen to play, it would give him a wonderful sense of belonging. I approached one of the boys in the field and asked if Shaya could play. The boy looked around for guidance from his teammates. Getting none, he took matters into his own hands, and said, "We are losing by six runs and the game is in the eighth inning. I guess he can be on our team, and we'll try to put him up to bat in the ninth inning." I was ecstatic and Shaya smiled broadly.

Shaya put on a glove and went out to play short-center-field. In the bottom of the eight inning, Shaya's team scored a few runs but was still behind by three. In the bottom of the ninth inning, Shaya's team scored again, and, now with two outs and the bases loaded with the potential winning run on base, Shaya was scheduled to be up. Would the team actually let Shaya bat at this juncture and give away its chance to win the game? Surprisingly, Shaya was given the bat. Everyone knew that it was all but impossible because Shaya didn't even know how to hold the bat properly, let alone hit with it.

However, as Shaya stepped up to the plate the pitcher moved a few steps closer to lob the ball softly so Shaya could at least be able to make contact. The first pitch came, and Shaya swung clumsily and missed. One of Shaya's teammates came up to Shaya, and together they held the bat and faced the pitcher, waiting for the next pitch. The pitcher again took a few steps forward to toss the ball softly toward Shaya.

As the pitch came in, Shaya and his teammate swung at the ball, and together they hit a slow ground ball to the pitcher. The pitcher picked up the soft grounder and could easily have thrown the ball to the first baseman. Shaya would have been out, and that would have ended the game.

Instead, the pitcher took the ball and threw it on a high arc to right field, far beyond the reach of the first baseman. Everyone started yelling, "Shaya, run to first. Run to first!" Never in his life had Shaya run to first. He scampered down the baseline, wide-eyed and startled. By the time he reached first base, the right fielder had the ball. He could have thrown the ball to the second baseman who would tag Shaya out, as Shaya was still running. But the right fielder understood what the pitcher's intentions were, so he threw the ball high and far over the third

---

PIECES SENT BY OTHERS

baseman's head. Everyone yelled, "Run to second, run to second." Shaya ran towards second base as the runners ahead of him deliriously circled the bases towards home. As Shaya reached second base, the opposing short-stop ran to him, turned him in the direction of third base and shouted, "Run to third." As Shaya rounded third, the boys from both teams came and ran behind him, screaming, "Shaya run home."

Shaya ran home, stepped on home plate, and all eighteen boys lifted him on their shoulders and made him the hero, as he had just hit a "grandslam" and won the game for his team.

"That day," concluded the father softly, *"those eighteen boys reached their level of God's perfection."*

DROPS OF NECTAR

ABOUT THE AUTHOR

His Holiness Pujya Swami Chidanand Saraswatiji

Spiritual and Academic Education: H.H. Swami Chidanand Saraswatiji's motto in life is, "In the Service of God and humanity." Touched by the hand of God at the tender age of eight, Pujya Swamiji left His home to live a life devoted to God and humanity, spending His youth in silence, meditation and austerities high in the Himalayas. At the age of seventeen, after nine years of unbroken, intense *sadhana*, He returned from the forest—under the orders of His guru—and obtained an academic education to parallel His spiritual one. Pujya Swamiji has master's degrees in Sanskrit and Philosophy as well as fluency in many languages.

The Teaching of Unity: Unity, harmony, and the belief in infinite paths to God are the foundation of Pujya Swamiji's "religion." His goal is to bring everyone closer to God, regardless of what name one uses. "If you are a Hindu, be a better Hindu. If you are a Christian, be a better Christian. If you are a Muslim, be a better Muslim. If you are a Jew, be a better Jew," He says.

In this line, He has been a leader in numerous international, inter-faith conferences and parliaments, including the **Parliament of World Religions**; the **Millennium World Peace Summit of Religious and Spiritual Leaders at the United Nations**; the **World Economic Forum**; the **World Council of Religious Leaders at the United Nations**; the **World Conference of Religions for Peace**; the **Global Youth Peace Summit at the United Nations**; the **Hindu-Jewish Summit**; and the **Hindu-Christian Dialogue initiated by the Vatican**. He is also a leader of frequent pilgrimages for peace across the world.

MORE INFORMATION

286

Spiritual Leader and Inspiration: Pujya Swamiji is the President and Spiritual Head of Parmarth Niketan Ashram in Rishikesh, one of India's largest and most renowned spiritual institutions. Under His divine inspiration and leadership, Parmarth Niketan has become a sanctuary known across the globe as one filled with grace, beauty, serenity and true divine bliss. Pujya Swamiji has also increased several-fold the humanitarian activities undertaken by Parmarth Niketan. Now, the ashram is not only a spiritual haven for those who visit, but it also provides education, training, and health care to those in need.

He is also the founder and the spiritual head of the first Hindu-Jain Temple in America. This beautiful, three-domed masterpiece is located on the outskirts of Pittsburgh, Pennsylvania, and has paved the way for unity between Hindus and Jains across America. Pujya Swamiji is also the founder and inspiration behind many other temples in the USA, Canada, Europe and Australia.

Guide to Youth: Pujya Swamiji knows that the youth are our future, and He is forever changing the course of that future through His profound effect on every youngster with whom He comes in contact. Children and adolescents seem to bloom like flowers under the rays of His light. Additionally, He gives pragmatic tools to help them unite in the spirit of peace, harmony and global change. Pujya Swamiji runs youth sessions and camps in the USA, Europe and throughout Asia.

Ceaseless Service: "Giving is Living" is Pujya Swamiji's motto; He is always in the midst of dozens of projects, each one a noble and tenaciously dedicated effort to make the world a better place for all of humanity. He is the Founder/Chairman of the India Heritage Research Foundation (IHRF), an international, non-profit, humanitarian organization dedicated to providing education, health care, youth welfare, and vocational training to the needy population. IHRF also, under the guidance and inspiration of Pujya Swamiji, is compiling the first *Encyclopedia of Hinduism* in history. Pujya Swamiji is also the Founder/ Chairman of the Divine Shakti Foundation, a non-profit organization dedicated to using the energy, strength and capability of women to help bring the light of life, hope, education and assistance to the abandoned, orphaned babies and young girls, as well as widowed and impoverished women.

Ganga Action: Pujya Swamiji is also the Founder of Ganga Action Parivar (GAP), a worldwide family of scientists, engineers, specialists, volunteers and devotees who are dedicated to working to make Mother Ganga's waters not only nirmal (clean) but also aviral (free-flowing). The work being undertaken by GAP is multi-faceted and extensive. See the separate GAP section and also www.gangaaction.com for more details.

Awards and Recognitions: Pujya Swamiji is the recipient of innumerable awards for both His role as spiritual leader as well as for His unparalleled humanitarian work. Some of the more noteworthy are as follows:

1. Mahatma Gandhi Humanitarian Award, given by the Mayor of New Jersey, USA for outstanding charitable and interfaith work

2. Hindu of the Year, 1991, by the international magazine *Hinduism Today*, for masterminding the project of the next millennium, the *Encyclopedia of Hinduism*

3. Uttaranchal Ratan ("Jewel of the State of Uttaranchal") Award

4. Bharat Vikas Parishad 1st Utkrishtta Samman Award

5. Devarishi Award, by Sandipani Vidya Niketan, under the guidance of Pujya Sant Rameshbhai Oza, for promoting Indian culture and heritage across the world

6. Bhaskar Award, 1998, by Mystic India and Bharat Nirman, for Outstanding Humanitarian Service

7. Prominent Personality Award, by Lions' Club

8. Diwaliben Mohanlal Mehta Charitable Trust Award for Progress in Religion

9. Best Citizens of India Award

Further, He has been given the title of Patron of the Russian Indian Heritage Research Foundation, Moscow, and is also a Patron of the Centre for Religious Experience in Oxford, UK.

The True *Sanyasi*: Pujya Swamiji seems unaffected by this incredible list of accomplishments and remains a pious child of God, owning nothing, draped in saffron robes, living a life of true renunciation. His days in Rishikesh are spent offering service to those around Him. Thousands travel from America, Europe and Australia as well as from all over India, simply to sit in His presence and receive His *darshan*. To them, the journey is an inconsequential price to pay for the priceless gift of His *satsang*. He travels the world, bringing the light of wisdom, inspiration, upliftment and the divine touch to thousands across the world.

India Heritage Research Foundation

Pujya Swami Chidanand Saraswatiji is the founder and chairman of the India Heritage Research Foundation, a non-profit, charitable organization dedicated to humanitarian and cultural projects. Founded in 1987, IHRF is committed to preserving the timeless wisdom and ageless grandeur of Indian culture. By weaving together ancient tradition, cultural history, a wide range of non-discriminatory charitable services, and inspiring youth programs, IHRF has created a tapestry of true, universal beauty.

The Encyclopedia of Hinduism

IHRF has completed the revolutionary project of compiling the first *Encyclopedia of Hinduism* in history. The *Encyclopedia* will mark the first time that the urgent need is met for an authentic, objective and insightful well of information, capturing both the staples and the spices of Indian tradition and culture. This eleven-volume work was previewed and blessed by the hands of the Dalai Lama and many other revered saints at a large function during the Maha Kumbha Mela in Haridwar in 2010, and will be available internationally by the end of 2011.

The *Encyclopedia of Hinduism* will be a significant landmark, encompassing the entire spectrum of the land called Bharat.

IHRF is dedicated to youth, education, spirituality, culture, inter-faith harmony, health care and ecology. To this end, it sponsors medical care programs, schools, *gurukuls*/orphanages, training centers, large-scale spiritual and cultural events, tree-plantation and clean-up programs, conferences geared toward inter-faith harmony, summer camps, and international youth awareness programs. Additionally, IHRF sponsors (both financially and otherwise) educational institutions that are already established but suffering from lack of resources.

Following are examples of only a few of the numerous ways that IHRF's arms embrace humanity:

Y.E.S. – Youth Education Services

Many villages throughout India are oceans of poverty and illiteracy. The influx of technology, commerce, education and metropolitanism that  has flooded most of India's cities since independence seems to have not even touched these villages. They exist as they did centuries ago. However, one crucial change has occurred. Now, basic education and marketable skills are absolute necessities in order to subsist in even the smallest communities. Hence, those who lack this education and training go to sleep hungry each night.

In the midst of this ocean of destitution, there are islands of light, islands of knowledge, islands of hope. The Y.E.S. schools are some of these islands. The Y.E.S. program encompasses dozens of children's schools, women's vocational training programs (including sewing, handicrafts, tailoring and fashion designing as well as adult literacy education), and two orphanages/*gurukuls*. These schools are located in Rishikesh, Swargashram, Rani Pokhri, Lucknow, Himachal Pradesh, Orissa, Uttarkashi, as well as other areas of the Himalayas and North-East India.

The children and women in the Y.E.S. program are given not only an education, but they are also given the priceless gifts of hope and faith.

The Y.E.S. program is dedicated to providing poor and orphaned children a positive, nurturing environment, and to giving them the chance to live a life free from destitution or despair.

Gurukuls/Orphanages

One visit to India is sufficient to see the urgent, dire need for orphanages and homes for underprivileged children. However, simple shelters with food, beds and babysitters are not sufficient.

These children need not only to be fed and sheltered. Rather, they also need to be educated and trained so they can become productive members of society. They need to be inculcated with values, ethics and spirituality which will make them torchbearers of Indian culture.

Our three *Gurukuls*/Orphanages serve as places where nearly 500 children are housed as well as educated, cultured and filled with crucial values such as non-violence, truth, and *seva*.

Their days are filled with academic and computer studies, *yoga*, meditation, Vedic chanting, reading of scriptures, *seva* and special programs, such as the performance of dramas based on Indian spiritual history, designed to instill in them essential *sanskaras*. Renamed *rishikumars*, the children travel on *yatra* to the Himalayas and perform *yagna* and prayers every night on the banks of Mother Ganga.

Looks of hopelessness have become looks of optimism and hope. Lightless eyes have become bright, shining eyes. Feelings of destitution and despair have become feelings of pride, faith and enthusiasm.

MORE INFORMATION

Mansarover Ashrams and Clinic

Under the guidance, inspiration and vision of Pujya Swami Chidanand Saraswatiji, IHRF has built three ashrams and a medical clinic in the holy land of Lake Mansarovar and Mt. Kailash in Tibet.

Prior to this project, there were no indoor lodging facilities nor medical facilities for hundreds of kilometers. People frequently suffered from basic, treatable ailments due to lack of medical attention. Therefore, after undertaking a *yatra* to the sacred land in 1998, Pujya Swamiji took a vow that – by the grace of God – He would do something for the local people (who don't even have running water) and for all the pilgrims who travel there.

The ashram (tourist rest house) and clinic on the banks of Lake Mansarovar were officially inaugurated in July 2003. We have also built two halls there where *satsang*, meditation and many other divine activities can take place.

Additionally, we have built an ashram in Paryang, Tibet, on the way to Mansarovar, the place where every yatri stays one day prior to reaching Mansarovar. This ashram was inaugurated in June 2006.

A third ashram has been built in Dirapuk, on the sacred Mt. Kailash *Parikrama* route, at the unprecedented altitude of 17,000 feet, and

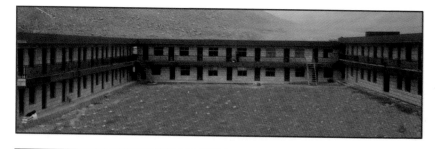

was inaugurated in September 2009. Dirapuk is the place where all pilgrims spend the first night of the two-night, fifty-two kilometer, treacherous *parikrama*. At this location, the *darshan* of Mt. Kailash is the clearest, closest, and most spectacular.

Additionally, we have pledged our support and assistance to the local villagers of Mansarovar.

The project is truly the grace of God and is a divine gift to this holy land, to all Tibetans who live there, and to all the pious pilgrims who cross oceans and continents in order to have a glimpse of the abode of Lord Shiva.

Tsunami Relief

On the 30th of December, 2004, Pujya Swamiji, Vivek Oberoi, Sadhvi Bhagwati, *Rishikumars* from Parmarth Niketan's *Gurukul* and Vivek Oberoi's family traveled down to South India in the wake of the devastating tsunami. Upon seeing the devastation wrought upon the land, they decided to stay and offer both short-term and long-term assistance. The relief work ranged from immediate, emergency measures to the permanent reconstruction of entire villages.

Phase I – Immediate, Emergency Relief Measures

1. Construction of 100 new, temporary homes

2. Establishment and running of seven community kitchens where thousands of families received fresh, hot meals, including milk for children

3. Medical Relief Centers operated at each of the kitchens

4. Playground for the children

5. Free Eye and Cataract Operation Camp for hundreds of villagers

6. Wide-scale distribution of necessities to thousands of people, including food, water, clothing, cooking supplies, shoes, and sheets

7. Repair of over 100 boats and purchase of 15 new boats

8. Purchase of over 600 new fishing nets

Phase II – Permanent Village Reconstruction in Pondicherry

Project Hope undertook the reconstruction of villages Pannithittu and Pattincheri in Pondicherry, totalling over 350 homes. Pannithittu, built through the generosity of Rotary International, Sadeh Lok, UK, Himjyoti Foundation and many other generous donors, was inaugurated in December 2005 by the hands of the Honorable Governors of Tamil Nadu, Pondicherry and Uttarakhand.

The village of Pattincheri, sponsored by Shri LN Mittal of London, was inaugurated in April 2007.

Phase III – Cuddalore Town, Cuddalore District, Tamil Nadu: Orphanage and Women's Center

The final stage in the work was completed and inaugurated on May 12, 2007. The orphanage which we built for the tsunami orphans as well as facilities for over 300 children who had been orphaned prior to the tsunami was inaugurated by H.E. the Honorable Governor of Tamil Nadu, Shri Surjit Singh Barnalaji with Pujya Swamiji.

The orphanage includes dormitory facilities, school rooms, a computer center, medical room, beautiful kitchen and dining facilities, a vocational training center and more. It has been built on the same land as the previously existing home for approximately 200 widowed/abandoned women, which we also beautified. In this way, the orphaned children

MORE INFORMATION

will receive, in addition to the staff, mothers, aunts, grandmothers and older sisters; the women will receive the priceless gift of caring for orphaned children. We have also built a vocational training center for the women, and the new huge dining/kitchen facilities are shared by both the children and the women.

Rural Development Program

We are running a rural development program in a town called Veerpur, on the banks of the Ganges, three kilometers south of Rishikesh.

The following are components of the rural development program:

Water facilities – Although the town lies on the banks of the Ganga River, most people had no running water or water for their farms. We dug a boring well and have brought running water to this village.

Tree plantation program

Construction of a proper road in the village

Organic Gardening program – We have started a special organic farming program as well. We have brought in trained organic farmers and scientists to teach the local farmers alternative, chemical-free methods of farming. Further, we will have a special "buy back" program with them where we will buy back from them all of their crops. In addition, the ashram at

Veerpur has its own organic farm.

Women's Vocational training program

Sewage Control and Sanitation programs – We have laid sewage lines in the village and constructed toilets for the villagers so that no pollution goes into Ganga.

Spirituality and Culture – We have started an evening devotional ceremony there on the banks of the Ganges, called *Aarti*. It is a way for the villagers to come together in a spirit of peace, culture & piety.

Gurukul/**orphanage** – The second of the three *gurukuls*/orphanages is here in Veerpur, and we have plans to open an orphanage for girls here as well.

Project Give Back

With the motto *"Give Back, Feel Good,"* Project Give Back is working to bring medical, environmental and engineering *seva* to the people of rural India by experts and professionals from around the globe. So far, we have been active in organizing and running various free medical camps in the villages of the Himalayas themselves, bringing medical care to the people. Doctors from all over the world of all different specialities come to beautifully donate their skills and expertise to the patients, who usually cannot afford such care, as well as distribute free medicines, glasses and other medical equipment to the patients.

There is also an effort to better educate people to maintain health

and hygiene. We are also working on the establishment of a model village in Veerpur which can serve as a model of environmental preservation and integrity, and which we will then expand into other rural areas.

IHRF is dedicated to bringing food to the hungry, medicine to the sick, and peace to the troubled.

IHRF does not discriminate on the basis of race, religion, caste, gender or nationality.

All of its services are open to all & free to all.

GANGA ACTION PARIVAR

Ganga Action Parivar (GAP) is a world family dedicated to serving Mother Ganga. GAP intends to restore, protect and maintain the River Ganga and Her tributaries in their *aviral* (free-flowing) and *nirmal* (unpolluted) states. Under Pujya Swamiji's guidance and leadership, numerous organizations, scientists, environmentalists, activists, government officials and volunteers are coming together to bring this noble goal to fruition.

GAP was first launched on April 4th, 2010 at a special "Sparsh Ganga" event at Parmarth Niketan Ashram by the hands of Pujya Swamiji, H.H. the Dalai Lama and many revered saints. The event raised awareness about the need for collective and holistic, solution-based action to address the crucial issues facing the holy river. Many were present to show their support and share their love and dedication towards our environment, and the massive event included participants pledging to help protect and restore the Ganga.

A similar event was held several weeks later in Gangotri, the source of the river Ganga, with Shri L.K. Advaniji and the Hon'ble Chief Minister of Uttarakhand Ramesh Pokhriyal in which thousands more took pledges to help clean and protect Ganga also.

MORE INFORMATION

Under Pujya Swamiji's guidance and leadership, numerous organizations, scientists, environmentalists, activists, government officials and volunteers are coming together to bring this noble goal to fruition. Several conferences have been held to bring these different groups

together. On October 27th, 2010, an Aviral Nirmal Ganga Conference was held at Parmarth Niketan Ashram where prominent spiritual leaders, scientists and experts came to discuss the next steps for addressing the issues facing Ganga, and it was in this conference that the official name "Ganga Action Parivar" was created.

On April 23-24th, 2011, the National Aviral Nirmal Ganga Conference was held at Parmarth Niketan Ashram once again. During this conference, scientists, environmentalists, activistis, government officals and many more came together to find sustainable, implementable solutions for the various issues facing Ganga and her tributaries. The conference was graced by many who are prominent in the movement to clean Ganga, including Shri R.K. Pachauriji, a leading environmental activist who won the Nobel Prize for his work.

Activities of GAP range from working to create sustainable, environmentally-friendly solutions for the various, complex problems facing Ganga and implementing such problems, to holding local clean-ups along Her banks, to educating people about the important and urgent need to live green. *(To learn more, please see www.gangaaction.com.)*

PARMARTH NIKETAN ASHRAM
RISHIKESH (HIMALAYAS), INDIA

H.H. Swami Chidanand Saraswatiji is the President of Parmarth Niketan Ashram in Rishikesh, India, a true, spiritual haven, lying on the holy banks of Mother Ganga, in the lap of the lush Himalayas.

Parmarth Niketan is the largest ashram in Rishikesh. Parmarth Niketan provides its thousands of pilgrims – who come from all corners of the Earth – with a clean, pure and sacred atmosphere as well as abundant, beautiful gardens. With over 1,000 rooms, the facilities are a perfect blend of modern amenities and traditional, spiritual simplicity.

The daily activities at Parmarth Niketan include morning universal prayers, daily *yoga* and meditation classes, daily *satsang* and lecture programs, *kirtan*, world renowned Ganga *aarti* at sunset, as well as

full Nature Cure, and Ayurvedic treatment available on the premises.

Additionally, there are frequently special cultural and spiritual programs given by visiting revered saints, acclaimed musicians, spiritual and social leaders and others.

Further, there are frequent camps in which pilgrims come from across the world to partake in intensive courses on *yoga*, meditation, *pranayama*, stress management, acupressure, Reiki and other ancient Indian sciences. Parmarth Niketan hosts the annual International Yoga Festival from the 1st-7th of March every year, in cooperation with the Government of Uttarakhand.

Parmarth Niketan's charitable activities and services make no distinctions on the basis of caste, color, gender, creed or nationality. Instead they emphasize unity, harmony, peace, global integrity, health, and the holistic connection between the body, mind and spirit.

True to its name, Parmarth Niketan is dedicated to the welfare of all. Everything is open and free to all.

Praise for Drops of Nectar

I am writing to let you know how much I enjoyed reading your book. It was one of the most enlightening books I've ever read. I've skimmed/read through many of [books on Hinduism, meditation, Self-realization, etc.], however none of them has impacted me the way that your book did. I felt as though this book was specially written for young Indian Americans such as myself. The thing I found most incredible, was that I could identify with all the issues you mentioned. Further, the solutions which were presented were logical and seemed to be a happy medium between the Eastern and Western culture. As I read the book, I could see myself practicing what was taught. I learned so much from the book. Thank you for such an insightful peace of work.

Florida, USA

Thank you very much for giving us such good guidelines and bringing a drastic change in our life. I feel your presence every moment. Your books are really a great gift to us and are helping in changing our nature and behavior.

Jakarta, Indonesia

Each word that Swamiji writes pours from his divine heart and truly touches ours to illuminate.

Brisbane, Australia

MORE INFORMATION

I am reading *Drops of Nectar* again. I like it because the book opens up my eyes wider each time and surely my heart will be just as wide as the ocean one day.

Bangkok, Thailand

I started reading [*Drops of Nectar*] and have found so many answers for myself. It is truly God's gift to whoever may read it..

Pujya Swamiji changed my life with a simple touch and a glance. In Him, the Divine shines brightly and clearly, illuminating all those who come near Him. Even though I live far away from Him, I still feel His presence and am grateful for His continual guidance.

New Jersey, USA

Swamiji came into our lives when we need Him the most. He has shown us there is a balance to be achieved in life and that religion is about our relationships with people and God. He inspires us to seek the truth and see goodness.

UK

Since meeting Pujya Swamiji I have incorporated spirituality into every aspect of my life. Pujya Swamiji's advice and guidance have helped me discover my life's mission to serve humanity with my thoughts, words and actions. Pujya Swamiji's presence has made this world a better place for all of us.

Winnipeg, Canada